MW00388610

The Vegan Cookbook

200 Healthy & Delicious Recipes for The Beginner Vegan

Jared Bangerter

Introduction

I want to thank you for purchasing this in-depth vegan recipe book and, if you are a new vegan, congratulate you on taking the initiative to live in a way that is friendlier to the environment and the other creatures who we share our beautiful planet with. I furthermore would like to congratulate you on taking your first step to a whole new life full of radiant health and meaning.

This is the perfect cookbook for any vegan, new and experienced alike. This is also the perfect cookbook for *anyone* who wants more variety – the spice of life – in their diet without compromising their health or violating their moral obligation to the environment around them. This book contains an abundance of 200 different vegan recipes to keep YOUR taste buds satiated and your body rich in health. This book is just what you need to be able to live the vegan way without feeling deprived. As you read through this book, uncover a whole new world full of flavors from full on stand-alone meals to smoothies and desserts that are bound to delight even the most discriminating of taste buds!

In addition to recipes, you will find scientific evidence suggesting *why* you and everyone who you care about and love should convert to veganism – for your own and their own health and longevity.

Everything you could ever hope for and more from a vegan cookbook is all present here. May this book prove to be a blessing for yourself and those who you love the most.

Jared G. Bangerter

© Copyright 2017 by Seeker Publishing - All rights reserved.

This document is geared towards providing exact and reliable information regarding the topic and issue covered. The publication is sold with the idea that the publisher is not required to render accounting, officially permitted, or otherwise, qualified services. If advice is necessary, legal or professional, a practiced individual in the profession should be ordered.

From a Declaration of Principles which was accepted and approved equally by a Committee of the American Bar Association and a Committee of Publishers and Associations.

In no way is it legal to reproduce, duplicate, or transmit any part of this document in either electronic means or in printed format. Recording of this publication is strictly prohibited and any storage of this document is not allowed unless with written permission from the publisher. All rights reserved.

The information provided herein is stated to be truthful and consistent, in that any liability, in terms of inattention or otherwise, by any usage or abuse of any policies, processes, or directions contained within is the solitary and utter responsibility of the recipient reader. Under no circumstances will any legal responsibility or blame be held against the publisher for any reparation, damages, or monetary loss due to the information herein, either directly or indirectly.

The health and fitness advice in this book is by no means intended as a replacement for medical advice. By using this book, you acknowledge that you are solely responsible to seek the advice of your doctor or medical counselor before following any advice herein. The author nor the publisher will not be held liable for any damages resulting from the use of the information in this book.

Respective authors and photographers own all copyrights not held by the publisher.

The information herein is offered for informational purposes solely, and is universal as so. The presentation of the information is without contract or any type of guarantee assurance.

The trademarks that are used are without any consent, and the publication of the trademark is without permission or backing by the trademark owner. All trademarks and brands within this book are for clarifying purposes only and are the owned by the owners themselves, not affiliated with this document.

Table of Contents

Introduction...

Chapter 1: The Science of Veganism.................1

Chapter 2: How to Use This Cookbook to Burn Fat & Lose Weight.......................................5

Chapter 3: Adjusting to a Vegan Diet...............9

Chapter 4: Breakfast Recipes...........................13

Chapter 5: Lunch Recipes.................................77

Chapter 6: Dinner Recipes..............................143

Chapter 7: Desserts, Smoothies & Treats......219

Chapter 8: Testimonials...................................275

Conclusion...321

About the Author..323

Index..325

Chapter 1: The Science of Veganism

What if I told you that there is a *science* to optimized veganism? Sure, simply eliminating meat and all animal products from your diet will significantly boost your health and prevent disease, but there is so much more you can do for your body than the simple basics. If you're going to go vegan, you might as well do it in a way that will optimize your health to its maximum potential. That's exactly what this chapter of the book is about – taking basic veganism to the next level and tapping into the touted vegan super powers you always hear so much about. The key to doing this is incorporating what I have coined *The Perfect Seven*. In this chapter, you will learn what exactly The Perfect Seven is and why they are so important to a well-balanced, fully optimized vegan nutrition plan. Before we get into The Perfect Seven, it's important to understand the basics of veganism. What science is there that has shown its superiority to a standard omnivore diet?

In 1999, EPIC conducted a study that sought to discover whether there was any difference in the prevalence of heart disease between three distinct populations: vegans, standard vegetarians and meat-eaters. For the first time ever, the results of this study showed an edge of superiority in veganism over vegetarianism. Vegans were shown to be a whopping 26% less likely to develop heart disease than meat eaters, while vegetarians were only 24% less likely.

Another study was conducted in 2009. This study examined differences in mortality between vegetarians and vegans in comparison to non-vegetarians. The study examined the population of the Christian denomination 7th Day Adventists, as they preach the benefits and principles of a vegetarian diet in their faith. The 7th Day Adventist study found that vegetarians and vegans do live a few years longer than their meat-eating counterparts. To be specific, 7th Day Adventist women were found to live 2.52 years longer than meat-eating women and the men were found to live 3 years longer than meat-eating men. In addition to differences in lifespan, it also revealed that meat-eaters are ~50% more likely to develop hypertension and diabetes. The study also looked at general differences in average Body Mass Index (BMI) between the two groups and found that the average vegan BMI was 23.6, while the average non-vegan BMI was a whole 5.2 points higher at 28.8! For reference, a BMI between 20 and 25 is considered to be in the healthy range. Anything higher than 25 is considered to be overweight and anything higher than 30 is counted as obese.

A study on cholesterol ratings found vegans on average are ranked at 160, while non-vegans are ranked at 180. A whopping 20-point difference in cholesterol, which is correlated to a host of various life-shortening diseases, should be more than enough reason alone for anyone to consider switching to a full vegan diet.

In 2002, EPIC Oxford conducted yet another study. This time, the study was on the prevalence of hypertension between vegan and non-vegan populations. They found that the age-adjusted prevalence of self-reported hypertension of vegan males was only 6% and females was only 8%, while non-vegan males was 15% and females was 12%.

Cross sectional rates in AHS-2 (Type-2 Diabetes) found that vegans are more than 50% less likely to be diagnosed with Type-2 Diabetes! Furthermore, naturopathic doctors have shown great success in treating their patients who have Type-2 Diabetes with the use of a properly balanced vegan diet.

With all of these scientifically proven benefits supporting a vegan diet, is it any wonder more and more people are waking up to the facts and converting to veganism every day? There is a catch though, and this is unfortunately the pitfall most new vegans fall into: deficiencies.

It is perfectly possible to be rich in all of the nutrients your body needs for optimal health, radiant skin and a super-charged metabolism while on a vegan diet, but you have to know what you are doing to achieve this. That's where The Perfect Seven comes into play! The Perfect Seven are seven key vitamins and nutrients that most people on vegan diets are completely deficient in. Without these vital components, you will find your energy plateaus as does your weight loss and general sense of wellbeing.

The first of The Perfect Seven is Vitamin B12. There are two types of Vitamin B12 deficiency. Overt Vitamin B12 deficiency causes nerve and blood problems. This results in neurological issues like multiple sclerosis and restless leg and perhaps even the onset of Parkinson's disease. If you have any of these symptoms, then you are already in dire need of more Vitamin B12! The second type of Vitamin B12 deficiency is mild Vitamin B12 deficiency. Even if you are just mildly deficient, you still need to supplement with more because prolonged deficiency may result in heart disease and stroke, Alzheimer's disease and an early death. When you select your B12 supplement, make sure it is the type made from methylcobalamin and *not* cyanocobalamin! This is very important as the latter type has been linked to causing acne breakouts and even rosacea.

The second of The Perfect Seven is Omega 3. You can't just take a ton of flax seeds, walnuts, canola oil and hemp seeds though, because those contain the wrong kind of Omega 3 that's lacking in a vegan diet. Those Omega 3's are what we know as ALA Omega 3's, which are the precursor to the DHA and EPA Omega 3's that we want. The problem is that it takes *months* for your body to convert ALA Omega 3's into the desired Omega 3's. The reason you need EPA and DHA Omega 3's so badly is because they play a crucial role in your body's ability to reduce inflammation and regulate blood clotting and cholesterol. As an added bonus, proper levels of DHA prevents depression. If you are depressed, a deficiency in this component of The Perfect Seven could be why!

Thirdly, you need to take a look at your consumption of Vitamin D3. Most of us don't have the necessary amount of time to spend in the sun that we need for a proper dose of Vitamin D3. Even though most meat-eaters are deficient in Vitamin D3, vegans tend to be significantly more deficient. A prolonged deficiency in Vitamin D3 may result in the development of fibromyalgia, psoriasis, rosacea, muscle weakness, multiple sclerosis, lower back pain, diabetes and upper respiratory tract infections. It is absolutely critical you supplement with this daily. Fortunately, Vitamin D3 as well as the rest of The Perfect Seven are extremely cheap to afford!

The fourth component is calcium. There is calcium in spinach and other greens, but unfortunately those same sources of calcium also contain oxalates. Oxalates bind to calcium, which reduces your body's ability to absorb and make proper use of it. In order to keep and maintain strong bones and prevent injury, you need a quality calcium supplement as part of your daily vitamin repertoire.

The fifth key to The Perfect Seven is adequate protein intake. This is absolutely possible to get on a standard vegan diet without the addition of protein supplements, but it may not always be convenient for you to have to make sure you are reaching your daily protein requirement from meals. The amount of protein you need a day for optimal health is .5 x (your body weight in pounds). For example, if someone weighed 190 lbs., they would multiply 190 x .5 and get the end result of 95 grams of protein per day as their requirement. You *can* get all of this easily from vegan foods such as beans or nuts. In fact, I have listed the protein, carbs, and fats in grams for each of the recipes included in this book to make that easier for you to do. However, it may not be practical for you if you have a busy schedule and are always rushing to and fro. If that's the case for you, it is recommended that you use a good quality hemp or chia protein powder. You can even make consuming it a breeze by adding it to any of the smoothie recipes contained in Chapter 7 of this book!

The sixth nutrient you need to make sure you are getting enough of is iodine. Iodine is usually abundant in non-vegan foods and is necessary for healthy thyroid function. The thyroid regulates your metabolism. If you have been struggling to burn fat and lose weight no matter how hard you try, you more than likely have an iodine deficiency. When it comes to being a vegan, there are two options to get your iodine:

1) Eat seaweed every day.

2) Take an iodine supplement.

Seaweed also contains a lot of other beneficial vitamins and nutrients, so if you can stand the taste of it, I recommend the first option. If seaweed isn't your cup of tea, however, you can always take a supplement.

The seventh and final of The Perfect Seven is iron. Iron is most often found in red meat – something you *never* eat! It regulates blood consistency and prevents anemia, promotes quality sleep and digestion as well. Long-term deficiency of iron can cause anemia, depression and other mood disorders.

You can choose to totally skip The Perfect Seven and still have a leg-up health-wise on the non-vegans of the world, but why would you want to settle for less than your full potential? Do you want to tap into the legendary vegan superpowers and unlock a new heightened state of wellbeing in your life? If you do, then take The Perfect Seven daily at the following dosages:

The Perfect Seven:

1. Vitamin B12 (1,000 mcg)
2. Omega 3 DHA (200-300 mg)
3. Vitamin D3 (1,000 IU)
4. Calcium (1,000 mg)
5. Iodine (75 mg)
6. .5 x (your body weight in lbs.) grams of protein
7. Iron (27 mg)

If you've been struggling with depression, anxiety, insomnia, fatigue, a lack of motivation or general weakness, then The Perfect Seven in tandem with a vegan diet just might be your be-all end-all cure!

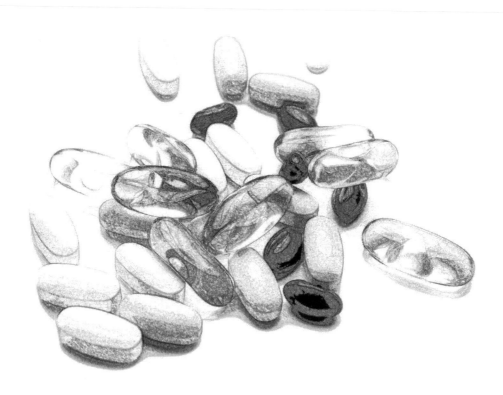

Chapter 2: How to Use This Cookbook to Burn Fat & Lose Weight

More than just a cookbook, this book is your complete and total guide to a body transformation that will drop the jaws of your friends and family. What if I told you that you could indulge yourself with *any* of the recipes in this book and continue to lose pound after pound, week after week? That's exactly what this portion of the book will teach you how to do!

The way weight loss works comes down to a simple equation of energy in versus energy out. You may recognize this as the law of thermodynamics. To put things simply, if you are consuming less calories per day and per week than your body needs to maintain its current weight, you WILL lose weight and nothing can stop you! It doesn't matter if you're eating the delicious vegan chocolate ice cream recipe or vegan pizza or whatsoever you choose. If you eat less calories than you need to maintain your weight, then you WILL lose weight – I guarantee it! You don't even have to exercise, if you don't want to.

The question remains, however, exactly how many calories do YOU need per day in order to maintain or lose weight? This is different from person to person, because everyone's body is unique to themselves and there is not one number that fits everyone. However, in this chapter you will learn how to calculate the exact number of calories YOU need to transform your body into a slim, fit and sexy new you. It's really a lot simpler than it sounds!

To begin, grab yourself a sheet of paper, a pen or pencil and a calculator.

STEP 1 – RESTING METABOLIC RATE

The first step is to calculate your *resting metabolic rate (RMR)*. Your resting metabolic rate is simply how many calories a day your body expends to just breathe and lay still without moving. If you were to be a complete vegetable, this is how many calories a day you would need just to not starve to death. To calculate your RMR, multiply your body weight (in pounds) x 10. It is best if you measure your body weight completely naked. You would be surprised how much clothing weighs! Now write down the number you get on your piece of paper and label it as "RMR".

EXAMPLE: A person with a body weight of 210 lbs would multiply their body weight by 10 to get 2100 calories per day as their resting metabolic rate. They would then write this number down for future reference.

STEP 2 – DAILY ACTIVITY EXPENDITURE

Now you need to calculate your *daily activity expenditure (DAE)*. If you wish to exercise or workout, don't add that number in just yet – we'll get to that in a moment. Your daily activity expenditure is the energy your body needs to use throughout the day and is not counting calories burned from your additional exercise. It has more to do with how much of your day you spend walking and talking, playing with your kids or whatever else your lifestyle includes. This number is ever so *slightly* different from person to person, because all of our lifestyles are quite varied. A safe rule of thumb is to use a 20% modifier. What do I mean by a 20% modifier? That is the number you multiply your RMR (from STEP 1) by in order to get your daily activity expenditure.

EXAMPLE: The aforementioned person in STEP 1, would then multiply their RMR (2100 calories) by .20 (for 20%) to get the number of 420 calories as their daily activity expenditure. They would then write this number down below 2100 on their paper and label it as "DAE" for future reference.

STEP 3 – EXERCISE EXPENDITURE

If you exercise daily, then include this step. If you are not on an exercise program and don't care to start one, skip this step and proceed to STEP 4.

This step is probably the easiest one. If you work out for approximately an hour a day, then a safe estimation of the number of calories you burn is going to be around 600 calories total for your complete workout. If you work out only 30 minutes a day, then 300 would be a safe number for you to use here. If you have a Fitbit or other calorie burning measurement device, feel free to use a more accurate number for this step. Write this number down below your daily activity expenditure and label it as "exercise expenditure" or "EE" for short.

STEP 4 – ADD IT ALL UP

At this point, you need to add up the numbers you calculated from steps 1 and 2 (and 3, if you are on an exercise program) in order to get your total daily expenditure of calories.

Once you have this number, it's incredibly easy to burn fat. Simply eat 100 to 200 calories less than this number per day and your body will be forced to lose fat. It doesn't matter which foods you choose from this recipe book – you *will* lose fat if you stick to this number. If you find you aren't burning fat and losing weight fast enough with a 100 to 200 calorie deficit after a couple of weeks, then try increasing the deficit by reducing your calorie count even further. I do not recommend using a calorie deficit of any more than 600 per day, however, as it can be dangerous.

You may feel hungry with a higher deficit, but you will be able to eat whichever foods you want – it's just a matter of the quantity that you must restrict.

MAKING LIFE EASIER

In order to make your life easier, I have calculated the exact calorie count of each of my 200 recipes that are included in this book. All you have to do is keep track of the number of calories you are consuming per day, from the recipes in this book, and make sure you don't go over your limit!

Divide the total yield of each recipe by the number listed next to "Servings" for the proper portion of food that corresponds with the calories and macronutrients listed. If the serving size says, "4", for example, then the calorie count listed is for *one-fourth* of the WHOLE dish. If you are splitting it with others, simply divide the total calorie count for the meal by the number of people you are splitting it equally with in order to get the number of calories you are consuming.

Using this book to burn body fat and lose weight, without depriving your taste buds, is *really* that simple!

Chapter 3: Adjusting to a Vegan Diet

If you haven't yet taken the plunge and committed to a full vegan diet, or even if you are still in the early days of the journey, this chapter is your guide to the exciting changes you will begin to experience.

DETOX SYMPTOMS

As you may have already discovered is true with anything worthwhile in life, there is usually rain before sun, night before dawn and darkness before light. It's no different when converting to veganism.

There are so many great benefits to be had by ceasing your consumption of animal products, but first your body has to essentially *relearn* how to thrive without them. When it does relearn how to thrive without meat and dairy, you will find yourself feeling superhuman! You will tap into an unlimited source of physical, mental and spiritual energy that will transform your health, your mental state and your very soul.

The key to understanding how detoxing from animal products works lies in understanding how the body builds up and stores toxins over time. Store bought meat and dairy is loaded with a vast variety toxins, hormones, antibiotics and other drugs that you ingest when you consume them. Over the course of time as you continue to ingest these harmful materials, your body's elimination pathways become clogged up and your body begins to store them wherever it can. This is why the diseases you are presently struggling with today seemed to have come on so gradually and slowly that you probably didn't even realize it at first! These hormones and toxins are commonly known to cause and promote the following diseases and health concerns:

1. Heart disease
2. Acne and Rosacea
3. Type-2 Diabetes
4. Multiple Sclerosis
5. Chronic insomnia
6. Restless Leg Syndrome & PLMD
7. Constipation
8. Anemia
9. Colon cancer
10. High blood pressure
11. High cholesterol
12. Migraines and Headaches
13. Chronic Fatigue Syndrome
14. Low energy
15. Obesity

16. Allergies
17. Halitosis
18. Irritable Bowel Syndrome
19. Psychotic disorders
20. Anxiety and depression

All of the above symptoms and more have already been linked to the very hormones, chemicals and toxins that you have been consuming from your animal products. Just imagine how many more diseases and health conditions exist that are yet to be discovered to be in correlation with the consumption of these substances! If you know anyone who is suffering from the above conditions, they should highly consider switching to a vegan diet right away.

When you cease consumption of these hazardous industrial poisons, your body's elimination pathways (such as the skin, the liver, the intestines, etc.) begin to clear up and your body receives the signal that it's time to clean house! When this happens, the built-up poisons that are in your body right now will begin to be pulled from the tissues they are stored in and sent to the elimination pathways. Make no mistake, this is a good thing! However, it will seem like your symptoms get so much worse at first. This is because suddenly your body will be pushing all of the toxins into the very areas that they have been causing problems, during the process of flushing them out of your system.

The silver lining in the mushroom cloud is that the worse your detox symptoms are, the more promising your end results from eating a vegan diet will be! In other words, someone who has very little detox symptoms will see very little benefit in terms of health from following a vegan diet. On the other hand, if your detox symptoms practically knock you sick into bed, you are going to have a mind-blowing transformation when this stage has finished! People probably won't even recognize you, you'll look and feel so much better!

When you begin to detox, expect whatever conditions you have on the prior list to temporarily get worse before they get better or, in most cases, go away completely. In addition to that, other detox symptoms are the following.

A bloated, gassy feeling with frequent farting:

Your body is suddenly having to process a lot of built up poison that's being pulled into your liver, spleen and intestines. There should be no doubt that this will cause gas!

Skin rashes:

Many of the toxins you are eliminating have a tendency to stimulate your immune system and cause it to over-react. When this happens, you can expect the formation of some itchy rashes. There is no reason to fear as this is completely normal and temporary.

Insomnia or difficulty sleeping:

When your body is working so hard to digest, process and remove these substances, you are more than likely going to be hard pressed to sleep adequately. Use an over-the-counter sleeping aid during this stage, if you absolutely must, but be careful not to become addicted to it.

Extra trips to the bathroom:

This is one of the clearest signs that your body is eliminating stored up waste! When you have to rush to the restroom once or twice an hour, you can rest assured that the body is tapping into the reservoir of poison that has been making you sick and doing its absolute best to flush it out. Drink at least a gallon of water a day during this stage to assist the body with removing waste from its preferred elimination channels so you can minimize the severity of the other detox effects.

POSITIVE SIDE EFFECTS

Do not fear. This initial stage of switching to a vegan diet is not all earthquakes and tsunamis! There is actually a lot to be enjoyed during this stage, even in the face of the horrible yet temporary detox symptoms. The following is a list of what you can expect in terms of positive changes that you will experience within the first few weeks.

1. Weight loss
2. Better fingernails and toenails
3. A healthy glow to your skin
4. Less body odor and an overall cleaner smell
5. Gradual, yet consistent increases in your energy
6. Less severe PMS symptoms
7. Fruits taste more intense and vivid
8. A happy and positive outlook on life
9. Increased sexual desire
10. Increased athletic performance
11. Improved mental functioning
12. Cravings for healthy foods

To conclude, yes there are going to be a few unpleasant experiences at the onset of this journey, but in the long run, it will pay dividends for the quality of your life! At the end of the day, you must choose your suffering. You are faced with two choices. The first is to continue living exactly as you have been and suffer the continued and gradual decay of your health without remedy. The second option is to pick up your vegan sword and join the fight to reclaim your health today. It is a battle for sure, but if you stay persistent, your body will inevitably eliminate the last of these industrial toxins and your mind, body and soul will be completely transformed. Your old life of sickness, suffering and misery will pass away and you will be reborn in the image of your wildest dreams.

Chapter 4: Breakfast Recipes

This section of the cookbook is dedicated to hearty vegan breakfast recipes to kickstart your day! You'll find an abundance of fruits, breakfast grains like oatmeal and millet for fiber and a host of other sweet and delectable ingredients. You know what they say – breakfast is the most important meal of the day!

You will notice that the calories as well as the grams of protein, fat and carbohydrates per each recipe are listed right beneath the name. The macronutrients listed correspond with the designated serving size. For example, if a recipe has servings listed as 4, then the total yield should be divided into fourths. If a recipe has servings listed as 6, then divide the total yield of the recipe into six different portions.

Breakfast Fruit Salad

Ready In: 5-10 minutes

Servings: 6   Calories: 128   Protein: 1.7g   Carbs: 33.2g   Fat: 0.5g

If you're in a hurry and don't have time to spend on an elaborate breakfast, this is the one for you. It's sure to delight your taste buds and offer a vast array of powerful antioxidants from the blueberries and grapes. If you choose to combine this breakfast with your favorite vegan protein source, the bromelain in the pineapple will boost protein synthesis which will help you get even more health value out of it.

Ingredients:

- 1 cup red seedless grapes
- 1 cup green seedless grapes
- 4 plums, pitted and chopped
- 1 pint blueberries
- 15 oz. Canned pineapple chunks
- 1 peeled cantaloupe
- ½ watermelon

Directions:

1. If you bought your watermelon and cantaloupe whole, rather than in chunks, use a baller to hollow each of them out and mix them in a large bowl. I recommend buying them pre-chunked to save time.
2. Rinse and drain your blueberries, pineapple chunks, plums and grapes.
3. Add your drained and rinsed fruit to the bowl with the chunked watermelon and cantaloupe.

Popeye's Breakfast Quiche

Ready In: 45 minutes

Servings: 4   Calories: 259   Protein: 10.2g   Carbs: 22.9g   Fat: 15g

It's called Popeye's for a reason. This delicious little number is packed full of spinach which contains a broad spectrum of vitamins from Vitamin A, Vitamin K to Vitamin E. It's also rich in manganese, potassium, iron and copper. All of these are essential to building big strong muscles, just like Popeye's! Not only is this breakfast a healthy choice for bodybuilders, but it's also packed full of flavor from the soy cheese to the onion and garlic. Most importantly, this is a quiche without eggs – of course, it's completely vegan!

Ingredients:

- 1 9" pie crust (unbaked)
- 1 cup soy cheese (whichever flavor you choose, cheddar recommended)
- ¼ cup diced onions
- 1 tsp. Minced garlic
- 10 oz. Frozen, chopped spinach
- ½ tsp. Black pepper
- ½ tsp. Sea salt
- 1/3 cup 1% soy milk
- 8 oz. Tofu

Directions:

1. Set your oven to preheat to 350°F (175°C)
2. Mix your tofu and soy milk in a blender. Blend the two together until the texture is smooth. Add in your sea salt and pepper while blending.
3. In a bowl, prepare a mixture of your spinach (properly rinsed), tofu and soy milk mixture, soy cheese(s), garlic and onion. Mix evenly and then pour into your pie crust.
4. Bake for 30 minutes at 350°F (175°C). If after 30 minutes, the top is not a nice golden-brown color, continue to check every few minutes until it is.
5. Let sit and cool for 5 minutes.

Vegan Pancakes

Ready In: 15 minutes

Servings: 4   Calories: 197   Protein: 4g   Carbs: 36.75g   Fat: 3.9g

Why shouldn't people who care about the environment be able to enjoy pancakes? With this quick and easy recipe, now you can too! Chances are if you're going out to eat at your favorite breakfast restaurant, then their pancakes are not entirely vegan. With this simple recipe, you can enjoy all the flavor with none of the guilt. Bon Appetit!

Ingredients:

- 1 tablespoon olive oil
- 1 ¼ cups water
- ½ teaspoon sea salt
- 2 tsp. Baking powder
- 2 tbsp. White sugar
- 1 ¼ cups all-purpose flour

Directions:

1. Put your water in a small bowl and add your oil. Whisk the two together.
2. In a large bowl, sift in the baking powder, sugar, salt and flour. Sift it all together and mix well.
3. Create a hole in the ingredients in the large bowl and pour the water and oil mixture into said hole.
4. Stir the full mixture (wet and dry) together until it is fully blended and a bit lumpy.
5. On medium-high heat, heat a mildly oiled griddle. When the griddle is heated, place large spoonfuls of the batter on the griddle and allow to cook until the spoonfuls begin to bubble and the edges become dry. Flip over and repeat on the other side.
6. Continue until all of the batter is used up.

Vegan Crepes

Ready In: 2 hours, 25 minutes

Servings: 4   Calories: 266   Protein: 4.2g   Carbs: 34.8g   Fat: 12.2g

If you love crepes, these vegan variety are just as delicious as you remember non-vegan crepes being. The rich texture created by the blend of soy margarine and turbinado sugar will dance across your palette, waking up your tongue and singing good morning to your taste buds. Add maple syrup and this really does taste like the beginning of a great day!

Ingredients:

- ¼ tsp. Sea salt
- 1 cup unbleached all-purpose flour
- 2 tbsp. Maple syrup
- 1 tbsp. Turbinado sugar
- ¼ cup melted soy margarine
- ½ cup water
- ½ cup soy milk

Directions:

1. Prepare a large mixing bowl full of your soy milk, water, salt, flour, sugar, syrup and margarine. Blend well. Cover and let chill for 2 hours.
2. Grease a 6-inch skillet (5 inches is okay) with soy margarine. Place skillet over heat source and allow to become hot.
3. Once skillet is properly heated, pour 3 tbsp. of the batter into the center of skillet.
4. Use a spoon or spatula to swirl until the entire bottom of the skillet is covered.
5. Allow to sit until golden and then flip and repeat on the other side.

Southern Fried Potatoes

Ready In: 25 minutes

Servings: 5   Calories: 428   Protein: 7.5g   Carbs: 70g   Fat: 14.2g

These succulent taters make a great side dish for *any meal,* but especially for a hearty breakfast! They're so nourishing and filling that you can even make them a standalone breakfast, if you so choose. The paprika and garlic do well to complement the natural flavor of breakfast potatoes that we've all grown to know and love. Add maple syrup, vegan sour cream or both as a topping to add even more meaning to this luscious dish.

Ingredients:

- ½ tsp. Paprika
- ½ tsp. Garlic powder
- ½ tsp. Ground black pepper
- 1 tsp. Sea salt
- 6 large potatoes
- 1/3 cup shortening

Directions:

1. Heat your 1/3 cup of shortening over medium-high heat in a cast iron skillet.
2. Cut and peel your 6 large potatoes, while shortening is heating.
3. Add potatoes to shortening, in the skillet, and stir frequently allowing the potatoes to cook to a nice and crisp golden-brown color.
4. Add the paprika, garlic, pepper and sea salt for seasoning.

Scrambled Tofu

Ready In: 25 minutes

Servings: 4   Calories: 359   Protein: 17.6g   Carbs: 59.8g   Fat: 13g

One of the most requested breakfast dishes for vegans is an alternative to our beloved scrambled eggs. Who needs scrambled eggs when you can enjoy the same loaded flavor in a healthier dish with tofu and turmeric? Introducing scrambled tofu! Turmeric is a powerful antifungal, antibacterial and antiviral, so if you're coming down with a cold, give this breakfast a spin. You may even find this protein-packed breakfast is so pleasing to the bite that you never miss eating eggs again!

Ingredients:

- ½ cup shredded soy cheese (cheddar flavor recommended)
- Salt and pepper
- Ground turmeric
- 12 oz. Tofu (silken, drained and mashed)
- 14.5 oz. Peeled and sliced tomatoes (with juice)
- 1 cluster green onions (chopped)
- 1 tbsp. Olive oil (extra virgin preferred)

Directions:

1. Set a medium-sized skillet on medium heat and add your olive oil.
2. Sauté green onions in skillet to the point of tenderness.
3. Toss in the tomatoes with the juice included and also throw in your mashed tofu.
4. Add in your seasonings of salt and pepper and be extra generous with the turmeric.
5. Lower heat and allow dish to simmer until fully heated through.
6. Top with shredded soy cheese of your favorite flavor.

Celiac-Friendly Banana Bread

Ready In: 45 minutes

Servings: 16   Calories: 188   Protein: 2.8g   Carbs: 29.4g   Fat: 7.3g

Do you or a loved one have Celiac's disease or does consuming gluten give you issues? If so, treat yourself to this mouth-watering banana bread and feel deprived no more! Using the power of Flegg (1 tbsp. ground flax seed mixed with 3 tbsp. water), you can enjoy a belly full of banana bread without gluten issues and without violating your vegan conscience.

Ingredients:

- 6 bananas, mashed
- 3 tbsp. Maple syrup
- 2 eggs equivalent of Flegg, lightly beaten (2 tbsp. flax meal mixed with 6 tbsp. water)
- ½ cup turbinado sugar
- ½ cup vegan butter
- ½ tsp. Sea salt
- 1 tsp. Baking powder
- 2 cups gluten-free all-purpose baking flour

Directions:

1. Set your oven to preheat to 350°F (175°C) and grease a 9" bread loaf pan.
2. Create a mixture of your baking powder, flour and salt in a large sized bowl.
3. In a second bowl, create a creamy mixture of the butter and sugar. Add in the Flegg, maple syrup and mashed bananas. Mix well.
4. Add the contents of each bowl together and mix until the matter is just a tad bit moist.
5. Pour the resulting batter into your pre-greased 9" pan.
6. Bake at 350°F (175°C) for 20 to 30 minutes or until a toothpick poked into the center comes out without debris.

Breakfast Pudding with Raisins

Ready In: 20 minutes

Servings: 6   Calories: 484   Protein: 10.6g   Carbs: 95.4g   Fat: 7.3g

For just twenty minutes out of your morning, you can enjoy this creamy cinnamon and rice breakfast pudding with raisins. The sliced almonds are there for more than just a challenging crunch – they are also a great source of protein that ensures you're going to have the energy you need to power through the rest of your day.

Ingredients:

- ½ tsp. Ground cardamom
- 1 tsp. Ground cinnamon
- ½ cup toasted almonds, chopped
- 1 cup soy milk
- ¼ cup maple syrup
- ½ cup raisins
- 3 cups cooked brown rice
- 1 cup water

Directions:

1. In a pan on your stove, mix your almonds, cinnamon, cardamom, soy milk, maple syrup, raisins and rice.
2. Bring mixture to a boil over medium-high heat.
3. At point of boiling, reduce heat down to low and allow the dish to simmer.
4. Continuously stir, to prevent scorching, until the pudding has thickened.

Flax & Pumpkin Bread

Ready In: 1 hour, 20 minutes

Servings: 16   Calories: 132   Protein: 1.7g   Carbs: 31.1g   Fat: 0.5g

This recipe is a bit on the longer side, being an hour and twenty minutes, but it is so worth the wait. Reap all of the medicinal benefits of flax seed while enjoying the moist crumbly texture of this delicious pumpkin bread. Layer on some vegan butter and this recipe serves as a great side to a scrambled tofu and vegan pancake breakfast!

Ingredients:

- ¼ tsp. Ground cloves
- ½ tsp. Ground nutmeg
- ½ tsp. Baking powder
- ¾ tsp. Salt
- 1 tsp. Ground cinnamon
- 1 tsp baking soda
- 1/3 cup whole wheat pastry flour
- 1 1/3 cup all-purpose flour
- ½ cup applesauce
- 1 cup canned pumpkin puree
- 1 ½ cups sugar
- 6 tbsp. Water
- 2 tbsp. Flax seed meal

Directions:

1. Set your oven to preheat to 350°F (175°C) and grease a 9" bread loaf pan.
2. Mix your water and flax seed meal together in a whisking fashion.
3. Gradually add in your applesauce, sugar and pumpkin puree.
4. In a bowl, prepare a combination of your cloves, nutmeg, baking powder, salt, cinnamon, baking soda, whole wheat flour and all-purpose flour. Stir into a mixture.
5. Add the two mixtures (the pumpkin puree mixture with the flour mixture) together. Stir the two together until the resulting texture is smooth.
6. Allow to bake at 350°F (175°C) for 65 to 70 minutes. You'll know it is finished when a toothpick inserted at the center can be pulled out without debris.

Molten Hot Fava Spread

Ready In: 20 minutes

Servings: 5   Calories: 348   Protein: 23.1g   Carbs: 54.2g   Fat: 5.7g

Enjoy a well-seasoned spread that is loaded with protein and nutrients and overflowing with flavor. This delicious dish is great as a side for any breakfast, a topping for your favorite vegan bread *or* a standalone breakfast in and of itself. Feel free to sprinkle it with your favorite vegan cheeses, if you wish. This dish goes excellent in a pita!

Ingredients:

- Ground red pepper, or crushed
- Salt and pepper
- ¼ cup lemon juice, fresh
- ¼ cup chopped parsley
- 1 large tomato, diced
- 1 chopped-up large onion
- 1 ½ tbsp. Extra virgin olive oil, organic
- 15 oz. Fava beans

Directions:

1. In a large pot of water, add your beans and bring them to a boil.
2. Reduce heat to a low simmer.
3. Mix in your tomatoes, onions, olive oil, parsley, fresh lemon juice, cumin, black pepper and crushed or ground red pepper.
4. Bring your ingredients back to the boiling point and then reduce the heat once again, but to medium heat.
5. Allow your pot to cook for 5 more minutes.

Rosemary Potatoes

Ready In: 45 minutes

Servings: 4   Calories: 368   Protein: 7.1g   Carbs: 61.3g   Fat: 13.2g

Who even needs hash browns when you can enjoy these delicately flavored, superbly seasoned little mouthfuls of goodness? These are more than your standard breakfast potatoes. These are seasoned in such a way that they not only taste better than your average breakfast potatoes, but are also packing a load of medicinal benefits from the rosemary and organic extra virgin olive oil. If you can stand the challenging hint of apple cider vinegar, feel free to lightly drizzle the final product in it to maximize your fat burning capacity.

Ingredients:

- Salt and pepper for flavor
- ¼ cup organic extra virgin olive oil
- 1 tbsp. Rosemary, dried
- 8 Yukon gold potatoes, cut into quarter slices

Directions:

1. Set your oven to preheat to 350°F (175°C).
2. Grab a large bowl and place the rosemary, oil, pepper and salt in it on top of the quartered potatoes. Shake and toss bowl to coat the potatoes thoroughly.
3. Lay the coated potatoes out onto a cookie sheet.
4. Bake for 30 minutes at 350°F (175°C).

Eggplant Bacon

Ready In: 6 hours, 25 minutes

Servings: 5   Calories: 111   Protein: 1.9g   Carbs: 14.1g   Fat: 5.9g

Have you ever found yourself missing the taste of crispy bacon since you made your conversion to veganism? Have you ever wished there was such a thing as bacon that wouldn't cause animal grease to get all over your hands and face while eating it? Perhaps you like the grease. Either way, this is your solution. You won't believe how good this eggplant bacon tastes until you invest the time to try it!

Ingredients:

- 2 tbsp. Brown sugar replacement
- 2 tbsp. Organic extra virgin olive oil
- 1 Chinese eggplant, slice very thin in length (like bacon)
- 1 small dash of cayenne pepper
- ½ tsp. Chili powder
- ½ tsp. Paprika
- 4 drops liquid smoke
- 1 tbsp. Maple syrup
- 3 tbsp. Barbecue sauce
- ¼ cup low-sodium soy sauce

Directions:

1. Mix your marinade. Combine your barbecue sauce with your soy sauce, 1 tbsp. Olive oil (save the other tablespoon for later), liquid smoke, syrup, paprika, cayenne pepper and chili powder in a dish.
2. Add in your eggplant slices. Be sure to coat each slice as equally and evenly as possible.
3. Leave in the refrigerator to marinate for 6 hours. If you have time, 12 hours works better.
4. Set your oven to preheat to 400°F (200°C).
5. Warm up your second tablespoon of olive oil in a skillet on medium-low heat.
6. Add in your eggplant slices and cook until they are thoroughly browned. This should take approximately 5 minutes on each side.
7. Lay your eggplant bacon slices on a cookie sheet. Top generously with brown sugar replacement.
8. Allow to roast in oven at 400°F (200°C) until the color is dark brown. This should take approximately 5 to 10 minutes.

● ●

DID YOU KNOW?

The Japanese people have a proverb that says, "The happiest omen for a New Year is first Mount Fuji, then the falcon, and lastly the eggplant."

● ●

Tater-Cakes

Ready In: 50 minutes

Servings: 6   Calories: 519.8   Protein: 11.4g   Carbs: 81g   Fat: 18.38g

This recipe is yet another great substitute for hash browns. Why choose between potatoes and pancakes when you can more or less have both? The texture of these little numbers is delicate, crispy and crumbly and they tend to just melt in your mouth. As you would do with a normal pancake, top these with maple syrup to complete the effect. Best served hot.

Ingredients:

- Extra virgin olive oil
- Salt and pepper
- 2 cups dried bread crumbs
- 2 tbsp. All-purpose flour
- ¼ cup organic extra-virgin olive oil
- 2 tbsp. Fresh lemon juice
- 1 tbsp. Fresh dill, chopped
- 1 tbsp. Flat leaf parsley, chopped
- 5 cloves crushed garlic
- 1 onion, diced
- 1 peeled carrot, shredded
- 10 peeled russet potatoes, shredded

Directions:

1. Combine your potatoes with your dill, parsley, garlic, onion and carrots in a bowl. Mix the lemon juice in as well as ¼ cup of the olive oil, flour, salt, pepper and bread crumbs.
2. Work it with your hands until the mixture begins to hold together on its own.
3. Set a skillet on medium heat and add in the extra ¼ cup of olive oil.
4. Begin to drop spoonful-sized batches of the potato mix into the heated olive oil.
5. Allow to cook 5 minutes per side or until the pancakes become a nice golden-brown color.

Fruity & Tangy Oats

Ready In: 7 minutes

Servings: 2   Calories: 158   Protein: 4.5g   Carbs: 30.7g   Fat: 2.2g

The simplest breakfasts are often the most enjoyable. It's no different for this nutrient-packed bowl of anti-oxidants and fiber. The sweet taste of blueberry, cranberry and orange do wonders to bring the otherwise-average flavor of oatmeal to life. If that isn't enough, ground cinnamon and ginger liven it up even further. This is the perfect breakfast for someone strapped for time and in a hurry.

Ingredients:

- ¼ cup orange juice
- 1 cup water
- 1 pinch ground ginger
- ¼ tsp. Ground turmeric
- ½ cup blueberries, frozen
- ¼ cup cranberries, dried
- ½ tsp. Ground cinnamon
- ¾ cup old-fashioned rolled oats

Directions:

1. Pour the oatmeal, turmeric, ginger, cinnamon, blueberries and cranberries into an adequate-sized bowl.
2. Pour your 1 cup of water into bowl of oats.
3. Microwave on high for about 2 minutes.
4. Add in orange juice and stir until you achieve the consistency you want.

Fat Guy Panikeke

Ready In: 40 minutes

Servings: 28   Calories: 514.7   Protein: 1.7g   Carbs: 23.6g   Fat: 46.89g

What's a panikeke you ask? It's essentially an orgasmic ball of deliciousness. It includes mashed bananas, flour and a whole ton of sugar – hence the name Fat Guy Panikeke. This may not be one of the recipes you choose to eat daily, if weight loss is your concern, but once-a-week or so, this makes for a delicious treat to go along with your breakfast! You read that right, by the way – 14,412 calories if you eat the whole batch! I don't use the prefix "fat guy" on a recipe's name lightly.

Ingredients:

- 6 cups vegetable oil
- 1 ½ cups water
- 1 tbsp. Vanilla extract
- 2 bananas, mashed
- 2 tsp. Baking powder
- 1 1/3 cup white sugar
- 3 ½ cups all-purpose flour

Directions:

1. Grab a large bowl and mix in the flour, sugar and baking powder until it is mixed completely.
2. In a stirring motion, mix in the bananas, water and vanilla extract until the resulting consistency of the dough is smooth and sticky.
3. In a large saucepan or deep fryer, heat your vegetable oil to 350°F (175°C). Use enough oil to fully immerse the panikekes while frying.
4. With a spoon, scoop up ¼ cup of the batter and use a second spoon to push it off into the vegetable oil.
5. The best results come from frying batches of 3 or 4 at a time. Fry until they turn golden-brown and float to the top of the oil. When this happens, then flip them over and fry their other sides.

Good Morning Millet

Ready In: 1 hour, 30 minutes

Servings: 4   Calories: 328   Protein: 7.6g   Carbs: 62.3g   Fat: 6.1g

Talk about a great source of fiber! If you choose Good Morning Millet as your breakfast, you are getting 17 grams of fiber at the start of your day. If you suffer with constipation, then this is your solution. Not only is this recipe great for keeping things moving, but it also tastes fantastic. Chopped dates and coconut add great flavor to the mixture.

Ingredients:

- 1 tsp. Vanilla extract
- ½ cup flaked coconut
- 2/3 cup chopped dates
- 5 ½ cups hot water
- ½ cup soy milk powder
- 1 cup dry millet

Directions:

1. Set your oven to 350°F (175°C) for preheating.
2. Add your soy milk powder, chopped dates, coconut, hot water and vanilla to the top of your millet in a 9" casserole dish.
3. Bake at 350°F (175°C) for 30 minutes.
4. Remove the casserole from oven and stir.
5. Place back in oven and let it cook an additional 30 minutes.

Avocado Toast

Ready In: 10 minutes

Servings: 4   Calories: 199   Protein: 5.2g   Carbs: 18.5g   Fat: 12.6g

If you're looking for a great source of healthy fats and flavor, look no further. In 10 minutes, you can be feasting upon a slice of toast topped with a savory, well-seasoned spread of avocado, parsley, onion and garlic. Not only does this topping go well on store-bought wheat bread, but it also goes great on any of the breads contained in this recipe book.

Ingredients:

- ½ tsp. Garlic powder
- ½ tsp. Onion powder
- ½ tsp. Ground black pepper
- ½ tsp. Salt
- ½ lemon, juiced
- 1 ½ tsp. Organic extra virgin olive oil
- 1 avocado, cut in half with pit removed
- 4 slices bread of your choice, wheat in calorie count

Directions:

1. Toast your bread in the toaster.
2. In a large bowl, mix well your avocado with garlic powder, onion powder, pepper, salt, lemon juice, olive oil and parsley.
3. Spread onto each slice of your toast.

Blueberry Pecan Granola

Ready In: 1 hour, 45 minutes

Servings: 4   Calories: 403   Protein: 8.7g   Carbs: 54.8g   Fat: 16.6g

Nothing beats good old-fashioned granola when it comes to breakfast or a snack on the hiking trail. The sweet marriage of blueberry and pecan, with brown sugar replacement and cinnamon, tango with a bit of applesauce and dried apricots in this incredible meal that makes for a great breakfast or a quick treat to stop and eat on your favorite hiking trail. Simply pour it from bowl to Ziploc baggy and you have yourself a snack to take to the great outdoors that won't go bad in the sun!

Ingredients:

- 3 tbsp. flax seeds, ground
- ¼ cup pecans, chopped
- ¼ cup diced and dried apricots
- 3 tbsp. Maple syrup
- ¼ cup applesauce
- 3 tbsp. Canola oil
- ¾ tsp. Ground ginger
- 1 tsp. Ground cinnamon
- ½ cup brown sugar replacement, packed
- ½ cup spelt flour
- 2 cups rolled oats
- 1 cup blueberries

Directions:

1. Set your oven to 300°F (150°C) for preheating.
2. In a large bowl, mix your spelt flour, flax seed, pecans, apricots, syrup, applesauce, canola oil, ginger, cinnamon and brown sugar with your rolled oats by tossing it together.
3. On a lined baking sheet, spread the granola mix as evenly as possible.
4. Allow to bake at 300°F (150°C) for 20 minutes.
5. Stir the granola and then bake for an additional 15 minutes.
6. Allow to fully cool and top with blueberries.

Super-Mangu

Ready In: 40 minutes

Servings: 4   Calories: 306   Protein: 2.1g   Carbs: 54.8g   Fat: 16.6g

You may have never heard of mangu before, but that's the whole point of this book – learning, discovering and growing while simultaneously pleasing your taste buds. Mangu is a popular breakfast in the Dominican Republic. Make no mistake though, this is no ordinary mangu. This is *super-mangu,* which has been named as such because it is vegan and therefore healthier and better equipped for someone who is environmentally conscious. Don't be afraid to explore and try new things. I promise this is a dish you will be glad you experimented with!

Ingredients:

- 1 cup sliced Anaheim peppers
- 1 ½ tbsp. Salt
- 1 cup sliced white onion
- ¼ cup organic extra virgin olive oil
- 1 quart water
- 3 plantains, green

Directions:

1. Take a saucepan and toss the plantains and water into it.
2. Bring the saucepan to a boil and allow to cook for 20 minutes or however long it takes for the plantains to be soft, but still slightly firm.
3. Drain the saucepan, keeping 1 cup of the liquid.
4. After the plantains have cooled off, peel each of them.
5. In a skillet on medium-heat, heat up your olive oil and then use it to sauté the onion until it is tenderized.
6. Mash the tenderized plantains with salt and the preserved liquid.
7. Put the mash in a blender with your puree and peppers and blend into a puree.
8. Lay the sautéed onions on top of the puree and it's ready to serve.

Face of Fasolia

Ready In: 40 minutes

Servings: 4   Calories: 475   Protein: 24.9g   Carbs: 70.8g   Fat: 12g

Fasolia is one of the more ethnic dishes in this book as it hails from the Arabic regions of the world. It is a traditional breakfast of the Arabic people, but it has also been known to be served at lunch or at dinner as well. Why would you limit such a delicious meal to *just* breakfast? This is one of those meals that are great at any time of the day. It's loaded with kidney beans, curry and a whole host of deeply flavored ingredients.

Ingredients:

- Salt and pepper
- 1 ½ tsp. Curry powder
- 1 ½ tsp. Ground cumin
- 15 oz. Dark red kidney beans, undrained
- 2 tsp. Tomato paste
- 1 chopped tomato
- 1 chopped jalapeno pepper
- 1 chopped large onion
- 3 tbsp. Organic extra virgin olive oil

Directions:

1. Put a large skillet on medium heat and add olive oil
2. Add in the onion and allow to cook till tender, while stirring frequently, until clear. This should take about 5 minutes.
3. Add the jalapeno and stir until it has become tender, which should take an additional 5 minutes.
4. Add the tomato and paste and stir together well with onion and jalapeno.
5. Dump the kidney beans and the kidney bean juice into the mixture.
6. Mix in the curry and cumin and stir well.
7. Bring the dish to a boil, then lower the heat down to medium-low and allow to simmer until the beans are fully hot and the sauce is thick. This should take about 10 to 20 minutes.

● ● ● ● ● ● ● ● ● ● ● ● ● ● ● ● ● ● ● ●

DID YOU KNOW?

While fasolia is more commonly eaten by Arabic populations today, it actually has its origins from Greek history. In fact, it used to be called the 'national food of the Greeks'.

● ● ● ● ● ● ● ● ● ● ● ● ● ● ● ● ● ● ● ●

Akki Rotti

Ready In: 1 day, 50 minutes

Servings: 6   Calories: 402.3   Protein: 4.68g   Carbs: 47.2g   Fat: 21.3g

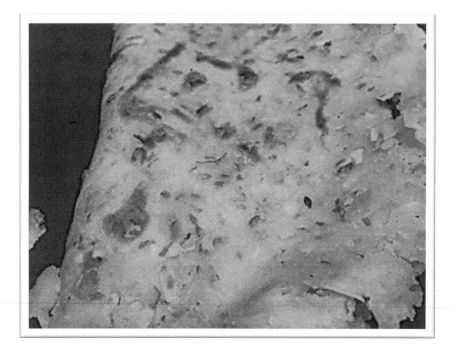

Akki Rotti is a southern Indian-style breakfast that is packed full of mung beans, carrots, cumin seeds, cilantro and a variety of other vitamin-loaded ingredients. If you think it sounds too healthy to possibly taste good, you're about to be proven wrong! This dish is best served while still hot and is complemented if you choose to serve it with a bowl of soup.

Ingredients:

- ½ cup vegetable oil, divided
- Salt
- ¼ cup carrots, shredded
- ½ cup coconut, shredded
- 2 tbsp. Cilantro, chopped
- ¼ tsp asafoetida powder
- 2 ½ tsp. green chili peppers, chopped
- 1 tsp. Cumin seeds
- 2 cups white rice flour
- 1 cup water
- ½ cup green mung beans

Directions:

1. Place the mung beans in a small bowl and immerse them in fresh water. Place bowl in the refrigerator to sit overnight.
2. The following day, drain the water from the beans and save the water they were soaking in for later.
3. Mix the mung beans with the rice flour, cumin seeds, salt, shredded carrots, shredded coconut, cilantro, asafoetida and green chili peppers.
4. Slowly begin to pour in the water you saved. Knead the mixture together with your hands in order to form a dough. Do not use too much water! ½ cup should be plenty.
5. With your hands, shape the dough into small ball-shaped chunks. The balls should be a little smaller than a baseball each.
6. Take a portion of the dough and flatten it into a thin circle shape.
7. Use your skillet to heat about 2 tablespoons of vegetable oil on medium heat.
8. Take the thin circle shape (the rotti) and put it in the oil and fry it about 30 to 40 seconds so it is golden-brown. Then flip it to the other side and repeat.
9. Repeat this process with the remaining balls of dough, while adding an additional 2 tablespoons of vegetable oil for each rotti.

Chocolate Vegan Scones

Ready In: 35 minutes

Servings: 5   Calories: 433.4   Protein: 5.8g   Carbs: 62.6g   Fat: 17.5g

What is tastier than scones? What is tastier than chocolate? Scones *with* chocolate, of course! These moist scones are riddled with chocolate chips and hazelnuts giving you a nice combination of chew and crunch. The key to these vegan scones is a balance between vegan butter, flour, sugar and baking powder among other ingredients. These sweet morsels make for an excellent breakfast or even brunch. There's no bad time for a scone – especially one with chocolate chips!

Ingredients:

- 1/3 cup dark chocolate chips
- 2/3 cup So Delicious Dairy Free Hazelnut Coconut Milk Creamer
- 6 tbsp. Vegan butter
- ½ tsp. Baking soda
- ½ tsp. Salt
- 1 ½ tsp. Baking powder
- ¼ cup sugar
- 2 cups all-purpose flour

Directions:

1. Set your oven to 425°F (218°C) for preheating.
2. Use parchment paper to line a cookie sheet.
3. Mix the flour, baking powder, sugar, baking soda and salt together in a bowl. Shake and toss to sift together.
4. Mix vegan butter into the concoction with your hands until the mixture becomes large and coarse crumbs about the size of granules of corn.
5. Sprinkle in your chocolate chips and your So Delicious creamer. Mix together until it is barely moistened.
6. Lightly flour a surface and put the dough on it. Work it together with your hands until the dough sticks together in the shape of a sphere.
7. Flatten the sphere of dough into a 2" thick circle with a 6" diameter.
8. Allow the dough to sit at room temperature for 20 minutes.
9. Cut it into 5 slices.
10. Top with the remainder of sugar.
11. Bake at 425°F (218°C) for 18 minutes or until it has become a golden-brown color.
12. Allow to cool off.

● ●

DID YOU KNOW?

According to the English Oxford Dictionary, the word 'scones' was originally used as a name for cake in 1513.

● ●

French Toast

Ready In: 20 minutes

Servings: 4   Calories: 133   Protein: 7.2g   Carbs: 20.8g   Fat: 2.2g

Who could have guessed you could have such delectable and authentic-tasting French toast without even needing eggs or cow milk? This overwhelmingly simple French toast recipe will surprise you as much as it delights you. This is the breakfast of choice if you are strapped for time, but still are in the mood for something more exciting than oatmeal or plain toast.

Ingredients:

- 4 slices of wheat bread
- 1/3 tsp. Ground cinnamon
- 1 tsp. Vanilla extract
- 1 tsp. Raw sugar
- 1 tbsp. Nutritional yeast
- 2 tbsp. All-purpose flour
- 1 cup soy milk

Directions:

1. In a small bowl, whisk together your soy milk with the cinnamon, vanilla extract, sugar, nutritional yeast and flour.
2. Pour the resulting mixture into a shallow dish.
3. Soak each side of each slice of bread in the mixture.
4. Place the soaked bread slices in an oiled skillet and cook on medium-low heat until each slice is golden-brown. This should take about 3 to 4 minutes on each side.

Choco-Cocoats

Ready In: 8 hours, 5 minutes

Servings: 2   Calories: 221   Protein: 4.5g   Carbs: 34.1g   Fat: 7.4g

If oatmeal is your jam and you have the time, this is the recipe I recommend. This recipe takes a bit longer to prepare, because these oats are overnight oats, but oh how the taste difference is so worth the extra eight hours! What you're looking at here might not look too impressive to the eye, but you will be completely caught off guard by how delicious this simple recipe is. Allow the chocolate to swirl together with the coconut shavings and chia seeds for a crunchy, yet soft and palpable way to start your day with a rush of sweetness.

Ingredients:

- 1 cup chocolate-flavored almond milk
- 1 splash vanilla extract
- 1 tbsp. Unsweetened cocoa powder
- 1 tbsp. Maple syrup
- 1 tbsp. Shredded and sweetened coconut
- 1 tbsp. Chia seeds
- ¾ cup old-fashioned rolled oats

Directions:

1. Prepare a 12 oz. Mason jar and fill it with your milk, vanilla extract, cocoa powder, syrup, shredded coconut, chia seeds and, of course, your oats. Stir and mix the ingredients together well.
2. Seal shut with a lid and place in refrigerator.
3. Refrigerate jar of oats overnight or for 8 hours.
4. In the morning, stir again with a spoon and eat cold.

Sweet Potato Biscuits

Ready In: 40 minutes

Servings: 6   Calories: 136.5   Protein: 2.8g   Carbs: 21.4g   Fat: 4.9g

These light fluffy sweet potato biscuits are a perfect side for any vegan breakfast and go great topped with vegan butter or vegan sour cream. If vegan butter and vegan sour cream are not available in your neck of the woods, they taste equally as incredibly when topped with maple syrup. Don't be afraid to get creative!

Ingredients:

- ¼ cup cashew milk
- 2 tbsp. Coconut oil
- ½ tsp. Ground cinnamon
- ½ tsp. Salt
- ½ tsp. Baking soda
- 2 tsp. White sugar
- 1 tbsp. Baking powder
- ½ cup whole wheat flour
- ½ cup white whole wheat flour
- 1 sweet potato

<u>Directions:</u>

1. Use a fork to punch holes over the entire surface of the sweet potato. Wrap it in plastic wrap and microwave on high for 2 minutes.
2. Turn the potato over and repeat another 2 minutes, so on and so forth until it is tender. This may take up to 10 minutes.
3. Allow sweet potato to cool.
4. Set your oven to 375°F (190°C) for preheating. Use parchment paper to line a cookie sheet.
5. Combine the whole wheat flour with the white whole wheat flour and the baking powder, baking soda, salt, cinnamon and sugar in a bowl. Using a pastry cutter, cut in the coconut oil until the mixture is about the size of granules of corn.
6. Peel the skin off of your potato and mash it up using a fork.
7. Scoop up ¾ cup of the sweet potato mash and stir it into the flour mixture.
8. Add in your cashew milk and mix it until the dough begins to become a bit adhesive.
9. Cover a surface with flour and manipulate the dough with your hands on the surface until it begins to come together. You may need to turn and knead it up to seven times for this to happen.
10. Cut the dough into rounds with a biscuit cutter and place them evenly spread apart on your cookie sheet.
11. Bake the biscuits at 375°F (190°C) for 13 to 17 minutes or until golden-browned.

● ●

DID YOU KNOW?

Vardaman, a town in Mississippi, is known as *The Sweet Potato Capital* and it holds an annual sweet potato festival every year in November.

● ●

Breakfast Oreo Donuts

Ready In: 35 minutes

Servings: 8   Calories: 576.2   Protein: 2.1g   Carbs: 64g   Fat: 36.5g

I couldn't decide whether this tasty recipe belonged in the Breakfast section or the Desserts section, but I realized more people eat donuts for breakfast than for dessert – so here it is! In order to win friends at the office, make enough to share with your co-workers and your boss. These vegan Oreo donuts are a great companion to a cup of your favorite coffee.

Ingredients:

- ¼ cup of crushed Oreos
- 2 tbsp. Coconut milk
- 4 oz. Shortening
- 4 oz. Vegan margarine of your choice
- 2 ½ cups confectioner's sugar
- ½ tsp. Vanilla extract
- 5 tbsp. Vegetable oil
- ½ cup water
- ¼ tsp. Salt
- ½ tsp. Baking soda
- ¼ cup cocoa powder
- ½ cup white sugar
- ¾ cup all-purpose flour
- Cooking spray

Directions:

1. Set your oven to 350°F (175°C) for preheating.
2. In a large enough bowl, prepare your mixture of sugar, flour, baking soda, cocoa powder and salt. Add in the vegetable oil, vanilla extract and water and stir until the consistency of the batter is smooth.
3. Pour the batter into a doughnut pan.
4. Bake in the preheated oven at 350°F (175°C) for 12 to 14 minutes.
5. Flip onto a wire rack and allow the donuts to cool for an additional 8 minutes.
6. In a second bowl, make a concoction of your vegan margarine, confectioner's sugar, coconut milk and shortening and beat it with an electric mixer. Continue until the resulting frosting is a fluffy and velvety texture.
7. Top your donuts with the frosting and sprinkle the Oreo crumbs on top.

Vegan Cinnamon Waffles

Ready In: 15 minutes

Servings: 8   Calories: 301   Protein: 4.8g   Carbs: 48.1g   Fat: 10.6g

This delicious waffle recipe can be prepared in as little as 15 minutes. Cinnamon is a great source of antioxidants, an excellent anti-inflammatory, fights diabetes and even protects your health. The addition of cinnamon to your ordinary waffles not only makes them taste a heck of a lot better, but it also promotes better health throughout your whole body. You can't go wrong taste or health-wise when you select this particular recipe for your breakfast!

Ingredients:

- ½ tsp. Salt
- 1 tbsp. Ground cinnamon
- 3 tbsp. Baking powder
- 3 tbsp. Apple cider vinegar
- 6 tbsp. White sugar
- 6 tbsp. Coconut oil, melted
- 2 cups water
- 3 cups all-purpose flour

Directions:

1. Fire up your waffle iron and allow it to heat up to full capacity.
2. Prepare a mixture of your salt, cinnamon, baking powder, apple cider vinegar, sugar, coconut oil and flour with the 2 cups of water.
3. Stir until the mixture forms a smooth batter.
4. Use a ladle to add the batter into your waffle iron and cook for about 5 minutes, or until the waffles become crisp.
5. Top with maple syrup and your selection of fresh fruit.

Chocolate Orange Muffins

Ready In: 40 minutes

Servings: 8   Calories: 331.2   Protein: 4.9g   Carbs: 62.1g   Fat: 7.9g

These vegan chocolate chip and mandarin orange-filled muffins have the perfect balance between moistness and crumbliness. The chocolate chips complement this further by adding a bit of crunch to keep things interesting. The best part is you don't even need a single egg to make a batch of these babies!

Ingredients:

- ¼ cup vegan milk chocolate chips
- ¼ cup vegetable oil
- 2 8 oz. Cans of mandarin orange pieces, drained, with juice saved
- ¼ tsp. Salt
- 2 tsp. Baking powder
- 1 cup uncooked quick oats
- 1 cup white sugar
- 2 cups all-purpose flour

Directions:

1. Set your oven to 375°F (190°C) for preheating.
2. Line a muffin pan with paper liners.
3. In a medium-sized bowl, beat your sugar, baking powder, flour and salt together.
4. Take 1 cup of the juice that you saved from your mandarin orange pieces and combine it with your vegetable oil. Stir well and then add it to your flour concoction.
5. Stir until well-mixed.
6. Add your chocolate chips and mandarin pieces into your batter mix.
7. Place spoonfuls of batter into the muffin cups.
8. Bake for 25 minutes or until golden-brown at 375°F (190°C).

Porridge of Quinoa

Ready In: 35 minutes

Servings: 4   Calories: 293   Protein: 5.1g   Carbs: 19.1g   Fat: 22.8g

Porridge of Quinoa actually has a leg up on most porridges in that quinoa is known to be a very high protein food. It is a bit tricky to get your daily requirement of protein on a vegan diet, so eating high protein choices like quinoa daily is essential. This healthy breakfast choice isn't just high in protein though! It's also jam packed with tasty goodness in the form of brown sugar replacement, cinnamon and whatever berries you decide to top it with.

Ingredients:

- 1 pinch of salt
- 1 tsp. Vanilla extract
- 2 tbsp. Brown sugar replacement
- ½ cup water
- 1 ½ cups almond milk
- ¼ tsp. Ground cinnamon
- ½ cup quinoa

Directions:

1. Set your stove top to medium heat and place a saucepan on top. Pour in your ½ cup of quinoa and water.
2. Add in your cinnamon and stir frequently for about 3 and a half minutes.
3. Add in your water, almond milk and vanilla and blend the brown sugar replacement and salt in evenly.
4. Bring the contents of the saucepan to a boil and then lower to low heat for about 25 minutes.
5. Add however much more water you need to, in order to prevent the liquid from drying up before it is finished.
6. Continue to stir so that it doesn't burn!

Lemon Scones with Poppy Seeds

Ready In: 35 minutes

Servings: 6   Calories: 480.8   Protein: 5.86g   Carbs: 61.5g   Fat: 24.8g

There's only ever one morning that you shouldn't eat one of these bad boys and that's the morning before a drug test! They contain poppy seeds which can cause your drug test to come back positive. Other than that, these lemon-flavored morsels are the perfect breakfast choice for any day of the week. Poppy seeds are a great source of calcium and iron, which makes this recipe a great way to meet two of the challenges of The Perfect Seven discussed in Chapter 1.

Ingredients:

- ½ cup water
- ½ cup soy milk
- 2 tbsp. Poppy seeds
- 1 lemon, juiced and zested
- ¾ cup vegan margarine
- ½ tbsp. Salt
- 4 tsp. Baking powder
- ¾ cup white sugar
- 2 cups all-purpose flour

Directions:

1. Set your oven to 400°F (200°C) for preheating.
2. Grease a cookie sheet.
3. Pour your sugar, flour, salt and baking powder together in a bowl and mix it all together by sifting it.
4. Begin adding in your vegan margarine until the consistency of your batter is similar to big granules of sand.
5. Dump in the lemon zest, lemon juice and poppy seeds and stir to blend.
6. In a glass, mix the water with the soy milk and then stir it into your batter until it is moistened, but has the consistency and thickness of dough. You probably won't need all of the water and soy milk that the recipe calls for!
7. Measure out ¼ cup-sized portions of batter and spread them out evenly on your baking sheet 2 to 4 inches apart from each other.
8. Bake at 400°F (200°C) for 12 to 15 minutes or until the color becomes golden.

Muesli

Ready In: 10 minutes

Servings: 6   Calories: 452   Protein: 16.6g   Carbs: 75.3g   Fat: 13g

Muesli is a recipe that you get to tap into your creative side when preparing! Feel free to choose whichever variety of dried fruit tickles your fancy, because any and all dried fruits taste incredible here. If you are a raw vegan, this is your dish as no cooking or baking is required. Simply mix the raw ingredients together and in just 10 minutes your muesli is ready-to-serve! This recipe makes for a great trail snack for you hikers out there.

Ingredients:

- 4 ½ cups rolled oats
- ½ cup toasted wheat germ
- ¼ cup raw sunflower seeds
- ¼ cup packed brown sugar replacement
- ½ cup walnuts, chopped
- 1 cup raisins
- ½ cup oat bran
- ½ cup wheat bran

Directions:

1. Prepare a large bowl
2. Fill the bowl with wheat germ, seeds, sugar, nuts, oat bran, wheat bran, rolled oats and whichever dried fruit you wish to add including raisins.
3. Mix well and store in an air-tight container. This muesli stores well at room temperature and can last from 6 to 8 weeks.

Oatmeal Pancakes with Chocolate

Ready In: 30 minutes

Servings: 6   Calories: 279   Protein: 6.3g   Carbs: 28.1g   Fat: 5.7g

This particular oatmeal pancake recipe is a vegan favorite throughout the community. It probably has earned the status of community favorite, because it is not only packed with fiber, but also contains a nice chocolatey crunch from the addition of vegan carob chips. Feel free to top with as much maple syrup as you wish!

Ingredients:

- 1 ½ cup soy milk
- ¼ cup vegan carob chips
- ¼ cup ground flax seeds
- ½ tsp. Sea salt
- ½ tsp. Baking soda
- 2 tsp. Baking powder
- ¾ cup pastry flour
- ¾ cup rolled oats

Directions:

1. Put a griddle on medium heat to allow it to preheat.
2. Mix your vegan carob chips, flax seeds, sea salt, baking soda, baking powder, pastry flour and rolled oats together in a bowl.
3. Use a ¼ cup measure to scoop up portions of batter and pour them onto the griddle.
4. Allow each portion of batter to cook for 1 to 2 minutes or until it begins to bubble, then flip the pancake and repeat on the other side.
5. Cook each pancake until golden-brown.
6. Top with maple syrup and serve!

Apple & Bran Muffins

Ready In: 40 minutes

Servings: 6   Calories: 318.5   Protein: 5.4g   Carbs: 67.1g   Fat: 5.7g

There is truly a lot of different flavors to be experienced when you pop one of these apple and bran muffins into your mouth: banana, apple, melted vegan butter, cinnamon, more apple, raisins, agave and did I mention apple? Apples are high in pectin, a powerful antioxidant. The cinnamon also has antioxidant properties which makes this delicious treat a surprising ally in clearing your body of toxic build-up. It tastes good and it's healthy – win / win!

Ingredients:

- ½ cup agave
- 1 ripe banana, mashed
- 1 apple, cored and shredded
- 2 tbsp. Melted vegan butter (whichever brand you choose)
- 1 tsp. Ground cinnamon
- 1 tsp. Baking soda
- 1 cup whole wheat flour
- 1 ½ cup bran breakfast cereal
- ¾ cup soy milk
- 1 egg's equivalent of Flegg (1 tbsp. flax meal mixed with 3 tbsp. water)
- ½ cup raisins

Directions:

1. Set your oven to 400°F (200°C) for preheating.
2. Line 12 muffin cups with paper.
3. Immerse your raisins in a cup of water and microwave on high for 1 minute. Drain the water from the raisins.
4. Beat your Flegg with the soy milk in a bowl and pour in the designated amount of bran cereal.
5. Let mixture sit alone to allow the cereal to absorb the Flegg and soy milk mixture. This should be finished in 6 minutes.
6. Add the plumped raisins along with the agave, mashed banana, shredded apple, melted vegan butter, cinnamon, baking soda and flour. Mix together by thoroughly stirring with a spoon.
7. Scoop the batter out of the bowl and into the muffin cups.
8. Bake at 400°F (200°C) for 20 minutes. You'll know they are finished if, after you stick a toothpick into the center, it comes out clean.

Fry Bread

Ready In: 20 minutes

Servings: 4   Calories: 321.2   Protein: 6.4g   Carbs: 49.4g   Fat: 10.8g

Fry bread is the perfect side for any breakfast and goes great when topped with syrup, agave or jam. You can even be creative and come up with your own variation of this simple recipe in order to turn it into a classy dessert. Not only is this vegan fry bread recipe quick to make, clocking in at 20 minutes preparation time, but it only requires 5 ingredients. It couldn't possibly get any simpler.

Ingredients:

- ¾ cup water
- 1 tsp. Salt
- 1 tbsp. Baking powder
- 2 cups all-purpose flour
- Vegetable oil

Directions:

1. Add an inch in depth of vegetable oil into a large-sized saucepan and heat it up to 350°F (175°C).
2. In a bowl, combine your salt, baking soda and flour and stir. Pour in some water a bit at a time for the dough to come together in a ball and to the point it no longer sticks in your hands. This should take about 6 minutes.
3. Rip out a tennis-ball-sized portion of the dough and flatten it into a ½" disk. Repeat until you have no more dough. You should have enough for several disks.
4. Fry the ½" disks in the vegetable oil until they cook to a nice golden-brown texture on each side. This should take 2 to 4 minutes.
5. Drain the oil on paper towels and it's ready to serve!

Tea-ah-Chia Pudding

Ready In: 8 hours, 20 minutes

Servings: 2   Calories: 427   Protein: 8.8g   Carbs: 19.9g   Fat: 37.6g

This recipe makes for a great standalone breakfast pudding, but it also surprisingly makes for a great topping on any old recipe of oatmeal! Chia seeds provide great protein value as well as an array of micronutrients. The sweet flavor of brown sugar replacement and maple syrup blend well with a hint of Earl Grey tea that complements the soft and creamy texture of this vegan pudding.

Ingredients:

- 1 tsp. Maple syrup
- 1 ½ tsp. Brown sugar replacement
- 1 tbsp. Vanilla extract
- ¼ cup chia seeds
- 1 Earl Grey tea bag
- 1 cup almond milk

Directions:

1. Place a saucepan on the stove and add the almond milk to it.
2. Bring it to a boil.
3. Add your Earl Grey tea bag.
4. Remove the saucepan from the stove and steep the tea for a good 6 minutes.
5. Throw the tea bag away.
6. In a bowl, combine your brown sugar replacement, vanilla extract and chia seeds. Pour your almond milk / tea mixture into the bowl and stir well.
7. Pour the resulting pudding into small cups and top with either vegan whipped cream or maple syrup or both.
8. Cover and set in refrigerator overnight or for 8 hours.

Chia Oatmeal (Overnight)

Ready In: 8 hours, 10 minutes

Servings: 4   Calories: 257   Protein: 5.7g   Carbs: 20.4g   Fat: 18.8g

You're looking at another delicious and nutritious overnight oatmeal recipe! This overnight oatmeal is loaded to the rim with chia seeds, shredded coconut, nutmeg and more wonderful flavors for you to soothe your taste buds with. As with every oatmeal dish, this breakfast makes for one great source of fiber and is one of the healthier recipes listed in this cookbook.

Ingredients:

- ¼ tsp. Nutmeg
- ¼ tsp. Ground ginger
- ¼ tsp. Vanilla extract
- ¼ tsp. Ground cinnamon
- ¼ tsp. Ground cardamom
- 2 tbsp. Shredded coconut
- 2 tbsp. Chia seeds
- 1 cup almond milk
- 1 cup oats

Directions:

1. Prepare a bowl of your oats.
2. Add in the almond milk, coconut, chia seeds, cardamom, vanilla extract, cinnamon, ginger and nutmeg. Stir and mix well.
3. Cover with plastic wrap and place in your refrigerator.
4. Let sit overnight or for 8 hours. Enjoy!

Vegan Drop Biscuits

Ready In: 20 minutes

Servings: 6   Calories: 319.8   Protein: 5.2g   Carbs: 35.5g   Fat: 18.3g

These are hands down the fluffiest, most moist and tender vegan drop biscuits on the market! Vegan drop biscuits make a great side to scrambled tofu, eggplant bacon or any other protein-centric dish that you'll find in this cookbook. If you're feeling bold, try dipping them in jam or peanut butter and see what you think! These biscuits are best served while still hot.

Ingredients:

- 1 cup almond milk
- 2 tbsp. Coconut oil
- 2 tbsp. Vegan butter
- 1 tsp. Salt
- 4 tsp. Baking powder
- 2 cups whole wheat flour

Directions:

1. Set your oven to 450°F (230°C) for preheating.
2. Prepare a bowl in which you mix your flour, salt and baking soda with each other.
3. Begin cutting coconut oil and vegan butter into the flour. Combine until the flour forms a crumbly-textured batter.
4. Pour in some almond milk and stir until combined.
5. Scoop out the batter onto a cookie sheet. Do not grease the cookie sheet.
6. Allow to bake for 12 minutes at 450°F (230°C).

58

Toasted Granola of Quinoa

Ready In: 45 minutes

Servings: 4   Calories: 238   Protein: 7.3g   Carbs: 33.1g   Fat: 8.3g

If it's a high protein granola recipe you're after, you just found it. Since this particular recipe uses quinoa in place of traditional granola grains, you're getting a tremendous serving of protein – as you can see in the calorie and macronutrient count above! You may even find that you prefer quinoa granola to the other varieties you have tried before.

Ingredients:

- ¼ cup flax seed
- 1 tsp. Ground cinnamon
- 1 tbsp. Olive oil
- 1 tbsp. Pure maple syrup
- 1 cup quinoa

Directions:

1. Set your oven to 350°F (175°C) for preheating.
2. Carefully and fully rinse the quinoa grains by running them under the faucet in a fine mesh strainer. This step is important! Quinoa grains naturally are covered in a protective, naturally occurring toxin called saponins. If you fail to thoroughly rinse them, you may get sick. Rinsing them should take about 5 minutes.
3. Pour your maple syrup, cinnamon and olive oil together in a large bowl and stir well.
4. Pour the rinsed quinoa and your flax seeds into the bowl of the maple syrup mixture and stir until the grains are evenly and completely coated.
5. Using a spoon, spread the resulting mixture out very thinly on a prepared cookie sheet.
6. Place the granola in the oven and allow to cook for 15 minutes at 350°F (175°C). Stir every 4 to 5 minutes.
7. Allow the granola to cool off and then store in a plastic airtight container.

Tasty Banana Muffins

Ready In: 50 minutes

Servings: 6   Calories: 349.9   Protein: 7.3g   Carbs: 54.5g   Fat: 14.9g

The combination of bran, chocolate chips and walnuts pack quite the crunch. You simply must try it out to believe it!

Ingredients:

- 1 cup raisins
- 1 cup dark chocolate chips
- 1 cup chopped walnuts
- ¼ cup peanut oil
- 10 ripe bananas, mashed
- 1 pinch ground nutmeg
- 1 pinch ground allspice
- 1 pinch ground sugar
- ¼ tsp. Salt
- 1 tsp. Ground cinnamon
- 1 tbsp. Baking soda
- 1 tbsp. Baking powder
- ¼ cup flax seeds
- ½ cup rolled oats
- 1 cup wheat bran
- 1 cup all-purpose flour

Directions:

1. Set your oven to 350°F (175°C) for preheating. In a large bowl, beat your bran, flour, nutmeg, allspice, ginger, salt, cinnamon, baking soda, baking powder, flax seeds and rolled oats together, mixing them well.
2. In a separate large bowl, mash your bananas and mix your peanut oil into them.
3. Stir the contents of the first bowl into your mashed banana and peanut oil mixture. Fold in the raisins, dark chocolate chips and walnuts into your batter.
4. Line muffin cups with paper.
5. Using a spoon, scoop the batter into your muffin cups, filling them about 2/3 of the way full.
6. Bake the muffins for about 30 minutes at 350°F (175°C), or until golden-browned. When you can stick a toothpick into the center and it comes out without debris, they are finished baking.

Vegan Energy Bars

Ready In: 40 minutes

Servings: 8   Calories: 189   Protein: 4.3g   Carbs: 35.2g   Fat: 4.3g

When you prepare this recipe, you will enjoy a vegan energy bar jammed with agave, ground cinnamon, almond butter, cashews, chocolate chips and, obviously, oatmeal. These bars are bound to satisfy your taste buds and your need for an energy boost.

Ingredients:

- ½ tsp. Vanilla extract
- 1/3 cup almond butter
- ½ cup warmed agave
- ¼ tsp sea salt
- ½ tsp. Ground cinnamon
- 1 tbsp. Wheat germ
- 1 tbsp. Ground flax meal
- 2 tbsp. Shelled unsalted sunflower seeds
- ½ cup ground unsalted cashews
- ½ cup all-purpose flour
- 1 1/3 cups rolled oats

Directions:

1. Set your oven to 350°F (175°C) for preheating.
2. Use aluminum foil to line a 9" x 11" baking dish.
3. In a small bowl, mix your oats, sea salt, cinnamon, wheat germ, flax meal, sunflower seeds, ground cashews and chocolate chips together by whisking them.
4. In a separate bowl, mix your almond butter with your warmed agave and vanilla extract. Stir well.
5. Combine the oat mixture with the agave mixture and stir until the batter is well-mixed.
6. Spread batter out in your prepared 9" x 11" dish.
7. Cover the batter with a sheet of wax paper and press down with great pressure to evenly distribute the batter across the entire dish. Throw away wax paper when done.
8. Place in the oven and allow to bake at 350°F (175°C) for 12 minutes.
9. Remove the aluminum foil from beneath the baked batter and allow it to cool for 15 minutes.
10. Cut into 8 bars.

Cornmeal Delight

Ready In: 12 minutes

Servings: 2   Calories: 276   Protein: 6.2g   Carbs: 58.6g   Fat: 2.7g

A delicious and nutritious breakfast recipe can't get a whole lot simpler than this – especially considering how versatile this cornmeal delight one is! You can eat it hot; you can eat it cold, but no matter how you eat it, it never gets old. No matter how you choose to eat it though, I recommend trying maple syrup as topping in order to enjoy it the way it was intended!

Ingredients:

- ½ tsp. Salt
- 2 ½ cups water
- 1 ¼ cups cornmeal

Directions:

1. Mix your water and salt together with your cornmeal in a medium-sized saucepan.
2. Cook on medium heat for 6 to 8 minutes, while stirring. You'll know you're done with this step when the mixture has thickened.
3. If you choose to eat this recipe as a cereal, use a spoon to scoop the mush into a bowl and serve it with soy or almond milk and a bit of added sugar.
4. If you wish to make *fried* cornmeal delight, then pour it into a loaf pan and allow it to chill in your refrigerator. When it is fully chilled, remove it from the pan and cut it into bars. Fry the bars in a little bit of olive oil on medium-high heat until both sides of each bar are brown. These fried cornmeal delight bars go great with your favorite sauces!

Slow Cooked Steel Oats with Pumpkin

Ready In: 6 hours, 5 minutes

Servings: 2   Calories: 282   Protein: 6.7g   Carbs: 47.7g   Fat: 3.3g

This recipe is incredibly easy to prepare and equally as delicious to eat. It requires six hours of time to slow cook, but it is so worth the wait! When you prepare this hearty and healthy slow cooked oatmeal, it feels like you are enjoying a plump slice of pumpkin pie for breakfast but there is no accompanying guilt! If you have a slow cooker and you have oatmeal, then there is no reason why you *shouldn't* give this recipe a spin.

Ingredients:

- 1 tbsp. Pumpkin pie spice
- 2 tbsp. Ground cinnamon
- 1 cup brown sugar replacement
- 1 ½ cups steel-cut oats
- 15 oz. Pumpkin puree
- 6 cups water
- Cooking spray

Directions:

1. Spray down the inside of the crock of your slow cooker with cooking spray.
2. Pour your pumpkin spice, cinnamon, brown sugar replacement, oats, puree and water into the slow cooker. Stir together.
3. Allow to cook on low heat for 6 hours.
4. Stir well and serve.

Protein-Packed Scones

Ready In: 1 hour

Servings: 8   Calories: 452.8   Protein: 10.5g   Carbs: 44.4g   Fat: 27g

This protein-packed scone recipe is the perfect breakfast for bodybuilders! It contains loads of protein from the included hemp seed hearts and chia seeds, not to mention a healthy dose of chopped almonds and pecans – both of which are highly rich in protein. I recommend eating these tasty morsels with a hemp protein smoothie drink, to even further increase a vegan bodybuilder's protein intake.

Ingredients:

- ¼ cup hemp seed hearts
- ¼ cup almonds, finely chopped
- ¼ cup pecans, finely chopped
- ½ cup cold coconut oil, divided into 8 equal-sized measurements
- ¾ tsp. Salt
- 1 tsp. Ground cardamom
- 1 tsp. Ground ginger
- 1 tsp. Baking soda
- ½ cup white sugar
- 2 cups all-purpose flour
- 1 tsp. Vanilla extract
- 2 tbsp. Chia seeds
- ¼ cup coconut milk
- 1 lemon, zested and juiced
- 1 orange, zested and juiced

Directions:

1. Set your oven to 300°F (150°C) for preheating.
2. Prepare a cookie sheet lined with parchment paper.
3. Prepare a small bowl in which you stir your lemon and orange juice together. Be sure to add water as necessary in order to produce a total of 7 tablespoons of fluid in the bowl.
4. Take the resulting juice mixture and combine it with your coconut milk, orange zest, lemon zest, vanilla extract and chia seeds. Stir together well. Allow it to sit on its own for the chia seeds to begin to gel. This should take no longer than 10 minutes.
5. Prepare a mixture of your flour, salt, cardamom, ginger, baking soda and sugar in a food processor. Pulse with the food processor until it has just-combined. Toss your 8 coconut oil measurements (taken from ½ cup cold coconut oil) into the food processor with your flour mixture and process until the resulting texture is like that of wet sand.
6. Pour the first mixture that has chia seeds, vanilla extract, lemon zest, orange zest and coconut milk into the second mixture containing flour. Pulse in food processor until the dough starts to form and come together.
7. Place your dough in a bowl and add your hemp seed hearts, almonds and pecan. Knead and work together with your hands until the nuts and seeds are evenly spread out throughout the dough.
8. Split the dough into two pieces. Flatten each piece into a 1" thin disk.
9. Cut each disk into 8 different slices (like you would do with a pizza).
10. Lay out the slices evenly on your prepared cookie sheet from step 2.
11. Bake in the oven at 300°F (150°C) for 33 minutes, or until the tops spring back when they are pressed.

Cinnamon-Quinoa & Oats

Ready In: 40 minutes

Servings: 2   Calories: 274   Protein: 10g   Carbs: 40g   Fat: 8.4g

This cinnamon flavored medley between quinoa and oatmeal can keep in your refrigerator for a whole week! If you are so busy that, on an average week day, you don't have time to prepare breakfast you may consider making a whole week's worth of this stuff in advance. Cinnamon-quinoa and oats is mighty tasty and only has six unique ingredients, meaning it is also a breeze to prepare!

Ingredients:

- 1 tbsp. Ground cinnamon
- 2 tbsp. Flax seed meal
- 2 tbsp. Almond meal
- ½ cup steel-cut oats
- ½ cup quinoa
- 3 cups water

Directions:

1. Set a saucepan on your stove and place your 3 cups of water inside of it.
2. Bring the water to a boil.
3. Add in your quinoa and your oats.
4. Lower heat to a simmer and continue stirring until the water is fully absorbed and the quinoa has softened. This should take 16 to 20 minutes.
5. Stir your flax seed meal and almond meal into the quinoa and oat mixture.
6. Pour it all into a glass mason jar and top with cinnamon.
7. Allow the oats and quinoa to cool for 20 minutes and then place in the refrigerator.

Mango-nut Breakfast Smoothie Bowl

Ready In: 10 minutes

Servings: 2   Calories: 288   Protein: 3.9g   Carbs: 61.7g   Fat: 5.3g

This exquisite breakfast smoothie bowl is ripe with frozen mango chunks, chopped bananas and goji berries. It is topped with coconut cream, coconut flakes and chia seeds. If you are on a raw vegan diet, this sweetly flavored breakfast will check off all of your requirements and then some. Prepare for a brain freeze if you eat it too fast though!

Ingredients:

- ½ tsp. Chia seeds
- 1 tsp. Goji berries
- 1 tbsp. Flaked coconut
- ¼ tsp. Vanilla extract
- 1 tbsp. Unsweetened coconut cream
- 1 frozen banana, chopped
- 1 cup vanilla-flavored almond milk
- 1 ½ cups frozen mango chunks

Directions:

1. Prepare your blender with the vanilla extract, coconut cream, chopped banana, almond milk and chunks of mango.
2. Blend into a puree until it becomes smooth and thick in consistency.
3. Pour into a bowl.
4. Top with your chia seeds, flaked coconuts and goji berries.

Cocoa Pancakes with Zucchini

Ready In: 35 minutes

Servings: 1   Calories: 427   Protein: 10.5g   Carbs: 86.4g   Fat: 6.8g

This is yet another great chocolate chip pancake recipe. This one uses shredded zucchini and mashed banana to mix things up a bit! Add chocolate chips to the equation and you've essentially just balanced a healthy breakfast out with some incredible sweet flavor. These cocoa pancakes with zucchini taste incredible when spread with and topped with agave. As a side note, these pancakes are completely *gluten-free!*

Ingredients:

- Cooking spray
- 1 pinch sea salt
- ¼ tsp. Ground cinnamon
- ¼ tsp. Baking soda
- ½ tsp. Baking powder
- 1 ½ tsp. Brown sugar replacement baking blend
- 1 tbsp. Unsweetened cocoa powder
- ½ cup gluten-free all-purpose flour
- ¼ tsp. Vanilla extract
- ¼ cup shredded zucchini
- 1 ripe and mashed banana
- ½ cup unsweetened almond milk
- 1 tbsp. Flax seeds
- 2 tbsp. water

Directions:

1. In a bowl, mix your flax seeds and water together. Place in the refrigerator and allow to sit for 15 to 30 minutes. You'll know when it's ready, because the mixture will thicken and have the consistency of eggs.
2. Remove from the refrigerator and add in your vanilla extract, zucchini, banana and almond milk. Stir contents together.
3. In a separate bowl, combine your flour, sea salt, cinnamon, baking soda, baking powder, brown sugar replacement baking blend and cocoa powder into a mixture. Stir well.
4. Pour in your flax mixture and stir together until the batter is just-combined.
5. Place a large griddle over medium heat and grease with cooking spray.
6. Measure out about 1/3 cup of your batter onto the griddle and cook until it becomes bubbly and the bottom becomes golden-brown. This should take about 5 minutes.
7. Flip it over to the other side and repeat.
8. Place the finished pancake on a rack to cool and repeat steps 6 through 8 until you have used up all of your batter.

● ● ● ● ● ● ● ● ● ● ● ● ● ● ● ● ● ● ● ●

DID YOU KNOW?

The very first pancake recipe appeared in an English cookbook during the fifteenth century.

● ● ● ● ● ● ● ● ● ● ● ● ● ● ● ● ● ● ● ●

Carrot Cake Muffins

Ready In: 55 minutes

Servings: 12   Calories: 370.3   Protein: 5.2g   Carbs: 50.7g   Fat: 18.1g

If you are a fan of carrot cake, these will probably be your favorite muffins in the whole cookbook. Imagine if a breakfast muffin and a carrot cake got together and made sweet, sweet love – emphasis on the *sweet*. These tasty little muffins would be their babies. It's like eating a carrot cake and a muffin at the same time!

Ingredients:

- ½ tsp. Ground cardamom
- 1 tsp. salt
- 1 tsp. Ground nutmeg
- 1 tsp. Ground cinnamon
- 1 ½ tsp. Vanilla extract
- 2 tbsp. Molasses
- ½ cup olive oil
- 2 tbsp. White sugar
- ¾ cup white sugar
- ¾ cup chopped walnuts
- ¾ cup raisins
- ¾ cup chopped pineapple, drained
- 1 ½ cups grated carrots
- 1 tsp. Baking soda
- 1 tsp. Baking powder
- ½ cup all-purpose flour
- 1 ¾ cup whole wheat flour
- 1 ½ tsp. Apple cider vinegar
- 1 cup almond milk

<u>Directions:</u>

1. Set your oven to 325°F (165°C) for preheating.
2. Prepare muffin cups with paper liners.
3. In a bowl, whisk your vinegar and your almond milk together. Allow it to sit for 10 minutes or until curdled.
4. In a second bowl, combine your baking soda, baking powder, all-purpose flour and whole wheat flour together.
5. In a third bowl, prepare a combination of your carrots, raisins, walnuts and pineapple.
6. In yet a fourth bowl, whisk your white sugar (¾ cup + 2 tbsp.), cardamom, salt, nutmeg, cinnamon, vanilla extract, molasses and olive oil together.
7. Combine your mixture of sugar and curdled milk into your flour mixture until the batter is mixed.
8. Fold in the carrot mixture.
9. Scoop enough of your batter into each muffin cup to completely fill it up.
10. Bake in the oven at 325°F (165°C) for 25 to 30 minutes. You'll know it is finished baking when you can stick a toothpick into the center and pull it out clean.

Breakfast Burrito

Ready In: 30 minutes

Servings: 2   Calories: 1,196   Protein: 40.1g   Carbs: 214.5g   Fat: 24.2g

Yes, this book is so diverse it even contains vegan breakfast burritos. I don't care what anyone says – a cookbook without a single burrito recipe is no cookbook at all! Who wouldn't want to start their day with a burrito every once in a while? With these vegan breakfast burritos, you're getting more than enough fiber and plenty of protein to boot. They are stuffed with delicately seasoned hash browns and onions, black beans, a spicy avocado spread and much more. Even though it has the most ingredients, this is probably my favorite breakfast recipe in the book!

Ingredients:

- Hot sauce
- ¼ cup salsa
- ½ ripe avocado
- 2 large vegan flour tortillas, wheat
- 1 pinch of seas salt
- 1 pinch of black pepper
- 1 sliced jalapeno, no seeds
- 1 cup sliced cabbage (mixture of purple cabbage, green cabbage and radish)
- 1 lime, juiced
- ¼ ripe avocado
- 1 cup cooked black beans, sea salt added
- ¼ tsp. Ground cumin
- ¼ tsp. Garlic powder
- ¼ tsp. Chili powder
- ¼ tsp sea salt
- ¼ tsp black pepper
- 2 tbsp. Vegan butter
- ½ red onion
- 4 small red potatoes
- ¼ cup chopped cilantro
- ½ lime, juiced
- ¼ tsp. Sea salt
- 1 ½ cups water
- ¾ cup white rice, cooked

<u>Directions:</u>

1. Stop complaining about how many ingredients are required for this recipe.
2. Bring a saucepan full of the rice and water to a boil. Add a pinch of salt.
3. After it comes to a boil, reduce the heat to a low simmer and cover. Let it sit for 20 minutes so that all of the water is fully absorbed by the rice.
4. Remove salted rice from the heat and let sit.
5. Wash and chop your red potatoes into small pieces. Slice your onion into rings about a fourth of an inch thick.
6. Heat a skillet on medium heat and place your vegan butter inside of it. Use a spoon to slide the vegan butter around and coat the entire surface of the skillet in it.
7. When the skillet is fully heated and the vegan butter has completely melted, toss in your red potato pieces on one half of the skillet and your slices of onions on the other half. Season both the potatoes and the onions generously with salt and pepper. Let them sit for 5 minutes or until golden on one side and then flip them over and repeat.
8. Place a small saucepan on medium heat and pour in the black beans. Use the chili powder, the garlic powder and the cumin to season the beans to your heart's content. When they start to bubble, lower the heat and keep them warm.
9. To prepare the avocado spread, mash the half of a ripe avocado (as called for in the ingredients) into the lime juice. Add the jalapeno and cabbage and toss to mix. Season with just a pinch of salt. Set the spread aside when finished.
10. Mix the cilantro and the lime juice into the cooked and seasoned rice. Toss together to combine.
11. Wrap your tortillas in a damp towel and heat in the microwave for 35 seconds.
12. Layer the avocado spread across the inside of each warmed tortilla and then stuff your burrito with the fillings you've prepared in the previous steps. Serve with the extra ¼ ripe avocado and your salsa or hot sauce. Enjoy!

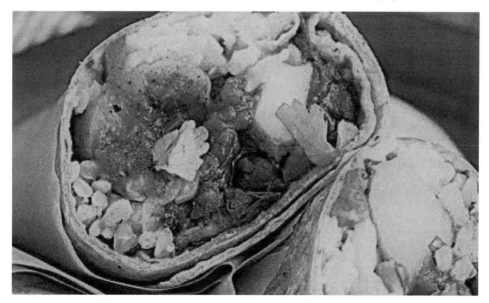

Cookie Dough Energy Balls

Ready In: 10 minutes

Servings: 8   Calories: 100   Protein: 3.1g   Carbs: 10.1g   Fat: 6g

Cookie dough balls for breakfast!? Sure! Why not? This is the ideal breakfast for someone who is going through a rough time. The mixture of agave, chopped walnuts, cooked oats, wheat bran and chocolate chips will lift anyone's spirits. Even if you're not going through hard times, these cookie dough energy balls will sweeten up your already sweet life even more.

Ingredients:

- ¾ cup quick cook oats
- 1 ½ tbsp. Mini chocolate chips
- 1 tbsp. Chopped walnuts
- 1 tsp. Vanilla extract
- 4 ½ tbsp. Almond butter
- 2 tbsp. Agave
- ¼ cup wheat bran

Directions:

1. Mix your oats and wheat bran together in a bowl.
2. In a second bowl, mix the agave, vanilla extract and almond butter together.
3. Combine the oat and wheat bran mixture with the liquid mixture from the second bowl.
4. Toss in the mini chocolate chips and the walnuts and stir to mix them together, so that everything is as evenly distributed as possible.
5. Roll the dough into 8 slightly-larger-than tablespoon-sized balls.

Fruity Parfait

Ready In: 6 hours, 5 minutes

Servings: 4   Calories: 249   Protein: 5.8g   Carbs: 24.2g   Fat: 16.1g

Not everyone out there wants to eat a huge filling breakfast. Some people aren't even hungry at breakfast time, but skipping breakfast altogether is detrimental to a person's health. If you are in the mood for something lighter, this is your breakfast. It only has 249 calories per serving, so you can save your daily caloric allowance for lunch and dinner – when you're probably the hungriest!

Ingredients:

- 1 cup fresh blueberries
- 1 cup fresh strawberries, sliced
- ½ cup sliced, canned peaches
- 1 pinch sea salt
- ¼ tsp. Vanilla extract
- 1 tsp. Lemon zest
- 1 tbsp. Maple syrup
- ¼ cup cold water
- 1 cup raw cashews

Directions:

1. Allow your cashews to sit in a bowl, completely immersed in warm water, for 6 hours.
2. Drain the water from the bowl of cashews and place them in a blender.
3. Add agave, lemon zest, water and salt to the blender as well.
4. Puree the mixture until it forms a smooth texture.
5. Place 2 tbsp. of your newly created cashew cream into a parfait glass. Cover the first layer of cashew cream with some of your sliced peaches, fresh blueberries and sliced up strawberries. Top that layer of fruit with another 2 tbsp. of cashew cream and then finish with another layer of fruit.
6. Add a spoon to the parfait glass and serve.

Chapter 5: Lunch Recipes

In this chapter, you will find all manner of gourmet lunch items, from sandwiches and soups to a variety of side items. If you are looking for the vegan burgers, pizzas, casseroles and other heavier duty recipes, turn over to the dinner recipes located in Chapter 6.

You will notice that the calories as well as the grams of protein, fat and carbohydrates per each recipe are listed right beneath the name. The macronutrients listed correspond with the designated serving size. For example, if a recipe has servings listed as 4, then the total yield should be divided into fourths. If a recipe has servings listed as 6, then divide the total yield of the recipe into six different portions.

Spicy Breaded & Fried Tofu

Ready In: 30 minutes

Servings: 4   Calories: 298   Protein: 18.8g   Carbs: 18.5g   Fat: 18.1g

The taste that the texture of breading on tofu creates is astounding! Considering the ample protein content in tofu, this is another dish I recommend vegan bodybuilders to incorporate into their diets a couple of times a week. -- at least.

Ingredients:

- 1/2 tsp. Cayenne pepper
- 1 tsp. Sage
- 1/2 tsp. Freshly ground black pepper
- 1 tsp. Salt
- 3 tbsp. Nutritional yeast
- ½ cup all-purpose flour
- 3 tbsp. Vegetable oil
- 2 cups vegetable broth
- 16 oz. Extra-firm tofu, drained and pressed

Directions:

1. Slice your pressed tofu into ½" thick slices.
2. Cut the same tofu slices again into ½" wide sticks.
3. Place the tofu sticks in a bowl and cover them in your vegetable broth. Move to the side and allow time to soak.
4. Stir your cayenne pepper, sage, pepper, salt, yeast and flour together in a second bowl.
5. Place a skillet on medium-high heat and warm up your vegetable oil in it.
6. Remove the tofu sticks from the vegetable broth they were soaking in and squeeze, not all, but the majority of the fluid out of them.
7. Roll the tofu sticks in the breading you created in step 4. You might need to roll the sticks in the breading twice to adequately cover them.
8. Place the breaded tofu sticks in the heated vegetable oil on your skillet and fry until crispy and golden-brown on every side. Add extra vegetable oil as needed during the frying process.

Spicy Soba Noodles with Kale & Sea Veggies

Ready In: 55 minutes

Servings: 8   Calories: 393   Protein: 13g   Carbs: 51.2g   Fat: 17.9g

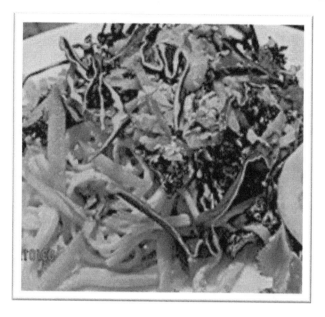

Spicy soba noodles abound in this recipe as does the flavor they are dripping with from the added rice vinegar, soy sauce, olive oil, Sriracha sauce, turmeric, seaweed, garlic and ginger! If you read Chapter 1, you'll recall that seaweed is a great way to get iodine – a key component of *The Perfect Seven!* Seaweed by itself may not be everyone's favorite, but I have yet to find someone who doesn't think this dish is one of the best vegan lunch dishes ever.

Ingredients:

- 1 bunch of kale, shredded into pieces
- 2 tbsp. Minced fresh ginger
- 2 cloves garlic, minced
- 1 tbsp. Olive oil
- 8 oz. Package dried soba noodles
- 1 packet arame seaweed
- 2 tbsp. Water
- ½ tsp. Ground turmeric
- 1/2 tsp. Chili-garlic sauce
- 2 tbsp. Olive oil
- 2 tbsp. Soy sauce
- 3 tbsp. Rice vinegar
- ¾ cup tahini

Directions:

1. Prepare a large bowl and use a fork to blend the 2 tbsp. of water with the turmeric, chili-garlic sauce, 2 tbsp. of olive oil, soy sauce, rice vinegar and your tahini. Add however much extra water you need in order to get the dressing to resemble the consistency of hummus. Set to the side when finished for later.
2. Prepare a pot of lukewarm water and allow the arame seaweed to soak therein for 12 minutes.
3. After the seaweed has soaked at a lukewarm temperature for 10 minutes, bring the pot of water to a boil at medium heat and then lower to a simmer on low heat and allow to simmer for 10 more minutes.
4. Drain the water from the pot of seaweed.
5. In a second pot, add lightly salted water and bring it to a boil.
6. Add in your soba noodles at the point it is boiling and allow them to cook until they are tender, yet still hard to bite. This should take about 8 minutes.
7. Drain the water from the pot of noodles and set to the side.
8. Place a large skillet on medium heat and add 1 tbsp. of olive oil into it. Stir the garlic in the olive oil, allowing it to cook, until the garlic becomes fragrant and you can smell it. This shouldn't take any longer than a minute.
9. Add the ginger and drained seaweed into the cooking garlic on the skillet. Allow another minute to cook while you continue to stir and blend these ingredients together.
10. Add your kale into the mix on the skillet. Stir the kale in with everything else for another minute and allow it to cook until it is slightly coated.
11. Reduce the heat to low, allowing your ingredients to simmer, and place a cover over the top of the skillet. Allow to simmer for 7 to 10 minutes or until the kale wilts.
12. Mix the soba noodles (having been drained) into the tahini sauce and stir until thoroughly coated.
13. Begin to fold the kale mixture and the seaweed into your noodles and toss about to continue coating it all together.

Vegan Seitan Makhani

Ready In: 1 hour, 5 minutes

Servings: 4   Calories: 327   Protein: 20.8g   Carbs: 21.7g   Fat: 18.9g

If you ever had chicken makhani before going vegan, there's not a doubt that you probably miss it. The good news is that you don't need chicken to enjoy makhani anymore! Introducing vegan seitan makhani. This tender recipe utilizes the power of seitan (not the power of Satan, don't worry!) in place of the traditional chicken. You can purchase seitan at your local health food store, buy it online or make your own from scratch.

Ingredients:

- ¼ cup cold water
- 1 tbsp. Cornstarch
- 1 pinch cayenne pepper
- 2 tsp. Garam masala
- 16 oz. Packaged chicken-style seitan, sliced into strips
- 1 ½ tsp. Peanut oil
- 1 pinch salt
- 1 pinch black pepper
- ¼ tsp. Cayenne pepper
- ¼ cup plain vegan yogurt
- 1 cup soy milk
- 1 cup tomato puree
- 1 bay leaf
- 2 tsp. Ground cumin
- 1 tsp. Chili powder
- 2 tsp. Curry powder
- 2 tsp. Garam masala
- 2 cloves of garlic, minced
- 1 tsp. Ground ginger
- 2 tsp. Lemon juice
- 2 tbsp. Vegan margarine
- ¼ cup onion, chopped
- 1 shallot, finely chopped
- 1 tbsp. Peanut oil

Directions:

1. Place a saucepan on medium heat and coat it in 1 tbsp. of peanut oil. Mix the onion and shallot in and stir until the onion has begun to soften and become more of a clear color. This should take approximately 5 minutes to achieve.
2. Layer in the lemon juice, bay leaf, cumin, chili powder, curry powder, garam masala, garlic, ginger and the margarine. Continue to stir while it cooks for 1 minute.
3. Add in the tomato puree and cook for an additional 2 minutes, while continuing to stir.
4. Lower the heat down to low and add in your soy yogurt and soy milk.
5. Allow to simmer for 10 minutes while you stir frequently and season to your preference with black pepper, salt and cayenne pepper.
6. Remove from the heat and set to the side.
7. Place a large skillet on medium heat and coat it with 1 ½ tsp. of peanut oil.
8. Add in your seitan and stir continuously while it cooks for 10 minutes.
9. Bring the heat to low and add your 2 tsp. of garam masala and a pinch of cayenne pepper to season the seitan.
10. Measure out ¼ cup of your tomato-yogurt sauce and stir it into the seitan. Allow it to simmer for 3 minutes before dumping the seitan mix into your saucepan.
11. Combine the cornstarch and cold water and stir them together.
12. Place your saucepan back on the stove on medium-high heat.
13. Stir the cornstarch and water mix into the sauce and bring it to a boil.
14. Reduce heat to a low simmer and wait 8 to 10 minutes until the sauce has become thick.

● ● ● ● ● ● ● ● ● ● ● ● ● ● ● ● ● ● ● ●

DID YOU KNOW?

The word seitan was originally coined by a Japanese man named George Ohsawa to describe a wheat gluten product created by one of his students.

● ● ● ● ● ● ● ● ● ● ● ● ● ● ● ● ● ● ● ●

Vegan Arepas

Ready In: 35 minutes

Servings: 6   Calories: 552.5   Protein: 17.3g   Carbs: 101.9g   Fat: 9.8g

If you're wondering what arepas are, they're essentially corn pancakes that are commonly eaten in the Venezuelan and Colombian regions of the world. They are usually served with avocado and various fruit spreads. I'll let you be creative on what else you want to serve them with!

Ingredients:

- 1 pinch of salt
- 1 minced jalapeno
- 1/4 cup diced onion
- 1 large mango, peeled and diced
- 1 peeled and pitted avocado, sliced
- 1 cup black beans, undrained
- 2 bananas, sliced lengthwise
- Olive oil
- 16 oz. Tube prepared polenta
- 8 oz. Tofu, drained

Directions:

1. Fire up your oven's broiler and allow it to preheat.
2. Position your oven rack about 6 inches away from the heat source.
3. Grease a cookie sheet.
4. Slice up your polenta as well as your tofu into slabs equal in terms of thickness. Coat in olive oil (with a baking brush or however else you choose to) and space them evenly apart on your cookie sheet.
5. Leave your slabs of tofu and polenta in your preheated broiler, allowing them to cook for approximately 5 minutes. You'll know they are finished when the tops of them become crispy. Once finished remove them from the broiler and set them aside.
6. Place a skillet over medium-high heat and heat up your olive oil, coating the surface of the skillet in it. Cook the bananas in the olive oil until they become crispy on the outside and soft and tender on the inside. This should be about 5 minutes. Remove the bananas from the olive oil and set them aside.
7. Pour the full cup of black beans into a blender and blend however long you need to until they become a thick sauce.
8. In a bowl, combine and stir the salt, jalapeno pepper, diced onion and mango together.
9. To put your arepas together, place a single slice of the polenta on each plate and cover each with about a ¼ of the total bean sauce you created in step 7. Then place a slice of your tofu on top of the layer of bean sauce. Then a few slices of the prepared banana, a bit of avocado and topping it all off with a ¼ of the total mango salsa on each.

Fajitas

Ready In: 1 hour, 10 minutes

Servings: 4   Calories: 494   Protein: 13.5g   Carbs: 64.4g   Fat: 23.4g

This is a mouthwatering meatless version of the common fajita! It is pleasing to the taste with its combination of red and green bell pepper strips, corn, black beans, squash and zucchini. For seasoning, delight your taste buds with garlic, chili powder, oregano, red wine vinegar and salt! You really *don't* need meat to enjoy a savory fajita for lunch.

Ingredients:

- 15 oz. Can black beans, drained
- 8.75 oz. Can whole kernel corn, drained
- 2 tbsp. Olive oil
- 1 red bell pepper, sliced into strips
- 1 green bell pepper, sliced into strips
- 1 large onion, sliced
- 2 medium yellow squash, julienne-style
- 1 tsp. White sugar
- Salt and pepper
- Garlic seasoning
- 1 tsp. Chili powder
- 1 tsp. Dried oregano
- ¼ cup red wine vinegar
- ¼ cup olive oil
- 4 whole wheat tortillas

Directions:

1. Mix together your sugar, pepper, salt, garlic seasoning, chili powder, oregano, vinegar and olive oil in a large bowl.
2. Marinade your zucchini, yellow squash, onion, green peppers and red peppers by adding them into the mixture.
3. Set the bowl in the refrigerator to give time for your vegetables to be marinated. You should at least marinate them for an hour, but no longer than 24 hours.
4. Place a large skillet on medium-high heat and heat up your oil in it. Drain the veggies and sauté them in the skillet until they become a bit tender. This shouldn't take any longer than 15 minutes.
5. Add in the beans and corn and stir. Increase the heat to high for 5 more minutes in order to turn your vegetables a brown color.
6. Scoop your fajita fillings into your whole wheat tortillas and serve!

Curried Chickpeas

Ready In: 40 minutes

Servings: 4   Calories: 350   Protein: 12.2g   Carbs: 56.1g   Fat: 9.5g

The delicious curry seasoning that plays out in tandem with turmeric, cayenne pepper, ground coriander, cumin, garlic and even crushed cinnamon sticks creates a bold taste in this exciting lunch recipe! Chickpeas are rich in Vitamin K, zinc, manganese and calcium which make them an essential part of a balanced vegan diet. If you enjoy dishes with curry, this is one you absolutely must try.

Ingredients:

- 1 cup chopped cilantro
- 2 x 15 oz. Cans of garbanzo beans
- 1 tsp. Ground turmeric
- 1 tsp. Cayenne pepper
- Salt
- 1 tsp. Ground coriander
- 1 tsp. Ground cumin
- 2 x 2" cinnamon sticks, crushed
- 6 whole cloves
- 2 tsp. Fresh ginger root, chopped
- 2 cloves of garlic, minced
- 2 onions, minced
- 2 tbsp. Vegetable oil

Directions:

1. Heat your vegetable oil in a skillet on medium heat.
2. Throw in your onions and allow them to fry until tenderized.
3. Mix in your turmeric, cayenne pepper, salt, coriander, cumin, crushed cinnamon sticks, cloves, ginger and garlic and stir for 1 minute.
4. Add in your garbanzo beans and the liquid they came in. Continue stirring as the ingredients cook until everything is blended well and completely heated through.
5. Remove the skillet from the heat.
6. Add cilantro right before you serve!

Ginger Stir-Fry

Ready In: 40 minutes

Servings: 2   Calories: 368   Protein: 7.8g   Carbs: 25.9g   Fat: 27.9g

This is hands down one of the best vegan stir-fry recipes you could find. It's also one of the healthiest, containing chunks of julienned carrots, green beans, onion, broccoli and fresh garlic and ginger. If you're looking for a healthy lunch that won't bloat you or give you that dreaded afternoon brain fog, this is it!

Ingredients:

- ¼ cup onion, chopped
- 2 ½ tbsp. Water
- 2 tbsp. Soy sauce
- ½ cup halved green beans
- ¾ cup carrots, julienned
- ½ tbsp. Salt
- ½ cup snow peas
- 1 small head of broccoli, cut into florets
- ¼ cup vegetable oil, divided
- 2 tsp. Chopped fresh ginger root, divided
- 1 ½ cloves crushed garlic
- 1 tbsp. cornstarch

Directions:

1. Combine 2 tbsp. of your vegetable oil with 1 tsp. of your ginger, your garlic and your cornstarch. Blend it all together until the cornstarch has dissolved.
2. Add your green beans, carrots, snow peas and broccoli to the mix and toss lightly to allow them to be coated.
3. Place a large skillet on the medium heat and coat it in 2 tbsp. of oil.
4. Cook your veggie mix in the oil for about 2 minutes. Continuously stir your veggies while cooking so that they don't burn.
5. Mix in your water and your soy sauce as well as the onion, remaining 1 tsp. of ginger and salt.
6. Continue to cook and stir until the veggies become crisp, yet tender.

Indian Lentils

Ready In: 1 hour, 5 minutes

Servings: 2   Calories: 321   Protein: 18.3g   Carbs: 47.2g   Fat: 8.2g

If you are a fan of Indian recipes, here is another great one for you to sink your teeth into! While this recipe doesn't include rice, it tastes mind-blowingly good when you use it to top a bowl of curried basmati rice – I highly recommend trying this! That said, if you are trying to keep calories and carbs to a minimum, this dish also tastes great completely on its own without the addition of rice. Enjoy!

Ingredients:

- 2 cloves garlic, crushed
- Black pepper for flavor
- 1 tsp. Ground cumin
- 1 tsp. Salt
- 10 oz. Frozen spinach
- 2 cups water
- ½ cup lentils
- 3 cloves garlic, minced
- 2 white onions, halved and sliced into ½ rings
- 1 tbsp. Vegetable oil

Directions:

1. Place a skillet on medium heat and cover the surface of it in oil.
2. Dump your onion slices into the oiled skillet and allow them to sauté for 10 minutes.
3. Add in your garlic and allow to sauté for an additional 1 minute.
4. Pour your water and lentils into the skillet. Bring to a boil.
5. Once the contents are boiling, lower the heat and allow to simmer and cover the skillet with a top to trap the heat. Allow simmering for up to 35 minutes. You'll know this stage is complete when the lentils have softened and have become tender.
6. While the skillet is simmering, microwave your frozen spinach in the manner suggested on its packaging directions. Once microwaved, add the spinach along with some cumin and salt into your skillet.
7. Cover the skillet back up and allow it to continue simmering until it is completely heated. This should take approximately 10 more minutes.
8. Season with your desired amount of black pepper and additional garlic.

Black Beans Matter

Ready In: 25 minutes

Servings: 4   Calories: 305   Protein: 9.9g   Carbs: 57.8g   Fat: 4.4g

This recipe proves that black beans and white rice *really can* live together in peace and harmony! This racially diverse dish hails from the southern region of Mexico and is incredibly popular among the vegans there – you'll see why when you take your very first bite. This lunch is so good it could probably cure someone of racism!

Ingredients:

- 1 1/2 cups uncooked instant white rice
- 1/2 tsp. Garlic powder
- 1 tsp. Dried oregano
- 14.5 oz. Can stewed tomatoes
- 15 oz. Can black beans, undrained
- 1 onion, chopped
- 1 tbsp. Vegetable oil

Directions:

1. Place a large saucepan on medium-high heat and spread oil to cover the surface of it.
2. Add in your onion and stir while allowing it to cook until tender.
3. Pour in your beans, garlic powder, oregano and stewed tomatoes.
4. Bring the contents of the saucepan to a boil and stir in your white rice.
5. Cover the saucepan and lower the heat down to a low simmer. Let sit for 5 minutes.
6. Remove the saucepan from the heat source and let sit an additional 5 minutes before you serve.

Avo-Tacos

Ready In: 25 minutes

Servings: 12   Calories: 211   Protein: 3.7g   Carbs: 27g   Fat: 11.1g

This vegan taco recipe is based all around the number one vegan commodity: the amazing avocado! If you've been a vegan for any significant length of time, surely, you've eaten your fair share of avocados. If you're beginning to get tired of eating stand-alone avocados, continue to reap their excellent health benefits while mixing it up enough to keep it fresh and interesting with this new and delicious recipe!

Ingredients:

- Jalapeno pepper sauce
- 1 bunch cilantro, finely chopped
- 12 6" corn tortilla shells
- ¼ tsp. Garlic salt
- ¼ cup onions, diced
- 3 avocados, mashed

Directions:

1. Set your oven to 325°F (165°C) for preheating.
2. Mix your mashed avocado, garlic salt and onion together in a bowl.
3. Spread out your 12 tortilla shells evenly apart on a cookie sheet and place in the oven for 4 or 5 minutes. They should be heated through.
4. Take your avocado spread from step 2 and spread it out onto your heated tortillas.
5. Top the spread with jalapeno pepper sauce and as much cilantro as you would like.

Vegan BBQ Sandwiches

Ready In: 25 minutes

Servings: 4   Calories: 429   Protein: 16.7g   Carbs: 65.7g   Fat: 12.1g

Despite what you're probably thinking, this is *not* another tofu recipe. Instead, it relies on the delicious texture and flavor of barbecue-style tempeh! The combination of barbecue sauce, chopped bell peppers and onion create an exquisite blend of seasoning and flavor that really makes tempeh taste better than you ever thought it could.

Ingredients:

- 4 Kaiser rolls, cut in half and toasted
- 1 medium-sized onion, chopped
- 1 green bell pepper, chopped and seeded
- 1 red bell pepper, chopped and seeded
- 1 tbsp. Vegetable oil
- 8 oz. Package of tempeh, crumbled
- 1 cup of barbecue sauce

Directions:

1. In a medium bowl, combine the barbecue sauce and the crumbled tempeh. Let sit to marinate for 10 minutes.
2. Place a skillet on medium heat and coat with oil.
3. Add the chopped peppers (both green and red) to the skillet as well as the onion.
4. Stir frequently while allowing to cook until tenderized.
5. Pour the barbecue / crumbled tempeh sauce into the skillet and mix well with vegetables to coat. Allow time to heat through completely.
6. Scoop the mixture out and spread onto Kaiser rolls to create your sandwiches.

Aloo Matar

Ready In: 45 minutes

Servings: 4   Calories: 446   Protein: 9.5g   Carbs: 73.1g   Fat: 14.3g

Aloo Matar is a delightful Indian dish that is rich in paprika, garam masala, ginger, garlic, onions and – you guessed it, mouthwatering flavor! The seasoning packs a punch of flavor onto the warm potatoes and peas in a Diwali of deliciousness.

Ingredients:

- 2 tbsp. Chopped cilantro
- 1 tsp. Salt
- 1 tsp. White sugar
- 1 1/2 tsp. Paprika
- 1 1/2 tsp. Garam masala
- ½ cup tomato puree
- 1 cup frozen peas
- 4 large potatoes, chopped and peeled
- 1 bay leaf
- 1 tbsp. Ginger and garlic paste
- 2 medium onions, chopped finely
- ¼ cup vegetable oil

Directions:

1. Put a wok on medium heat and coat it with your oil.
2. Stir the bay leaf, ginger and garlic paste and onions together on the wok. Allow to cook until the onions tenderize.
3. Add the potatoes and peas into the mixture.
4. Cover the wok and allow to cook until the potatoes have become delicate and tender. This should take 15 minutes.
5. Take the bay leaf out of the wok.
6. Pour in your garam masala, paprika, sugar, tomato puree and salt and blend with the veggie mixture. Allow to cook for another 10 minutes.
7. Sprinkle your cilantro in and continue to cook for an additional 2 minutes.
8. Dish out into bowls and serve!

Coconut-Curry Quinoa

Ready In: 1 hour

Servings: 10   Calories: 409   Protein: 16.7g   Carbs: 53.6g   Fat: 15.4g

This quinoa is topped with a delicious curry composed of coconut flavor, coriander and red lentils among other things. Not only is this hearty dish vegan, but it is also gluten-free, which means it's great for someone suffering from celiac disease or even just gluten-intolerance!

Ingredients:

- 1 bunch of cilantro, chopped
- Salt and pepper
- 2 cups red lentils
- 2 tbsp. Ground coriander
- 3 tbsp. Curry powder
- 1 4" cinnamon stick
- ¼ cup coconut powder
- 1 tbsp. Molasses
- 14 oz. Can coconut milk
- 1 cup water
- 5 large tomatoes, chopped
- 6 cloves garlic, minced
- 1 small onion, chopped
- 2 tbsp. Coconut oil
- 1 tbsp. Salt
- 3 ½ cups water
- 2 cups quinoa

<u>Directions:</u>

1. Using a fine mesh strainer, thoroughly rinse your quinoa under a running faucet for 5 to 10 minutes to ensure you completely remove the naturally occurring saponin. This is important, because if you fail to rinse it completely then the saponins will make you sick.
2. Put your 3 ½ cups of water and 1 tbsp. of salt into a saucepan and bring it to a boil.
3. Add in the quinoa and stir well.
4. Cover the saucepan and reduce heat to medium-low and allow to simmer for about 15 minutes. You'll know this step is complete when the liquid has absorbed into the quinoa and it has become tender. Set the quinoa aside for later.
5. In another large saucepan on medium heat, melt your coconut oil and toss in your garlic and onion. Stir continuously until the onion has become translucent and has softened a bit. This should take 5 or 6 minutes.
6. Pour in the tomatoes and stir for another 5 minutes to cook.
7. Add the coconut milk and water to the saucepan, along with the coconut powder, molasses, cinnamon, curry powder and coriander.
8. Bring the saucepan to a simmer over medium-high heat.
9. When it has begun to simmer, stir in the lentils and allow to continue cooking until they are just tender. This may take 10 to 15 minutes. Be sure to stir continuously so that the lentils do not stick. Be extra careful not to overcook them though.
10. When finished, season with your salt and pepper and sprinkle in the chopped-up cilantro. Pour over your prepared quinoa and enjoy!

Sweet-Ginger Tofu Wedges

Ready In: 1 hour, 25 minutes

Servings: 4   Calories: 344.5   Protein: 11.7g   Carbs: 13.2g   Fat: 27.7g

These delicious tofu wedges are sweet and spicy at the same time! They are bathed in red pepper flakes, ginger, soy sauce, chili pepper and even orange juice. It may sound like an interesting combination and one you hadn't thought of before, but trust me when I say they taste a whole lot better than they sound. No description I give can ever do these tofu wedges justice, but your taste buds can!

Ingredients:

- 2 dried chipotle chili peppers
- ¼ cup chopped cilantro
- 1 green onion, cut into 1" strips
- ¼ tsp. Red pepper flakes
- 1 tbsp. Minced fresh ginger root
- 3 cloves garlic, minced
- 4 tsp. Dark sesame oil
- 1/3 cup canola oil
- 1/3 cup soy sauce
- ¼ cup rice vinegar
- 1 cup fresh orange juice
- 1 pound firm tofu

Directions:

1. Position your tofu on its side and slice it into 4 thin pieces.
2. Reposition the tofu flat on its surface again and cut it in a diagonal fashion to create 8 different wedges.
3. While carefully still holding the pieces together so they do not separate, place your tofu on a cutting board and cover it with a paper towel. Set a heavy skillet on top of it and allow it to sit on its own for 30 minutes, to allow the extra water to be drained from the tofu.
4. Whisk your oils, garlic, ginger, red pepper flakes, soy sauce, vinegar and orange juice together in a bowl.
5. Separate your tofu wedges and nicely and evenly arrange them together in a baking dish forming only one layer.
6. Cover the layer of tofu wedges with the marinade you created in step 4 and garnish them with cilantro and your green onion.
7. Remove the stems from your chili peppers and place them in the dish with the tofu.
8. Cover the dish with plastic wrap and set in the refrigerator for at least about 30 minutes or up to as long as overnight, if you have the time. The longer you allow them to sit, then the more they will marinate.
9. Set your oven to 350°F (175°C) for preheating.
10. Drain a bit of the excess marinade from your dish to allow the tofu to only be covered about half way.
11. Bake for 45 minutes, without turning, at 350°F (175°C).
12. You will know it is finished, when the tofu becomes golden and the majority of marinade is absorbed.

Mac Without Cheese

Ready In: 1 hour, 15 minutes

Servings: 6   Calories: 429   Protein: 10.9g   Carbs: 40.4g   Fat: 25.7g

The 100% tried and true vegan version of macaroni and cheese that is bound to please your whole family's taste buds. This mac without the cheese is so much healthier than regular mac and cheese and tastes just as great! The secret to the flavor this recipe offers is the combination of vegetable oil with nutritional yeast and canola oil, along with a few other bells and whistles you can see in the ingredients below. Spread this macaroni in between two slices of toast and you have a delicious mac without cheese sandwich!

Ingredients:

- 1 tsp. Onion powder
- 1 tsp. Garlic powder
- 3 tbsp. Nutritional yeast
- 1/3 cup canola oil
- Salt
- 1 1/3 cups water
- 1/3 cup lemon juice
- 1 cup cashews
- 1 medium onion, chopped
- 1 tbsp. Vegetable oil
- 8 oz. Package uncooked elbow macaroni

Directions:

1. Set your oven to 350°F (175°C) for preheating.
2. Place a large pot with lightly salted water on your stove and bring it to a boil.
3. Pour in your elbow macaroni and allow to cook for 10 minutes.
4. Drain the water and pour the macaroni into a baking dish.
5. Place a saucepan on medium heat and cover with vegetable oil.
6. Add in your onion and stir until tender and gently browned.
7. Mix the onion with the macaroni.
8. Use a food processor to process together your salt, water, lemon juice and cashews.
9. Slowly begin to blend in the onion powder, garlic powder, nutritional yeast, roasted peppers. Continue blending until a smooth texture is formed.
10. Mix the processed ingredients together with the macaroni and onions.
11. Place the baking dish of macaroni, onions and the processed ingredients into the oven and bake for 45 minutes at 350°F (175°C). When finished, it should be lightly golden-browned.
12. Allow to cool for 15 minutes.

Hummus Sandwich Spread with Tapenade

Ready In: 2 hours, 20 minutes

Servings: 4   Calories: 131   Protein: 5.3g   Carbs: 10g   Fat: 8.7g

This hummus and tapenade-based sandwich spread is the perfect partner for any of the sandwiches in this cookbook! From the abundance of Kalamata olives, hummus and tahini, it has a great deal of the healthy kind of fat that your brain and your body need to function at their maximum potential. This sandwich spread is also perfectly cut out to serve as a dip for crackers!

Ingredients:

- 1/8 tsp. Ground black pepper
- 1/8 tsp. Onion powder
- 1/8 tsp. Garlic powder
- 1/2 tsp. Ground coriander
- 1 tsp. Rosemary, minced
- 1 tsp. Italian parsley, minced
- 1 tbsp. Tahini
- 8 oz. Hummus
- 2 tbsp. Green olives, pitted
- ¼ cup pitted Kalamata olives

Directions:

1. Use a food processor to pulse your green olives and your Kalamata olives together until perfectly minced.
2. Mixed your minced olive combination with your onion powder, pepper, garlic powder, coriander, rosemary, parsley, tahini and your hummus and stir in a bowl until they are completely combined.
3. Cover the bowl and place it in your refrigerator to sit and chill for two hours minimum.
4. Uncover the bowl and prepare to serve!

Avocado & Tomato Sandwich

Ready In: 10 minutes

Servings: 1   Calories: 372   Protein: 8.5g   Carbs: 39.9g   Fat: 22g

An avocado sandwich, topped with a few slices of tomato, makes for a fantastic lunch for those who are strapped for time! In as little as 10 minutes, this healthy sandwich featuring ciabatta bread, avocado and sliced tomato can be ready to eat.

Ingredients:

- 1 pinch ground black pepper
- 3 slices of tomato
- 1 slice ciabatta bread
- 1 tsp. Garlic salt
- 1/2 avocado, mashed

Directions:

1. Mix your garlic into your mashed avocado in a small bowl. Stir and mix thoroughly.
2. Layer your avocado spread onto your slice of ciabatta bread.
3. Dress with your tomato slices and sprinkle on a pinch of black pepper!

No-Tuna Salad Sandwich

Ready In: 10 minutes

Servings: 4   Calories: 492   Protein: 11.3g   Carbs: 53.1g   Fat: 27.4g

There may not be tuna on this no-tuna salad sandwich, but your taste buds don't have to know that! There is no fishy taste, but the creamy and luscious texture of tuna salad is very much present here. The Dijon mustard and the rice vinegar combine to form a very pleasant taste!

Ingredients:

- 1 tsp. Dried dill weed
- ¼ cup dried onion, chopped
- 1 stalk celery
- ½ cup chopped dill pickles
- 1 cup drained canned chickpeas
- 1 tsp. Rice vinegar
- 1 tsp. Dijon mustard
- 1 tsp. White sugar
- 1 tsp. Sea salt
- ¼ cup soy milk
- ½ cup olive oil
- 8 slices sourdough bread

Directions:

1. Pour your soy milk and olive oil into a blender and blend together until it becomes a thick consistency.
2. Add mustard, sugar and salt.
3. Start the blender back up and, as it's still blending, pour your vinegar through the opening in the top of the lid. Continue adding however much vinegar you need to in order for the texture to become smooth.
4. Pour your pickles, celery, chopped onion, dill and chickpeas into the blender and blend until everything is evenly chopped and blended together.
5. Layer the spread onto one of your slices of sourdough bread and top with another.

Zucchini Wrap

Ready In: 40 minutes

Servings: 4   Calories: 350   Protein: 8.1g   Carbs: 42.7g   Fat: 16.2g

These zucchini wraps are absolutely packed to their very edges with seasonings, spices and mouthwatering flavors. This heart-healthy and vegan-friendly lunch selection is light on your stomach and won't give you a mid-afternoon energy flatline, like many of the other heavier-duty options might.

Ingredients:

- ½ cup sour cream
- 4 fresh chives
- 4 10" flour tortillas
- Salt
- ¼ tsp. Ground cinnamon
- ¼ tsp. Ground cloves
- ¼ tsp. Ground black pepper
- ½ tsp. Chili powder
- 4 cups grated zucchini
- 1 tbsp. Grated fresh ginger
- 1 small red onion, sliced
- 1 tsp. Cumin seeds
- 1 tsp. Mustard seeds
- 1 tbsp. Vegetable oil

Directions:

1. Heat a wok to medium-high heat and cover the surface of it with your oil.
2. Mix in your cumin seeds and mustard seeds. When they start to pop, reduce the heat to a low simmer and toss in the ginger and onion. Allow the onions to sauté until they are soft and being a very light pinkish hue.
3. Mix the zucchini in and increase the heat just a little bit, as you continue to stir for 5 to 10 minutes or however long it takes for the zucchini to become soft.
4. Mix and stir in your salt, cinnamon, clove, pepper and chili powder.
5. Heat up your tortillas in the microwave for 30 seconds or until they are just warm. Measure out a ¼ of the total zucchini filling you have prepared and place it in the middle of each tortilla.
6. Roll the wrap up and tie it together with a chive. Repeat steps 6 and 7 for each of the 4 tortillas.
7. Serve with vegan sour cream, if you wish!

Sweet Potato PETA Pitas

Ready In: 35 minutes

Servings: 6   Calories: 537   Protein: 26.4g   Carbs: 95g   Fat: 7.6g

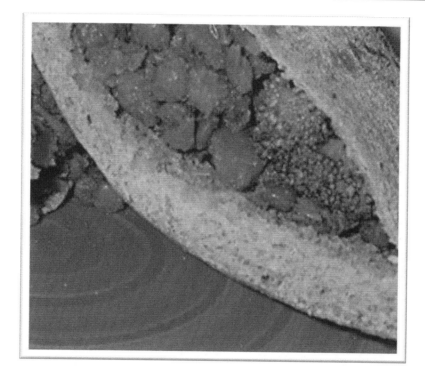

If PETA were hypothetically ever to endorse a pita, this would be the one! No animals were harmed during the creation of this recipe. This scrumptious vegan pita is stuffed with peeled, cut and well-seasoned slices of sweet potato, tomatoes and broccoli – all of which are complemented by your favorite brand of barbecue sauce!

Ingredients:

- 6 whole wheat Lebanese-style pita bread rounds
- 6 tbsp. Barbecue sauce, divided
- 2 tomatoes, chopped
- 1 tsp. Garlic salt
- 1 ½ tsp. Cayenne pepper
- 1 tbsp. Cumin
- 15 oz. Canned lentils, drained and rinsed
- 1 cup broccoli florets
- 2 tbsp. Organic extra virgin olive oil
- 2 sweet potatoes, cut into bite-sized portions and peeled

Directions:

1. Prepare a large pot of water and immerse your sweet potatoes in it.
2. Bring the pot to a boil and then immediately lower the heat down to a nice, low simmer and cook for 8 minutes.
3. Drain the water from the pot and set to the side.
4. Place a skillet on medium-high heat and cover its surface with some olive oil.
5. Stir the broccoli in the skillet's heated oil until it becomes crispy, but still maintains some tenderness. This should take no more than 5 minutes.
6. Mix the cayenne pepper, cumin, lentils and sweet potatoes into the skillet with the broccoli and stir them all together. Allow to cook until fully heated through, which should also take no more than another 5 minutes.
7. Toss in your diced tomatoes and cook for an additional 3 minutes or until they are hot.
8. Pour about 1 tbsp. of barbecue sauce inside of each pita round. Measure out 1 cup of the sweet potato mixture from your skillet for each pita shell and fill each of them up.
9. Fold or wrap your pitas however you would like and secure with toothpicks as needed.

Ta'ameya Falafel Balls

Ready In: 8 hours, 30 minutes

Servings: 8   Calories: 485.7   Protein: 13.9g   Carbs: 28.8g   Fat: 37g

This falafel recipe originated from Egypt, where they refer to it as *Ta'ameya!* Ta'ameya, as the Egyptians call it, is a widely popular street food in their culture. The difference between their falafel balls and the variety you usually find elsewhere throughout the world is that the Egyptians make their Ta'ameya with dried fava beans as opposed to chickpeas. I believe you'll agree that Ta'ameya is even tastier than common falafel balls, once you try this recipe out for yourself!

Ingredients:

- Vegetable oil for frying
- 1 cup sesame seeds
- 1 tsp. Ground cumin
- 1 ½ tsp. Salt
- 1 ½ tsp. Ground coriander
- 3 cloves garlic
- ½ cup fresh dill
- 1/2 cup fresh cilantro
- 1/2 cup fresh parsley
- 1 red onion, quartered
- 2 cups dried and split fava beans

Directions:

1. Prepare a large bowl full of your fava beans and cover them with a few inches of water. Allow the beans to soak in the water for 8 hours or overnight.
2. Drain the water from the fava beans and mix them with your cumin, salt, coriander, garlic, dill, cilantro, parsley and red onion in a food processor. Process until it becomes a thick doughy consistency.
3. Place a skillet over medium heat and add your sesame seeds. Stir frequently as they cook, until they are toasted. This may take up to 5 minutes.
4. Transfer your toasted sesame seeds to a plate.
5. Work your fava bean dough into balls and roll them in the sesame seeds until adequately coated.
6. Put a large-sized saucepan on medium heat and fill it ¼ of the way full with oil.
7. Fry your fava bean dough balls together in a series of batches, until they turn golden-brown. This may take up to 5 minutes.
8. Drain with paper towels.

Vegan Pate

Ready In: 1 hour, 15 minutes

Servings: 9   Calories: 219   Protein: 6.5g   Carbs: 16.1g   Fat: 15.4g

This vegan pate is an amalgamation of whole wheat flour, sunflower seeds, nutritional yeast, potatoes, carrots, onions, celery, garlic and much more! It forms a wonderful spread that can be used to top crackers, sandwiches or anything else you can think of. It is a pate that will add to and improve almost any lunch!

Ingredients:

- ½ tsp. Ground dry mustard
- ½ tsp. Black pepper
- ½ tsp. Dried savory
- 1/2 tsp. Dried sage
- 1/2 tsp. Dried basil leaves
- ½ tsp. Dried thyme
- 1 ½ cups water
- 1 clove garlic, peeled
- 1 stalk celery, chopped
- 1 onion, chopped
- 1 large carrot, peeled and sliced
- 1 potato, peeled and chopped
- 2 tbsp. Lemon juice
- ½ cup vegetable oil
- ½ tsp. Salt
- ½ cup nutritional yeast
- ½ cup whole wheat flour
- 1 cup sunflower seeds

Directions:

1. Set your oven to 350°F (175°C) for preheating. Grease an 8" x 8" baking dish.
2. Blend your dry mustard, pepper, savory, sage, basil, thyme, water, garlic, celery, onion, carrot, potato, lemon juice, vegetable oil, salt, nutritional yeast, whole wheat flour and sunflower seeds together in a food processor until the texture becomes almost smooth.
3. Pour the mixture into your 8" x 8" baking dish and bake for up to 1 hour at 350°F (175°C). You will know it is done when it has browned lightly and becomes bubbly.

Roasted Mushrooms & Eggplant

Ready In: 55 minutes

Servings: 1   Calories: 256   Protein: 15.5g   Carbs: 50.2g   Fat: 1.4g

Imagine zucchini, mushrooms and eggplant all roasted together with a hint of tomato and a variety of savory seasonings. That's what you can expect to enjoy when you invest the 55 minutes needed to put this incredible lunch together! I recommend melting your favorite vegan-certified cheeses as a topping to this already incredible meal, but that's just a tip. Feel free to enjoy this dish however you wish.

Ingredients:

- Salt and pepper
- ½ tsp. Dried basil
- 1 clove of garlic, minced
- ½ cup water
- 1 ½ tbsp. Tomato paste
- 8 oz. Package of mushrooms, sliced
- ½ small yellow onion, chopped
- 2 small zucchinis, cubed
- 1 medium eggplant, cubed and peeled

Directions:

1. Set your oven to 450°F (230°C) for preheating.
2. Prepare a 2-quart casserole dish in which you place your mushrooms, onion, zucchini and eggplant.
3. Mix your tomato paste with your water in a small bowl and stir in the basil, salt, pepper and garlic. When well-mixed, pour it over your vegetables in the casserole dish and mix together well.
4. Bake at 450°F (230°C) for 45 minutes or until the eggplant becomes soft and tenderized. Remember to stir occasionally. Add however much extra water you need if your vegetables begin to stick or clump together. Vegetables should be slightly browned and relatively dry when finished.

1-Hour Hot & Sour Soup

Ready In: 1 hour

Servings: 2   Calories: 329   Protein: 24g   Carbs: 28.6g   Fat: 12.5g

This hot and sour soup recipe comes out tasting just like the top-of-the-line stuff that you can order from a high-end oriental restaurant! This soup contains bamboo fungus (phallus indusiatus), which is *extremely* healthy for you. Studies have shown that bamboo fungus is good for your lungs and your eyes and it can even help you lose weight, reduce your cholesterol and prevent cancer!

Ingredients:

- 1 cup Chinese dried mushrooms
- 1 green onion, sliced
- ½ tbsp. Sesame oil
- ½ tsp. Chili oil
- ¾ tsp. Ground white pepper
- 1/2 tsp. Ground black pepper
- ¼ tsp. Crushed red pepper flakes
- 1 quart of vegetable broth
- 8 oz. Firm tofu cut into ¼ inch strips.
- 5 tbsp. Rice vinegar
- 3 tbsp. Soy sauce
- 1/3 oz. Bamboo fungus
- 2 cups hot water
- 12 dried tiger lily buds
- 4 dried shiitake mushrooms
- 1 oz. Dried wood ear mushrooms

<u>Directions:</u>

1. Mix your wood mushrooms, lily buds and shiitake mushrooms together in a small bowl and pour in 1 ½ cups of hot water. Allow it to soak for 20 minutes to re-hydrate.
2. Drain the water from the mushroom / lily bud mix and save the water for later.
3. Remove the stems from the mushrooms and cut them all into very thin strips.
4. Cut the lily buds into halves.
5. Soak the bamboo fungus in ¼ cup of slightly salted hot water in a second bowl. Allow about 20 minutes of soaking time. Drain and mince.
6. Blend the soy sauce and the rice vinegar with 1 tbsp. of cornstarch in a third bowl. Place half of the tofu strips into this mixture.
7. Put a medium saucepan on the stove to boil and combine the lily bud / mushroom liquid you saved from step 2 with the vegetable broth in the saucepan. Stir continuously.
8. Once it's boiling, lower the heat to a dull simmer for about 5 minutes. While it's simmering, you should begin to season it with your white pepper, black pepper and red pepper.
9. In yet another separate bowl, combine your leftover cornstarch and water and stir well.
10. Add the leftover cornstarch and water mixture into the broth mixture on the saucepan and stir until it becomes a thick consistency.
11. Combine the soy sauce mixture and remaining tofu pieces with everything else, in the saucepan.
12. Bring the saucepan back to a boil and stir in the sesame oil, chili oil and the bamboo fungus.
13. When finished, removed the saucepan from the heat source and allow to cool for 20 minutes. Pour into bowls and serve.

Black Bean Soup

Ready In: 1 hour

Servings: 8   Calories: 426   Protein: 25g   Carbs: 72.5g   Fat: 6.4g

This zesty black bean-centric soup combines the hearty flavor of seasoned black beans with crushed tomatoes in a perfect blend! Black bean soup is one of the healthier soup options contained in this book as well as one of the simpler ones to prepare.

Ingredients:

- 14.5 oz. Can of crushed tomatoes
- 15 oz. Can of whole kernel corn
- 4 x 15 oz. Cans of black beans
- 4 cups vegetable broth
- 1 pinch black pepper
- 1 tbsp. Ground cumin
- 2 tbsp. Chili powder
- 4 cloves garlic, chopped
- 2 carrots, chopped
- 1 stalk celery, chopped
- 1 large onion, chopped
- 1 tbsp. Organic extra virgin olive oil

Directions:

1. Place a large pot on medium-high heat.
2. Heat your oil up in the pot.
3. Sauté your garlic, carrots, celery and onion in the pot. This should take 5 minutes.
4. Season your veggies with black pepper, cumin and chili powder. Allow to cook 1 additional minute.
5. Mix your vegetable broth, corn and 2 of your cans of beans into the pot. Stir to mix well.
6. Bring the pot to a boil.
7. Use a food processor to blend together your 2 remaining cans of black beans and your tomatoes. Process and blend until the texture is smooth.
8. Stir the blend from your food processor into the boiling soup mixture.
9. Reduce the heat to medium to a simmer. Simmer for 12 to 15 minutes.

Red Lentil Soup

Ready In: 55 minutes

Servings: 4   Calories: 462   Protein: 15.7g   Carbs: 42.5g   Fat: 27.8g

Red lentils help stabilize your blood sugar, improve digestive health, promote weight loss, are packed full of protein and help lower cholesterol! What more could you ask for from the main ingredient in a delicious soup? The butternut squash, red lentils, garlic and other succulent flavors you will delight in with this soup make it a must have lunch for anyone on a vegan diet!

Ingredients:

- Salt and pepper
- 1 pinch ground nutmeg
- 1 pinch cayenne pepper
- 1 tsp. Curry powder
- 2 tbsp. Tomato paste
- 14 oz. Can coconut milk
- 2 cups water
- 1/3 cup finely chopped fresh cilantro
- 1 cup butternut squash, peeled, seeded and cubed
- 1 cup dry red lentils
- 1 pinch fenugreek seeds
- 1 clove garlic, chopped
- 1 tbsp. Minced fresh ginger root
- 1 small onion, chopped
- 1 tbsp. Peanut oil

Directions:

1. Place a large pot on your stove and set it to medium heat. Heat your oil.
2. Add the onion, ginger, fenugreek and garlic into the pot and allow to cook until the onion becomes tenderized.
3. Add in your cilantro, squash and lentils. Pour in the water, coconut milk and tomato paste and stir well.
4. Season the mix with your pepper, salt, cayenne pepper and curry powder.
5. Bring the pot to a boil and then reduce the heat to a nice, low simmer for 30 minutes. You'll know your soup is done and ready to eat when the squash and red lentils become tender.

Broccoli Soup

Ready In: 35 minutes

Servings: 4   Calories: 355   Protein: 16.2g   Carbs: 37g   Fat: 18.1g

This broccoli soup recipe is one of the quicker-to-prepare soups in the book. It has a creamy taste complete with nutmeg and coconut milk that creates a sweet, nutty flavor to be enjoyed. This particular soup tastes just as good cold as it does when it's hot!

Ingredients:

- ¼ tsp. Black pepper
- 1 tsp. Sea salt
- 1 tsp. Dried basil
- 4 ½ cups broccoli, chopped
- 1 onion, chopped
- 2 Yukon gold potatoes, cut into ½" cubes
- 5 cups vegetable broth, divided
- 1 cup raw cashews

Directions:

1. Blend your cashews with 1 cup of your vegetable broth together in a food processor until the texture is smooth. This should take 1 minute.
2. With the additional 4 cups of vegetable broth, place your potatoes and onions in a large pot and cover. Place the covered pot on the stove and allow to simmer for 5 minutes.
3. Mix your broccoli and basil into the pot and stir well. Return the pot to a simmer.
4. Cover the pot once again and allow to cook for 10 more minutes or until the potatoes have become tender.
5. Pour and stir your cashew mix into the soup. Season with salt and pepper. Bring to simmer again and then immediately remove the pot from the heat source.
6. Pour half of the soup into your food processor and blend until it becomes smooth in texture.
7. Return your blended soup back to the pot and stir everything together to mix well.

Garbanzo Bean & Kale Soup

Ready In: 45 minutes

Servings: 4   Calories: 343   Protein: 13.6g   Carbs: 36.3g   Fat: 17.1g

Garbanzo beans and kale come together in a delicious union of glory in this curried soup! Enjoy a bowl of high-fiber and high-flavor soup that is complete with a broad spectrum of vitamins and other beneficial nutrients. The combination of garbanzo beans and kale provide iron, zinc, Vitamin A, Vitamin B6, Vitamin C, Manganese, Calcium and a whole lot more!

Ingredients:

- 1 cup almond milk
- ¼ tsp. Curry powder
- 1 cube vegetable bouillon
- 15 oz. Can garbanzo beans, drained and rinsed
- 4 cups kale leaves, chopped
- 1 quart vegetable broth, divided
- ¼ cup minced onion
- 1 tsp. Minced garlic
- Cooking spray

Directions:

1. Use your cooking spray to prepare the inside of a stockpot.
2. Place the stockpot on medium heat and cook and stir in the garlic until it has become lightly browned. This should take 3 minutes or less.
3. Pour in 2 tbsp. of vegetable broth and your onion into the stockpot. Continuously stir while cooking for 5 to 10 minutes or until the onion is translucent.
4. Add in your kale and stir well. Continue to cook until the kale wilts slightly, which should be about 4 minutes.
5. Mix in your remaining vegetable broth, garbanzo beans, curry powder and vegetable bouillon.
6. Bring the stockpot to a boil.
7. Reduce the heat and allow to simmer until fully heated through. This should take 15 more minutes.
8. Stir in almond milk and cook until heated through, for about 3 minutes.

Carrot Curry Soup

Ready In: 35 minutes

Servings: 4   Calories: 408   Protein: 17.2g   Carbs: 52.2g   Fat: 14.9g

This is a simple and comforting soup! Carrot soup has long been used as a folk remedy to recover from the common cold and flu. If you wish to further augment this recipe for the purpose of healing, add the famous antibacterial, turmeric, to the dish at your leisure. Turmeric is not included in the base recipe, but it sure tastes great as an addition to it!

Ingredients:

- 1 tsp. Fresh cilantro, chopped
- 14 oz. Water
- 14 oz. Can of coconut milk
- 2 lbs. Carrots, peeled and chopped
- ½ tsp. Ground ginger
- ½ tsp. Ground cinnamon
- 1 tsp. Ground cumin
- 2 tsp. Curry powder
- 4 cups vegetable broth

Directions:

1. Place a soup pot on the stove and boil your vegetable broth in it over medium heat.
2. Stir in your carrots, ginger, cinnamon, cumin and curry powder.
3. Reduce the stove's heat to a simmer. Continue to simmer for 20 minutes or until the carrots become tender. Stir frequently.
4. Use a strainer to separate the carrots from the broth.
5. Pour carrots into a food processor and fill the pitcher no more than half of the way full.
6. Pour ¼ cup of your vegetable broth into the food processor and blend into a smooth puree.
7. When that has pureed completely, add in another batch of carrots and repeat until all of your carrots have been successfully pureed. Pour the pureed carrots back into the vegetable broth mixture.
8. Mix in the water and the coconut milk by stirring well.
9. Bring the soup pot back to a simmer and sprinkle the top with cilantro.

Tofu Soup for the Vegan Soul

Ready In: 55 minutes

Servings: 4   Calories: 325   Protein: 18.3g   Carbs: 36.6g   Fat: 14.3g

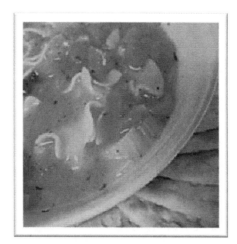

This chicken noodle soup alternative is incredible! Your taste buds will have no idea that you're *not* eating chicken noodle soup. The seasoning and texture of the tofu in this recipe is so convincing that you will actually feel like you're eating a hearty bowl of chicken noodle soup!

Ingredients:

- 3 tbsp. Cold water
- ¼ cup cornstarch
- ¼ tsp. Black pepper
- ¼ tsp. Dried marjoram
- ¼ tsp. Dried rosemary
- ¼ tsp. Dried thyme
- ¼ tsp. Poultry seasoning
- ½ tsp. Dried oregano
- ½ tsp. Dried basil
- ¼ cup raisins
- 14 oz. Container extra-firm tofu, drained and cubed
- 2 cups whole wheat noodles
- 12 cups vegan chicken-flavored broth
- 1 1/2 tsp. Minced garlic
- 1 1/2 cups celery, chopped
- 1 1/2 cups onion, chopped
- 2 cups carrots, sliced
- 2 tbsp. Vegan butter alternative

Directions:

1. Place a stockpot on medium heat and melt in your vegan butter alternative.
2. Stir in the garlic, celery, onion and carrots. Cook and stir frequently for 10 minutes.
3. Pour your vegan chicken-flavored broth into the stockpot and bring it to a boil on high heat.
4. At the point of boiling, reduce the soup to a simmer and add in your whole wheat noodles, pepper, marjoram, rosemary, thyme, poultry seasoning, oregano, basil, raisins and tofu.
5. In a small bowl, combine your water and cornstarch and allow it to dissolve.
6. Mix your cornstarch mixture into the soup and stir to mix well.
7. Bring the soup back to a boil and then reduce the heat to medium-low.
8. Cover and allow 30 more minutes to simmer.

Mushroom Salad

Ready In: 4 hours, 10 minutes

Servings: 10   Calories: 466   Protein: 5g   Carbs: 24.8g   Fat: 43.9g

Enjoy a salad of mushrooms marinated in a dressing of lemon and garlic! If you are trying to watch your calories, this is a great lunch selection to consider. It offers a satisfying taste with a moist and delicate texture, without causing you to splurge on your calorie limit!

Ingredients:

- 5 lbs. Whole, fresh mushrooms, thinly sliced
- 2 tbsp. Black pepper
- 8 cloves garlic, chopped
- ¼ cup salt
- 2 bunches curly-leaf parsley, chopped
- 1 cup lemon juice
- 2 cups vegetable oil

Directions:

1. Prepare a large serving bowl with your pepper, garlic, salt, parsley, lemon juice and vegetable oil. Whisk together.
2. Add your mushrooms to the bowl and stir thoroughly to coat the mushrooms in the dressing.
3. Use plastic wrap to cover your bowl. Place in the refrigerator for 4 hours while stopping by to toss together every once in a while.

Fava Bean Salad

Ready In: 1 hour, 20 minutes

Servings: 4   Calories: 333   Protein: 13g   Carbs: 35.3g   Fat: 17.5g

This fava bean salad will make for a perfect lunch on any day of the week! It has slices of chopped cucumber and Roma tomatoes, diced onions and, of course, fava beans. Flavored with balsamic vinegar, maple syrup and olive oil and garnished with a juiced lemon, this is a simple salad recipe that's hard to beat when it comes to sheer flavor!

Ingredients:

- 2 x 15 oz. Cans of fava beans, drained
- 2 Roma tomatoes, chopped
- 1 small sweet onion, diced
- 1 cucumber, diced
- 1/3 cup extra virgin olive oil
- 1 clove garlic, minced
- 1 tsp. Maple syrup
- 2 tbsp. Balsamic vinegar
- ½ lemon, juiced

Directions:

1. Prepare a small bowl full of your olive oil, garlic, maple syrup, balsamic vinegar and lemon juice. Whisk together to form a dressing.
2. In a large bowl, toss your fava beans, tomatoes and onions together with your cucumber.
3. Pour the dressing you prepared in the small bowl over the vegetable mix in the second bowl and toss to coat thoroughly.
4. Leave to chill in the refrigerator for 1 hour and then serve!

Jicama Salad

Ready In: 50 minutes

Servings: 4   Calories: 475   Protein: 14.1g   Carbs: 106.3g   Fat: 5.8g

Jicama salad is a refreshing lunch option for those who are looking for something sweet, spicy, low in calories and high in fiber! Enjoy a light salad consisting of jicama, navel oranges, red, orange *and* yellow bell peppers, cucumbers, radishes, Thai chili peppers and even jalapeno. The delightful range of flavors are pleasing to the tongue as the beautiful spectrum of colors created by this offering is visually pleasing to the eye!

Ingredients:

- Black pepper
- 1 lemon, juiced
- ½ bunch cilantro, chopped
- ½ jalapeno pepper, diced
- 3 Thai chili peppers, minced
- 4 radishes, thinly sliced
- 2 small sweet orange peppers, sliced
- 3 small sweet yellow peppers, sliced
- ½ hothouse cucumber, diced
- 1 large red bell pepper, cut into bite-size pieces
- 2 navel oranges, peeled and cut into chunks
- 1 large jicama, peeled and julienned

Directions:

1. Mix your black pepper, lemon juice, cilantro, jalapeno pepper, Thai Chile peppers, radishes, orange and yellow peppers, cucumber, red bell pepper, orange chunks and your jicama together in a large bowl.
2. Toss together to combine thoroughly.
3. Cover your newly mixed salad with plastic wrap and place in the refrigerator to allow the flavors to blend. This shouldn't take any longer than 30 minutes.

Sweet Potato & Black Bean Salad

Ready In: 40 minutes

Servings: 4   Calories: 383   Protein: 11.5g   Carbs: 59.8g   Fat: 12.2g

Sweet potato and black bean salad is an easy way to get a lot of carbohydrates in fast, which makes this a fantastic bodybuilder-friendly salad for any vegan who is looking to bulk up and get bigger! Chunks of sweet potato and black beans drizzled in olive oil and lime juice are seasoned with onion, black and red pepper and cumin and are just waiting to be enjoyed when you select this delectable lunch salad!

Ingredients:

- ½ cup fresh cilantro, chopped
- ½ red onion, finely chopped
- 14.5 oz. Can of black beans, rinsed and drained
- 2 tbsp. Freshly squeezed lime juice
- Salt and black pepper
- 1/4 tsp. Red pepper flakes
- ½ tsp. Ground cumin
- 3 tbsp. Olive oil, divided
- 1 lb. Sweet potatoes, peeled and cut into ¾" cubes

Directions:

1. Set your oven to 450°F (230°C) for preheating.
2. Prepare a cookie sheet and spread your sweet potatoes across it evenly.
3. Gently and slowly pour a tablespoon of olive oil over the tops of your sweet potatoes and season them to your taste with black pepper, salt and red pepper flakes.
4. Toss the sweet potatoes about a bit until they are evenly coated in the olive oil and seasoning.
5. Place cookie sheet on the lower rack of your oven and roast for 15 minutes at 450°F (230°C).
6. Stir the sweet potatoes and turn them over before roasting for an additional 15 minutes.
7. In a large bowl, whisk the leftover 2 tablespoons of olive oil with your lime juice and season this mixture with salt and pepper.
8. Add your roasted sweet potatoes into the dressing you created in the large bowl.
9. Add in your black beans, cilantro and onions.
10. Gently toss the bowl to coat its contents evenly. Enjoy!

Vidalia Salad Dressing

Ready In: 10 minutes

Servings: 16   Calories: 204   Protein: 0.2g   Carbs: 5.3g   Fat: 20.5g

Here is a quick 10-minute recipe for a *delicious and savory* salad dressing that goes great as a topping for any of the salads listed in this cookbook! The rich interchange between white vinegar, onion, ground mustard and garlic do wonders to liven up any salad recipe you can imagine. This dressing will give your typical salad a much-needed buzz!

Ingredients:

- 1 tbsp. Salt
- 1 tsp. Ground mustard
- 1/3 cup white sugar
- 1 clove garlic
- 1 large sweet onion, peeled and quartered
- 1 cup distilled white vinegar
- 1 ½ cups canola oil

Directions:

1. This recipe is incredibly simple. Literally all you do is combine all of the ingredients: the oil, vinegar, salt, mustard, garlic and onion into a blender and blend until the texture is smooth.
2. Drizzle over your favorite salad and enjoy!

DID YOU KNOW?

You can preserve your left over Vidalia onions longer by wrapping each bulb in paper towels, to absorb the moisture, and then placing them in the crisper compartment of your refrigerator with the vents closed.

Oatmeal Crackers

Ready In: 40 minutes

Servings: 6   Calories: 261.8   Protein: 4.8g   Carbs: 32g   Fat: 13.2g

This is the vegan lunch side-menu item you are looking for! These delicious crackers made out of oatmeal and wheat flour are a great and healthy choice to accompany any of my vegan sandwiches *or* to be dipped in any of my vegan soups. It also doesn't hurt that the preparation of these crackers is so simple anyone could do it!

Ingredients:

- 5 tbsp. Olive oil
- ½ cup water
- 1 tsp. Ground cinnamon
- 1 tbsp. White sugar
- ½ tsp. Salt
- 1 cup whole wheat flour
- 1 ½ cups rolled oats

Directions:

1. Set your oven to 350°F (175°C) for preheating and grease a cookie sheet.
2. Pour your rolled oats into a food processor and pulse a few times until they are ground into coarse flour.
3. Combine your newly created oat flour with your whole wheat flour, cinnamon, sugar and salt in a medium sized bowl.
4. Pour your olive oil and water into the bowl and stir to form a soft dough.
5. Once the dough is ready, place it onto your greased cookie sheet and roll it out to be about 1/8 of an inch thick.
6. Use a knife or pizza cutter to slice the dough into whatever shape of cracker you want.
7. Bake for 10 to 15 minutes in your oven at 350°F (175°C). Keep a close eye on them, because these crackers have a tendency to burn.
8. Allow to sit for 15 to 20 more minutes before breaking along the score lines and dividing the crackers.

Tomato Soup

Ready In: 1 hour, 25 minutes

Servings: 2   Calories: 288   Protein: 11.5g   Carbs: 62.8g   Fat: 2.8g

This is no ordinary tomato soup! It is tomato soup plus pasta and chunks of vegetables, with an extra dash of deliciousness or two thrown in for good measure. Enjoy tomato soup like you've never tasted it before with this custom modified recipe including hot red pepper sauce, Italian seasoning, garlic, chopped onion and more!

Ingredients:

- ½ cup cooked ditalini pasta
- 1 cup frozen corn
- 1 small zucchini, chopped
- 2 carrots, peeled and sliced
- 2 stalks celery, sliced
- 1/8 tsp. Hot red pepper sauce
- ¼ tsp. Pepper
- 1 tsp. Salt
- 1 ½ tsp. sugar
- 1 ½ tsp. dried parsley
- 1 tsp. Italian seasoning
- 2 cloves garlic, minced
- 1 small onion, chopped
- 1 bay leaf
- 3 cubes vegetable bouillon
- 5 cups water
- 28 oz. Can of tomato sauce

Directions:

1. Prepare a large pot with your 5 cups of water, tomato sauce, hot red pepper sauce, pepper, salt, sugar, parsley, Italian seasoning, garlic, onion, bay leaf and vegetable bouillon.
2. Bring the pot to a boil and then reduce heat to a low simmer for 30 minutes.
3. Stir in the corn, zucchini, carrots and celery and allow to simmer for an additional 30 minutes.
4. Mix in your ditalini pasta and cook for 10 more minutes.

Chickpea Sandwich

Ready In: 30 minutes

Servings: 4   Calories: 611   Protein: 28.4g   Carbs: 92.8g   Fat: 15.4g

This is a sandwich that's different than any sandwich you've probably ever eaten before. This chickpea sandwich is stuffed with a creamy mixture of mashed chickpeas, vegan mayonnaise, minced onion, dill relish, lettuce and nori. It's topped with a few slices of fresh tomato to finish it all off! If you'd like, go ahead and include a side of chips.

Ingredients:

- 8 tomato slices
- 8 lettuce leaves
- ¼ cup vegan mayonnaise
- 8 slices whole wheat bread, toasted
- Black pepper
- ½ tsp. Salt
- 2 tbsp. Dill relish
- 2 tbsp. Dried minced onion
- 1/3 cup finely diced celery
- 1/3 cup minced or finely grated carrot
- ¼ cup vegan mayonnaise
- 15 oz. Can of chickpeas, no salt added, drained and rinsed
- ½ sheet nori (dried seaweed)

Directions:

1. Place your nori in a blender or food processor and pulse until it becomes a fine powder. Set to the side and allow the dust to settle.
2. In a large bowl, mash your chickpeas up until they're in small pieces. Be sure not to over-mash them, as the chickpeas should retain some of their original texture.
3. Stir your vegan mayonnaise into the mash as you mash the chickpeas ever so slightly more.
4. Mix in your pepper, salt, dill relish, onion, celery, carrot and nori powder and stir well.
5. Cover the bowl with plastic wrap and place in your refrigerator for as little as 15 minutes or as long as 3 days. The longer you let it chill, the more the flavor will form. To put your sandwiches together, first spread a nice layer of vegan mayonnaise over your toast and top with lettuce and fresh tomato slices. Then spread on your chickpea mash and top with another slice of toast. Slice the sandwiches in half and serve with your favorite style of chips!

Green Chili Salsa

Ready In: 20 minutes

Servings: 2   Calories: 84   Protein: 2.8g   Carbs: 17.1g   Fat: 1.6g

This green and tangy salsa is great for dipping not only chips, but crackers into as well! It can also be used according to your own imagination and creativity as a topping for a large number of the delicious recipes included in this cookbook. For example, it goes particularly well as a topping on my *Black Beans Matter* recipe!

Ingredients:

- Salt
- 1 fresh jalapeno pepper, seeded
- ¼ cup chopped fresh cilantro
- 4 oz. Can of chopped green chili peppers
- 2 cloves of garlic, peeled
- 3 shallots
- 8 tomatillos, husked

Directions:

1. Place your salt, jalapeno pepper, cilantro, green chili peppers, garlic, shallots and tomatillos into a blender or food processor.
2. Use the pulse setting to coarsely dice and chop the ingredients up to a nice blend with the consistency you would expect from salsa.
3. Pour the salsa into a bowl and cover with plastic wrap.
4. Place in your refrigerator until you are ready to serve.

Tofu Nuggets with Maple-Mustard Dip

Ready In: 30 minutes

Servings: 24   Calories: 41   Protein: 1.7g   Carbs: 3.5g   Fat: 2.4g

These delicious slices of breaded and well-seasoned extra-firm tofu are very similar in flavor to what you would expect from chicken nuggets, but why stop there? Also included in this recipe is a side of maple-mustard dipping sauce! If the delicate and mouthwatering flavor of the tofu nuggets aren't enough on their own, the addition of this unique dipping sauce will ensure you are left satisfied.

<u>Ingredients:</u>

- 2 tbsp. Canola oil
- ¼ cup pure maple syrup
- ½ cup smooth Dijon mustard
- Olive oil cooking spray
- 1/2 tsp. Dried thyme, crumbled
- 1 tsp. Garlic powder
- 2 tsp. Onion powder
- ¾ cup dry fine whole-wheat bread crumbs
- 3 tbsp. Low-sodium soy sauce
- 14 oz. Package extra-firm tofu

Directions:

1. Gently press down on tofu with a paper towel to drain out the excess water and moisture. Use another paper towel to blot the surface of the tofu dry.
2. Crosswise, slice your tofu into 6 rectangular pieces. Slice these pieces in half to create a total of 12 tofu squares. Finally, cut these tofu squares diagonally to create 24 different wedges.
3. Prepare three plates. On one of your plates, combine your garlic powders, thyme, onion powder and bread crumbs and mix together. On the second plate, you should cover the surface with your soy sauce.
4. Take your 24 tofu wedges, one at a time, and dip each side of them into the soy sauce, making sure it's thoroughly coated. Then rub the slice of tofu into the bread crumb mixture being sure to cover both sides. Set the breaded tofu wedge on your third plate. Repeat this whole process with all 24 tofu triangles.
5. Spray down a cast iron skillet with your olive oil cooking spray and set it over medium-low heat.
6. With batches no larger than 8 tofu triangles at a time, cook the tofu in the skillet and flip with a thin spatula. Be sure to respray the skillet in between the batches. Each batch shouldn't take any longer than 5 minutes to cook. You'll know they're finished when they are crispy golden-brown on the sides.
7. To prepare the mustard-maple dip, prepare a small bowl. In the bowl, mix your oil, syrup and mustard together with a spoon or fork. Add warm water as necessary to prevent the sauce from becoming too thick.

Vegan Bagel Sandwich

Ready In: 15 minutes

Servings: 1   Calories: 184   Protein: 7.5g   Carbs: 36.9g   Fat: 1.3g

This vegan bagel sandwich is one of the healthiest lunches you could prepare for yourself and it only takes 15 minutes! It's stuffed with crisp veggies like romaine lettuce, green bell peppers, cucumbers, red onions, fresh tomato and alfalfa sprouts. To moisten it up, it's topped with delicious coarse-grain brown mustard. This nutrition-packed lunch will fill you up and keep you full until dinner!

Ingredients:

- ½ cup alfalfa sprouts
- 2 slices red onion
- Salt and freshly ground black pepper
- 2 slices tomato
- 4 slices cucumber
- 2 x ¼" thick rings of green bell pepper
- 1 leaf romaine lettuce
- 1 tbsp. Coarse-grain brown mustard
- 1 bagel, sliced in half

Directions:

1. Spread your brown mustard onto the cut sides of your bagel.
2. On one of your bagel halves, stack on the lettuce, followed by your green pepper rings, cucumber slices and your tomato slices.
3. Add some seasoning to your sandwich with your desired quantity of salt and pepper.
4. Layer on your onion slices and then the alfalfa sprouts. Close your sandwich with the other bagel half. Enjoy!

Avocado Tzatziki

Ready In: 5 minutes

Servings: 4   Calories: 112   Protein: 1.4g   Carbs: 6.9g   Fat: 9.9g

Tzatziki is a Greek sauce that is usually made with yogurt, but this vegan version uses a custom avocado blend instead! This delicious sauce goes great on just about any lunch meal, like the *Sweet Potato PETA Pita,* and it also goes great when layered into the *Breakfast Burrito.* You can alternatively use it as a dipping sauce!

Ingredients:

- Salt and pepper
- 1 tbsp. Fresh mint, chopped
- 1 tbsp. Fresh cilantro, chopped
- ½ tsp. Red pepper flakes
- 1/2 cup cucumber, chopped and seeded
- 1 lemon, juiced
- 2 cloves garlic, minced
- 1 large avocado, peeled and pitted

Directions:

1. Mash your avocado in a medium bowl. If it isn't ripe enough, use a food processor to blend it into a smooth and somewhat thick consistency.
2. Stir in the garlic, lemon juice and cucumber. Mash a little bit more.
3. Season well with pepper, salt, mint and cilantro. Stir together.
4. Cover the bowl with plastic wrap and set in the refrigerator for 1 hour.
5. Scoop into a small bowl and serve!

Portobello Stroganoff

Ready In: 1 hour, 10 minutes

Servings: 4   Calories: 568   Protein: 17.6g   Carbs: 92g   Fat: 13.3g

The creamy, rich marinade of this vegan stroganoff alternative is what makes it so delicious! The way the Portobello mushrooms are prepared make them incredibly tender and delicate. Enjoy plenty of seasoning from garlic powder, dried basil, black pepper, garlic and even a half cup of red wine.

Ingredients:

- ¼ cup water
- Cooking spray
- 2 large Portobello mushroom caps, stems and gills removed
- 2 cloves garlic, minced
- 1 tbsp. Balsamic vinegar
- 2 tbsp. Soy sauce
- 1 tbsp. Olive oil
- ½ cup dry red wine
- ¼ tsp. Ground black pepper
- ¼ tsp. Dried basil
- ¼ tsp. Garlic powder
- 2 tsp. Vegan no-beef bouillon
- 2 tbsp. All-purpose flour
- 3 tbsp. Dried onion, minced
- ½ cup water
- 8 oz. Vegan sour cream
- Vegan noodles of your choice (for stroganoff)

Directions:

1. Prepare a bowl and fill it with your black pepper, basil, garlic powder, vegan bouillon, flour, minced onion, 1/2 cup water and sour cream. Whisk the ingredients of the bowl together into a perfect mixture. Cover the bowl and place in the refrigerator.
2. Set your oven to 350°F (175°C) for preheating.
3. In a second bowl, whisk your red wine, balsamic vinegar, garlic, soy sauce and olive oil together.
4. Prepare a baking dish and evenly space apart your mushroom caps with gill-side-up in it.
5. Marinate the mushrooms in your baking dish by pouring the red wine mixture over the top of them. Allow them to sit to absorb the marinade for 20 minutes.
6. Cover the baking dish with aluminum foil.
7. Place the mushroom-filled baking dish into your oven and bake at 350°F (175°C) for 30 minutes.
8. Remove the foil covering of the dish and flip the mushrooms over to their other sides.
9. Continue baking for 10 more minutes. Set the dish aside to cool for 5 to 10 minutes.
10. Dice the mushrooms.
11. Spray down a saucepan with cooking spray and heat it up on medium heat.
12. Cook your mushrooms in the saucepan for 5 minutes while stirring continuously.
13. When the mushrooms have become slightly browned, reduce the heat to a low simmer.
14. Stir your vegan sour cream alternative into the mushrooms on the saucepan. Allow to continue cooking while you stir, until the mixture is thickened. This should take another 1 to 2 minutes. If the sauce thickens too much, then add ¼ cup of water.
15. Simply prepare the vegan stroganoff noodles of your choice and then mix in the mixture from step 1 to them and stir well.
16. Top the seasoned noodles with your creamy and well-prepared stroganoff mushrooms and serve!

Split Pea Soup

Ready In: 3 hours, 10 minutes

Servings: 6   Calories: 398   Protein: 20.6g   Carbs: 73.6g   Fat: 3.6g

This recipe creates a very thick and chunky split pea soup! If you wish to make it a bit thinner, reduce the amount of split peas that you use or increase the amount of water. I happen to enjoy split pea soup on the thicker and chunkier side, so I would prepare it just as listed below. Enjoy!

Ingredients:

- ½ tsp. Ground black pepper
- ½ tsp. Dried thyme
- ½ tsp. Dried basil
- ½ cup chopped parsley
- 3 potatoes, diced
- 3 stalks celery, chopped
- 3 carrots, chopped
- 7 ½ cups water
- 1 ½ tsp. Salt
- ½ cup barley
- 2 cups dried split peas
- 3 cloves garlic, minced
- 1 bay leaf
- 1 onion, chopped
- 1 tbsp. Vegetable oil

Directions:

1. Place a large pot on your stove at medium heat. Put your oil, garlic, bay leaf and onion in the pot and sauté it well for 5 minutes or until the onions have become translucent.
2. Add in your water, salt, barley and peas and bring the pot to a boil.
3. Reduce the heat to low and simmer for 2 hours. Stir occasionally.
4. Toss in your ground black pepper, thyme, basil, parsley, potatoes, celery and carrots and allow to simmer for 1 more hour. You'll know it's ready when the peas and vegetables have become tender.
5. Allow to cool for 20 minutes. Dish into bowls and serve!

Barley Party Salad

Ready In: 3 hours

Servings: 6   Calories: 463   Protein: 17.8g   Carbs: 86.7g   Fat: 7.4g

This is the perfect salad to serve at your fiesta! It's a rich blend of barley, black beans, various chopped peppers, onion, carrots and a whole variety of seasonings. For added creaminess, this recipe goes great topped with the avocado tzatziki you can find in this book!

Ingredients:

- Onion powder
- 1 tsp. Distilled white vinegar
- ¼ cup chopped cilantro
- 1 tbsp. Lemon juice
- 1 tbsp. Lime juice
- 1 tbsp. Canola oil
- 2 tbsp. Light corn syrup
- ¼ cup water
- ½ tsp. Ground cumin
- ½ tsp. Black pepper
- ½ tsp. Salt
- 1 tbsp. Canola oil
- ¾ chipotle pepper in adobo sauce, finely chopped
- 1 large carrot, chopped
- 1 small red onion, chopped
- 1 stalk celery, chopped
- 8.75 oz. Can of whole kernel corn, drained
- ½ red bell pepper, chopped
- ½ green bell pepper, chopped
- ½ 15 oz. Can of black beans, rinsed and drained
- 2 cups water
- 1 cup pear barley

Directions:

1. Pour your barley and water into a saucepan and bring to a boil on high heat.
2. Cover the saucepan and reduce the heat to a low simmer. Simmer for about 30 minutes or until your barley is tender. Remove the saucepan from the heat and place in your refrigerator to chill.
3. Mix your cooked barley with your cumin, black pepper, salt, 1 tbsp. of canola oil, chipotle pepper, carrot, red onion, celery, corn, bell peppers and black beans in a large salad bowl by stirring together.
4. Whisk your onion powder, white vinegar, cilantro, lemon juice, lime juice, 1 tbsp. of canola oil, corn syrup and water together in a second bowl to create a dressing.
5. Pour your newly created dressing over your barley mixture and continue to toss and combine.
6. Let the finished salad sit in your refrigerator until it's cold. Enjoy!

Carrot Dogs

Ready In: 3 hours, 30 minutes

Servings: 10   Calories: 206   Protein: 5.2g   Carbs: 29.2g   Fat: 7g

Holy smokes! Did someone say carrot hot dogs!? That's right! These delicious vegan hot dogs don't have any of the murder or nastiness of a normal hot dog and they taste amazing. Now you can show up to your neighborhood barbecues with an answer to both obesity and animal cruelty. Top these dogs with your favorite relish, mustard or ketchup just like you would with a normal hot dog!

Ingredients:

- Black pepper
- 2 cloves garlic, minced
- 1 tbsp. Ginger root, minced
- ¼ cup sesame oil
- ½ cup rice vinegar
- 1 cup water
- 1 cup soy sauce
- 10 carrots, ends trimmed to make hot dog-size shapes
- 10 hot dog buns

Directions:

1. Position a steamer insert on the inside of a saucepan.
2. Fill the saucepan with water to just below the bottom of the steamer.
3. Bring saucepan to boil over high heat on the stove.
4. Add carrots, cover and steam until the carrots are tender, but still have some snap-action. This should take 15 minutes.
5. Under the sink, run cold water over the carrots to cease the cooking and place them in a storage container.
6. In a bowl, whisk your black pepper, garlic, ginger, sesame oil, vinegar, water and soy sauce together. Pour this mixture over the top of your carrots and cover their storage container.
7. Place the marinating carrots in the refrigerator for a minimum of 3 hours to marinate. Feel free to marinate even longer to pack in even more flavor.
8. Heat up your outdoor grill to medium-high heat and oil it lightly.
9. Pull the carrots out of their marinade and set them on your grill.
10. Grill until they achieve the desired done-ness. This should take about 5 to 10 minutes.
11. Place them in your favorite hot dog buns and top with your favorite condiments.

Vegan Melted Cheese

Ready In: 15 minutes

Servings: 8   Calories: 177   Protein: 4.4g   Carbs: 17.2g   Fat: 10.4g

This vegan melted cheese recipe is one of the most versatile recipes in the whole book! When you prepare this creamy melted cheese alternative, you can creatively and strategically use it in so many different ways. For example, you can use it in fondue, macaroni, lasagna or as a topping to tacos, vegan burgers, fries or even as a dipping sauce for pizza and breadsticks! Let your imagination run wild with how you can incorporate this one into your dream breakfast, lunch *or* dinner.

Ingredients:

- 1 dash ground black pepper
- 1 tsp. Salt
- 1 clove garlic, minced
- 1/8 onion, minced
- 1/3 cup vegetable oil
- 1 tbsp. Flax seeds, milled
- 2 tbsp. Nutritional yeast flakes
- ½ cup glutinous rice flour
- ½ cup chickpea flour
- 1 ½ cups water

Directions:

1. Put a saucepan over low heat and combine your flax seeds, nutritional yeast flakes, rice flour, chickpea flour and water in it.
2. Stir the ingredients in the saucepan together until dissolved.
3. Add oil, onion and garlic to the mix.
4. Continue to cook and stir the mixture until it becomes the consistency of melted cheese. This should take 10 minutes. Add a little water if it becomes too thick.
5. When finished, add salt and black pepper to taste.

Seitan Pepperoni & Crackers

Ready In: 2 hours, 20 minutes

Servings: 4   Calories: 486   Protein: 24.6g   Carbs: 71.1g   Fat: 16.3g

Seitan pepperoni and crackers makes for a phenomenal lunch treat on days where you're in the mood for something lighter in calories, yet higher in protein. The preparation of the seitan in this recipe results in a flavor very much on par with regular pepperoni and, as such, makes it perfect for crackers. What makes this recipe taste even better is topping these seitan pepperoni and crackers with the vegan melted cheese found in the previous recipe!

Ingredients:

- 2 tsp. Liquid smoke flavoring
- 2 tbsp. Liquid amino acid
- 2 tbsp. Olive oil
- ¼ cup tomato paste
- ¾ cup cold water
- ½ tsp. White sugar
- ½ tsp. Crushed anise seeds
- 1 tsp. Cayenne pepper
- 1 tsp. Garlic powder
- 1 tsp. Ground black pepper
- 1 tsp. Salt
- 1 1/2 tsp. Crushed fennel seeds
- 2 tsp. Paprika
- 2 tsp. Mustard powder
- ¼ cup nutritional yeast
- 1 ½ cups vital wheat gluten flour
- 1 box Triscuit crackers

<u>Directions:</u>

1. Set your oven to 325°F (165°C) for preheating.
2. Prepare a large bowl within which you mix your sugar, anise seeds, cayenne pepper, garlic powder, black pepper, salt, fennel seeds, paprika, mustard powder, nutritional yeast and wheat gluten flour. Stir well and mix thoroughly.
3. In a second bowl, combine your liquid smoke flavoring, liquid amino acid, olive oil, tomato paste and water.
4. Stir your wet mixture into the flour mixture from step 1 and mix thoroughly until the dough has become evenly mixed together.
5. Knead dough on a work surface until it has become smooth.
6. Shape the dough into a 1 ½" to 2" diameter log shape.
7. Wrap the log dough in aluminum foil and twist it together at the ends, sealing and securing it.
8. Bake at 325°F (165°C) for 90 minutes.
9. Using a hot pad, remove the pepperoni log and unwrap carefully. Allow to sit at room temperature until cool.
10. Cut the pepperoni into slices and place on your crackers.

Popeye Bites

Ready In: 1 hour, 40 minutes

Servings: 4   Calories: 263.5   Protein: 8.3g   Carbs: 34.3g   Fat: 11.9g

These fantastic muscle-building bites are packed full of spinach to help you get big and strong! Made from Idaho potatoes, fresh spinach, minced garlic, flax seed meal and more, you can be sure these tasty little morsels are packed full of vitamins and nutrients, protein and *oodles* of flavor!

Ingredients:

- 1 lb. Idaho potatoes, peeled and cut into 2" chunks
- ¼ cup all-purpose flour
- ½ tsp. Salt
- 1 tsp. Baking powder
- 1 tbsp. Flax seed meal
- 3 tbsp. Water
- 3 cloves garlic, minced
- 1 onion, minced
- 3 tbsp. Canola oil, divided
- 2 bunches fresh spinach, divided

Directions:

1. Place a large pot of water on your stove and fill it with your potatoes. Bring the pot to a boil.
2. Reduce the heat to a medium-low simmer and allow to simmer for 20 minutes or until tender.
3. Drain the pot and move your potatoes into a large bowl. Allow 30 minutes for potatoes to properly cool.
4. Place 1/2 cup of spinach into a juicer and process.
5. Add juiced spinach to the potatoes and mash together until smooth.
6. Place your remaining spinach in a blender or food processor and process until it becomes finely chopped. Add to the top of your potato / spinach mash.
7. Place a large skillet over medium heat and heat up a tablespoon of oil in it.
8. Add garlic and onion to the skillet and stir until it becomes fragrant. This should take 5 minutes.
9. Allow onion and garlic to cool for 10 minutes.
10. Mix onion and garlic into your potato mash by stirring thoroughly.
11. In a small bowl, stir your flax seed meal with your water to produce well blended mixture. Allow to sit 5 minutes in order to thicken.
12. Mix your water / flax seed meal mixture with your mashed potatoes, baking powder and flax seed. Form the resulting combination into patties. Be sure to dust both sides with flour.
13. Set your oven to 425°F (220°C) for preheating. Cover a cookie sheet with parchment paper.
14. Heat another tablespoon of oil in your large skillet on medium heat. Cook your patties together in batches until they form a pale crust on their outside. This should take 3 minutes per side or so.
15. Pull the crusted patties out of the skillet and into the prepared cookie sheet.
16. Bake in the oven at 425°F (220°C) for 10 minutes or until golden-browned and thoroughly cooked through.

● ● ● ● ● ● ● ● ● ● ● ● ● ● ● ● ● ● ●

DID YOU KNOW?

American spinach growers in the 1930's gave credit to the popular cartoon character *Popeye* for a more than 30% increase in spinach consumption!

● ● ● ● ● ● ● ● ● ● ● ● ● ● ● ● ● ● ●

Japanese Turnip Curry

Ready In: 1 hour

Servings: 2   Calories: 406   Protein: 11.4g   Carbs: 65.3g   Fat: 14.6g

Don't dismiss this recipe on the presumption that the turnips you've tried are anything like Japanese turnips! If you haven't yet tried a Japanese turnip, then this is a recipe I absolutely insist that you try. A Japanese turnip is semi-sweet and very crunchy -- a lot like a radish! This delicious lunch option will provide you with plenty of healthy ingredients and leave your tummy satisfied.

Ingredients:

- 1 pinch salt
- ¼ cup peas
- 4 fresh curry leaves
- 1 x 1"-piece fresh ginger root, minced
- 2 cloves of garlic, minced
- 1 x 1" piece of cinnamon stick
- ½ tsp. Fennel seeds
- 1 tsp. Canola oil
- 1 tsp. Water
- 2 tbsp. Fresh mint, chopped
- 2 tbsp. Cilantro, chopped
- ¼ tsp. Cumin seeds
- ½ tsp. Fennel seeds
- 2 green cardamom pods
- 5 cashews
- 1 tbsp. Coriander seeds
- 2 tbsp. Unsweetened dried coconut
- 4 pearl onions
- 1 x ½ piece cinnamon stick
- 2 small Thai green chilis
- 2 dried red chilis
- 1 tsp. Canola oil
- ¼ tsp. Ground turmeric
- 1 cup water
- 1 tomato, diced
- 1 potato, peeled and cubed
- 2 cups cubed Japanese turnips

Directions:

1. Prepare a large saucepan with 1 cup of water and turmeric as well as your diced tomato, potato and Japanese turnips.
2. Bring the saucepan to a boil and then reduce heat to allow to simmer until your vegetables are tender. This should take 15 minutes.
3. Place a skillet on medium heat and heat up a teaspoon of canola oil in it.
4. Add your red and green chilis, cumin seeds, ½ tsp. of fennel seeds, cloves, cardamom pods, cashews, coriander, coconut, pearl onions and ½" cinnamon stick.
5. Stir constantly as your ingredients cook in the skillet. Cook until the spices have become fragrant and your coconut starts to toast. This should take around 3 minutes.
6. Remove the skillet from the heat and transfer its contents to a spice grinder.
7. Also add 1 tsp. of water, mint and your cilantro to the spice grinder. Grind it all together until a smooth paste forms. Add as much water as you need to.
8. Heat 1 tsp. of canola oil in a large skillet set on medium-low heat. Mix in your remaining ½ tsp. of fennel seeds and your 1" piece of cinnamon stick. Cook for no more than 30 seconds.
9. Add your minced garlic, curry leaves and ginger to the skillet and cook until the garlic and ginger have become fragrant. This process should be 2 minutes.
10. Combine your spice paste and cooked vegetables into the garlic-ginger mixture and bring it to a boil.
11. Mix in your salt and green peas. Reduce heat and let simmer for 10 minutes.
12. Pour into bowls and serve!

Chapter 6: Dinner Recipes

This is the chapter to read through if you're looking for vegan burgers, casseroles, pizzas and other elaborate recipes. The meals listed here are more along the lines of what you would want on the menu for a dinner, whereas Chapter 5 has lunch-based dishes such as soups, sandwiches, curries and side dishes.

You will notice that the calories as well as the grams of protein, fat and carbohydrates per each recipe are listed right beneath the name. The macronutrients listed correspond with the designated serving size. For example, if a recipe has servings listed as 4, then the total yield should be divided into fourths. If a recipe has servings listed as 6, then divide the total yield of the recipe into six different portions.

Shepherd's Pie

Ready In: 1 hour, 15 minutes

Servings: 8   Calories: 339   Protein: 20.8g   Carbs: 28.5g   Fat: 15.9g

This delicious dinner tastes just like you remember shepherd's pie tasting, but it's completely vegan! Russet potatoes, vegan mayonnaise, vegan cream cheese substitute, yellow onion, garlic, Italian seasoning and more come together in this incredible recipe that is enough to feed a whole family.

Ingredients:

- ½ cup shredded cheddar-style soy cheese
- 14 oz. Package vegan ground beef substitute
- 1 pinch ground black pepper
- 1 clove of garlic, minced
- 1 tsp. Italian seasoning
- 1 tomato, chopped
- ½ cup frozen peas
- 3 stalks celery, chopped
- 2 carrots, chopped
- 1 large yellow onion, chopped
- 1 tbsp. Vegetable oil
- 2 tsp. Salt
- 3 tbsp. Vegan cream cheese substitute
- ¼ cup olive oil
- ½ cup soy milk
- ½ cup vegan mayonnaise
- 5 russet potatoes, peeled and cut into 1" cubes

<u>Directions:</u>

1. Prepare a pot of your potatoes. Cover the potatoes in cold water and set the pot on the stove over medium-high heat.
2. Bring the pot to a boil, then lower the heat to medium-low and let simmer until tender. This should take around 25 minutes.
3. Drain the water from the pot of potatoes.
4. Mash the potatoes with a potato masher until smooth and fluffy. Stir the salt, vegan cream cheese, olive oil, soy milk and vegan mayonnaise into the mashed potatoes until it is a nice smooth and fluffy texture.
5. Set your oven to 400°F (200°C) for preheating. Spray a 2-quart baking sheet with cooking spray.
6. Put a large skillet on medium heat and heat your vegetable oil in it. Stir in your tomato, frozen peas, celery, carrots and onion with the oil on the skillet. This should take about 10 minutes until the mixture is softened. Blend in your pepper and garlic and Italian seasoning.
7. Reduce the heat of the skillet to a simmer on medium-low heat and crumble your vegan ground beef substitute into the skillet with your veggies.
8. Stir well, breaking up the meat substitute and thoroughly mixing it into your veggies for 5 minutes.
9. Transfer the mixture from the skillet into the bottom of your sprayed baking dish and cover with a layer of the mashed potatoes. Smoothly coat the potatoes evenly across the top of the vegan-meat mix.
10. Sprinkle the layer of mashed potatoes with the shredded soy cheese.
11. Bake in the oven for 20 minutes at 400°F (200°C).
12. Allow to cool before cutting and serving.

● ●

DID YOU KNOW?

A large number of vegans and vegetarians call the meat-free version of shepherd's pie 'shepherd-less' pie.

● ●

Vegan Lasagna

Ready In: 2 hours, 30 minutes

Servings: 12   Calories: 235   Protein: 14.5g   Carbs: 33.3g   Fat: 6.7g

If you've ever dreamed of a lasagna that was completely vegan, this is your dream come true! This flavorful 100% vegan lasagna is the perfect dinner for those who love Italian food, but are also looking out for their health. Enjoy the taste of fresh basil, minced garlic, spinach, parsley, tomato sauce and so much more in this healthy lasagna recipe and walk away satisfied.

Ingredients:

- 3 x 10 oz. Packages of frozen chopped spinach, thawed and drained
- Ground black pepper
- ½ tsp. Salt
- ¼ cup chopped parsley
- 1/4 cup chopped fresh basil
- 2 tbsp. Minced garlic
- 2 lbs. Firm tofu
- 16 oz. package lasagna noodles
- 1 tsp. Ground black pepper
- 1 tsp. Salt
- ½ cup chopped parsley
- ½ cup chopped fresh basil
- 1/3 cup tomato paste
- 4 x 14.5 oz. Cans of stewed tomatoes
- 1 ½ cups chopped onion
- 2 tbsp. olive oil

Directions:

1. To prepare your sauce, put a large saucepan over medium heat and heat up your olive oil. Add your onions into the saucepan and sauté them for 5 minutes or until they become soft.
2. Add your garlic and cook an additional 5 minutes, stirring frequently.
3. Add in the spinach and sauté for an additional 2 minutes.
4. Add your parsley, basil, tomato paste and tomatoes into your sauce pan. Stir thoroughly and then cover the saucepan and lower the heat to let the sauce simmer. Allow to simmer 1 hour. Add your salt and pepper to the saucepan.
5. As the sauce simmers, prepare a kettle or pot of salted water and bring it to a boil on the stove. Boil your lasagna noodles for 10 minutes. Drain the noodles and rinse thoroughly.
6. Set your oven to 400°F (200°C) for preheating.
7. Place your tofu blocks in a bowl. Mix in the parsley, basil and garlic. Add salt and pepper and mash the ingredients completely together as a mix by squeezing the chunks of tofu through your fingers.
8. To put your lasagna together, prepare a 9 x 13-inch casserole pan with 1 cup of tomato sauce spread over the bottom of it. Layer in an arrangement of lasagna noodles and sprinkle 1/3 of the tofu mixture over them. Scoop out 1 1/2 cups of tomato sauce with a ladle and cover the tofu with it. Place one more layer of noodles over the tomato sauce. Finish by topping the noodles with the remaining 1/3 of the tofu. Spread the remaining tomato sauce over everything.
9. Cover your casserole dish with aluminum foil and bake for 30 minutes at 400°F (200°C). Allow to cool before cutting and serving.

Pasta Mexicana

Ready In: 20 minutes

Servings: 8   Calories: 333   Protein: 15.9g   Carbs: 56.7g   Fat: 5.6g

When you choose pasta Mexicana as your dinner, enjoy the spicy and delicious union of Italian and Mexican! This recipe consists of seashell pasta, onions, green bell pepper, corn, black beans, diced tomatoes, salsa, black olive, taco seasoning, salt and pepper and olive oil. It also makes a great taco filling!

Ingredients:

- Salt and pepper
- 1 ½ tbsp. Taco seasoning mix
- ¼ cups sliced black olives
- ¼ cup salsa
- 14.5 oz. Can of peeled, diced tomatoes
- 15 oz. Can of black beans, drained
- ½ cup of sweet corn kernels
- 2 onions, chopped
- 2 tbsp. Olive oil
- ½ lb. Seashell pasta

Directions:

1. Fill a pot full of water and lightly salt it. Place the pot on the stove and add pasta. Bring pot to boil. Cook for 8 to 10 minutes.
2. As the pasta continues to cook, prepare a large skillet with olive oil and place on medium heat. Cook your pepper and onions in the oil until beginning to lightly brown. This should take 10 minutes.
3. Stir the corn into the skillet and heat all the way through.
4. Mix in your salt and pepper, taco seasoning, salsa, olives and black beans.
5. Cook an additional 5 minutes.
6. Toss your cooked pasta with your sauce to combine and serve.

Bean Burgers

Ready In: 30 minutes

Servings: 8   Calories: 286   Protein: 15.3g   Carbs: 54.2g   Fat: 1.7g

Save a cow and enjoy this delicious bean burger for dinner! This variety of vegan burger uses a home-made meat replacement created from black beans and flour. There's more magic in the recipe than just that, but if you follow the directions carefully, these will turn out great. Great for vegan barbecues!

Ingredients:

- 1 pinch chili powder
- Salt
- ½ tsp. Ground black pepper
- ½ cup whole wheat flour
- 1 cup dried bread crumbs
- 2 cups salsa
- ½ cup chopped onion
- ½ cup chopped green bell pepper
- 15 oz. Can of black beans

Directions:

1. Fill a bowl with your black beans and mash them together. Mix your whole wheat flour, bread crumbs, salsa, onion and green pepper together and stir into the bean mash.
2. Season with salt, pepper and chili powder.
3. Add more flour to make the texture firmer, if needed. Add more salsa if the mixture is too stiff.
4. Use your hands to work the mixture into 8 patties and place them on a greased cookie sheet.
5. Prepare a large skillet with cooking spray and place it over medium-high heat.
6. Fry your patties for 8 minutes per side, or until they become brown and firm.
7. Place your patties on hamburger buns. Decorate with your choice of burger toppings such as onion rings, pickles, ketchup and mustard. Serve.

Stuffed Zucchini

Ready In: 1 hour

Servings: 4   Calories: 484   Protein: 25g   Carbs: 77.9g   Fat: 10.8g

This zucchini-based dish is stuffed with garbanzo beans and mushrooms and is arranged in such a way that is very pleasing to the eye! This dish makes a great centerpiece at any festive vegan gathering. It's also very healthy and loaded with tons of fiber and protein!

Ingredients:

- Ground black pepper
- sea salt
- 2 tbsp. Chopped fresh parsley
- ½ lemon, juiced
- 15.5 oz. Can of garbanzo beans, rinsed and drained
- 1 1/2 tsp. Ground cumin
- 1 tsp. Ground coriander
- ½ 8 oz. Package of button mushrooms, sliced
- 1 onion, chopped
- 1 tbsp. Olive oil
- 4 zucchinis, halved

Directions:

1. Set your oven to 350°F (175°C) for preheating. Grease a baking dish.
2. Hollow out the center of each halved zucchini with a spoon, removing the flesh. Chop the flesh and set it to the side. Place the zucchini shells in the prepared baking dish.
3. Heat up your oil in a large skillet set on medium heat. Place your onions in the skillet to be sautéed for 5 minutes.
4. Add garlic and sauté for 2 more minutes.
5. Mix your chopped zucchini into the skillet along with your mushrooms and stir well. Sauté for 5 minutes.
6. Blend in your pepper, salt, parsley, lemon juice, garbanzo beans, cumin and coriander.
7. Scoop the mixture from the skillet to fill up your zucchini shells. Distribute evenly.
8. Bake in your oven for 35 minutes at 350°F (175°C).

Vegan Chili

Ready In: 40 minutes

Servings: 6   Calories: 525   Protein: 49.1g   Carbs: 49.2g   Fat: 19.7g

This chili is one of the best tasting chili recipes anyone can enjoy! The seasoning of garlic and onion combine with chili powder, black pepper and your desired amount of salt to create a flavor that packs boom with each bite. I recommend topping this chili with the vegan melted cheese recipe from the lunch recipes section!

Ingredients:

- 2 tsp. Chili powder
- Salt and pepper
- 2 tbsp. Vegan brown sugar substitute
- 4 cups water
- 14.5 oz. Can stewed tomatoes
- 4 x 16 oz. Cans of chili beans
- 8 oz. Textured vegetable protein
- 1 tbsp. Olive oil
- 1 stalk celery, chopped
- 5 cloves crushed garlic
- 1 onion, chopped

Directions:

1. Prepare a large saucepan over medium heat.
2. Sauté onion, celery and garlic in olive oil until the onions become soft.
3. Toss your textured vegetable protein, chili powder, salt and pepper, sugar, water, tomatoes and chili beans into the saucepan. Stir occasionally.
4. Allow the saucepan to simmer for 30 minutes.
5. Scoop into bowls and serve!

Paella

Ready In: 1 hour

Servings: 4   Calories: 313   Protein: 10.7g   Carbs: 57.5g   Fat: 5.2g

Paella is traditionally a Spanish dish consisting of rice and meat, whether it be seafood, chicken, or beef. This vegan twist does away with the animal cruelty and instead relies on your choice of seitan, tofu or tempeh to replace the protein. You don't have to add a protein source though – you can prepare it just as it is below and it will still taste incredible!

Ingredients:

- 1 cup drained quartered canned artichoke hearts
- 1 cup peas
- 1 tsp. Ground turmeric
- 1 tsp. Salt
- 1 tbsp. Paprika
- 2 cups vegetable broth
- 1 tomato, diced
- 1 red bell pepper, sliced
- 1 green bell pepper, sliced
- 3 cloves of garlic, minced
- 1 onion, chopped
- 1 tbsp. Olive oil
- 1 cup white rice
- 2 cups boiling water

Directions:

1. Prepare a bowl of your rice and pour in your boiling water. Let the bowl stand for 20 minutes to cool and then drain.
2. Heat up some olive oil in a skillet that you place on medium heat.
3. Throw in your onion and garlic and cook and stir until the onion becomes translucent. This should take no longer than 5 minutes.
4. Add your bell peppers (both green and red) and your tomato to the skillet and continue to stir as you cook for 2 to 4 more minutes or until the peppers become tender.
5. Mix your drained rice and vegetable broth into the onion and pepper mix. Bring to a boil.
6. Reduce the heat to a low simmer and add paprika, turmeric and salt. Cover your skillet and allow it to simmer for another 20 minutes to allow the rice to become tender.
7. Add your artichoke hearts and peas into the mixture and continue to cook and stir for 1 more minute.
8. Pour into bowls and enjoy!

● ● ● ● ● ● ● ● ● ● ● ● ● ● ● ● ● ● ●

DID YOU KNOW?

A restaurant owner in Valencia prepared the world's largest paella, with a team of workers in October of 2001, which fed around 110,000 people.

● ● ● ● ● ● ● ● ● ● ● ● ● ● ● ● ● ● ●

Vegan Pizza

Ready In: 1 hour, 30 minutes

Servings: 10   Calories: 756   Protein: 38.1g   Carbs: 58.7g   Fat: 48.8g

If you've been vegan for a while, you probably haven't had pizza in ages. Well, now you can! This completely vegan pizza recipe is free of cheese, meat and anything else that would violate your conscience. This is truly a guilt-free pizza!

Ingredients:

- 1 avocado – peeled, pitted, sliced
- ½ small red onion, thinly sliced
- 3 cups smooth tomato sauce
- 1 cup nutritional yeast
- 1 tsp. Dried sage
- 1 tsp. Dried marjoram
- 1 tbsp. Dried basil
- 1 tbsp. Dried oregano
- 2 cups olive oil
- 4 heads garlic, peeled
- 1 1/2 cups all-purpose flour
- 1 cup warm water
- 1 x .25 oz. Package active dry yeast
- 2 tbsp. White sugar

<u>Directions:</u>

1. Set your oven to 350°F (175°C) for preheating.
2. Prepare a large bowl of warm water and place your sugar and yeast in it to dissolve together. Allow bowl to stand until the yeast starts to soften up a bit and begins to form a creamy foam. This should take no longer than 5 minutes.
3. Pour your flour into the yeast mixture and stir until the dough begins to hold together well.
4. Knead your dough on a floured surface. Continue until it becomes a smooth texture and elastic in behavior. This should take 8 minutes.
5. Put your dough in a bowl and cover it up with a towel. Set aside for 30 minutes to allow it to rise slightly.
6. Prepare an 8" x 8" baking dish and fill it with your peeled garlic cloves, olive oil, oregano, sage and marjoram.
7. Bake the contents of the baking dish for 35 minutes at 350°F (175°C).
8. Remove the dish from the oven and allow time to cool off.
9. Coat a baking dish with the cooled ingredients of the dish you just pulled from the oven and spread out your dough on top of it.
10. Brush more of the oil and herbs on top of the dough.
11. In a separate bowl, mash the garlic cloves up using a fork. Stir the nutritional yeast into the mashed garlic. Add some of your herbed olive oil, if the mixture is dry. Stir your tomato sauce into the garlic mixture.
12. Spread the newly created sauce over the top of your dough. Place your red onion slices on top of the sauce.
13. Bake for 15 to 20 minutes at 350°F (175°C).
14. When your pizza is done, decorate it with your peeled avocado slices.
15. Use a pizza cutter to slice and serve your pizza.

Potato & Zucchini Bake

Ready In: 1 hour, 15 minutes

Servings: 4   Calories: 335   Protein: 6.9g   Carbs: 49g   Fat: 13.8g

When it comes to a healthy, zesty and extravagant dinner, this is the easiest one to prepare! When you choose to prepare this recipe, you will enjoy the flavor of baked potatoes, zucchini and red bell pepper seasoned to the limits with breading, garlic, paprika, salt and pepper and olive oil. If you had a stressful day and need something that requires minimal effort on your part, try this out!

Ingredients:

- Ground black pepper
- Salt
- Paprika
- ¼ cup olive oil
- ½ cup dry bread crumbs
- 1 clove garlic, sliced
- 1 medium red bell pepper, seed and chopped
- 4 medium potatoes, peeled and cut into large chunks
- 2 medium zucchinis, quartered and cut into large pieces

Directions:

1. Set your oven to 400°F (200°C) for preheating.
2. Prepare a medium baking pan in which you toss your pepper, salt, paprika, olive oil, bread crumbs, garlic, red bell pepper, potatoes and zucchini together. Make sure it's all evenly and equally distributed.
3. Bake for 1 hour at 400°F (200°C). Occasionally stir. When the potatoes have become lightly golden-brown and tender, you are finished.

Great Northern Bean Quesadillas

Ready In: 55 minutes

Servings: 8   Calories: 467   Protein: 25.6g   Carbs: 76g   Fat: 7.6g

Considering these vegan quesadillas don't have cheese, they hardly have any of the fat you would be consuming with a regular quesadilla! These quesadillas consist of great northern beans, black beans, diced tomatoes, chili powder and garlic among other things. They really do deliver a great deal of flavor and are an excellent dinner! Serve with a side of the *Avocado Tzatziki* recipe contained in the lunch portion of this cookbook.

Ingredients:

- Cooking spray
- 1 tbsp. Olive oil
- ¼ cup diced tomatoes
- ½ cup black beans, drained and rinsed
- 1 pinch cayenne pepper
- Salt
- ¼ tsp. Chili powder
- 1 tsp. Ground cumin
- 1/3 cup nutritional yeast
- 1 clove garlic
- ¾ cup diced tomatoes
- 15 oz. Can of great northern beans, drained and rinsed
- Red pepper flakes
- 8 whole grain tortillas

Directions:

1. Pour your garlic, ¾ cup of tomatoes and your great northern beans into a food processor and process until smooth.
2. Mix in your red pepper flakes, salt, chili powder, cumin and nutritional yeast and blend until smooth again.
3. Pour your mixture from the food processor into a bowl. Stir ¼ cup tomatoes and black beans into the food processed mixture.
4. Heat olive oil in a skillet that you set on medium high.
5. Place one of your 8 tortillas into the skillet. Evenly spread ¼ cup of your filling onto the surface of the tortilla.
6. Layer another tortilla on top of the filling.
7. Allow to cook for 10 minutes.
8. Spray down the top most tortilla with your cooking spray and flip it over to cook the alternate side for 3 to 5 minutes.
9. Repeat the process with your remaining tortillas.

Cauliflower Alfredo

Ready In: 1 hour, 35 minutes

Servings: 4   Calories: 289   Protein: 23.9g   Carbs: 28.4g   Fat: 11.6g

This perfectly viable chicken alfredo alternative has a nice and creamy texture created by the blending of soy milk, shredded mozzarella-style vegan cheese, nutritional yeast and tofu! It is seasoned beyond-belief with so many delicious seasonings and hosts a variety of healthy vitamin-rich veggies.

Ingredients:

- 1 cup cherry tomatoes, halved
- 3 large kale leaves, minced
- 1 tsp. Ground black pepper
- 1 tsp. Garlic powder
- 1 tbsp. Dried parsley
- 1 tbsp. Dried oregano
- 1 tbsp. Dried marjoram
- 1 tbsp. Dried basil
- 1 tbsp. Lemon juice
- 2 tbsp. Onion powder
- ¼ cup nutritional yeast
- ½ 8 oz. Package shredded mozzarella-style vegan cheese
- 14 oz. Package firm tofu, cut into cubes
- Canola oil cooking spray
- 2 cloves of garlic, chopped
- 2 large red onions cut into wedges
- 2 large heads cauliflower cut into pieces

159

Directions:

1. Set your oven to 350°F (175°C) for preheating.
2. Prepare a baking sheet and spread your onions, cauliflower and garlic out across its surface.
3. Bake for 30 to 45 minutes at 350°F (175°C).
4. When finished baking, transfer your veggie mixture from the current baking dish into a 9" x 13" baking dish and reduce the oven's temperature to 300°F (150°C).
5. Pour your garlic powder, black pepper, parsley, oregano, marjoram, basil, lemon juice, onion powder, nutritional yeast, vegan cheese alternative, tofu and soy milk into a food processor and process into a creamy sauce.
6. Pour your sauce into a saucepan and cook it on medium to low heat until it has sufficiently warmed. This should take 5 minutes.
7. Toss some kale into the sauce and let it cook until it begins to wilt. This should take another 5 minutes.
8. Pour your sauce over the top of your cauliflower / veggie mix and add in your tomatoes. Mix together well.
9. Once again, bake it in the oven for 40 minutes at 300°F (150°C).
10. Allow it to sit to cool for 15 to 20 minutes and serve.

Cornbread

Ready In: 30 minutes

Servings: 9   Calories: 208   Protein: 4g   Carbs: 27.6g   Fat: 9.6g

Cornbread is, in my opinion, the best kind of bread to go as a side for dinner. However, most corn bread contains animal products. Introducing completely vegan cornbread! This is some great tasting corn bread that's even healthier macronutrient-wise than traditional cornbread, due to the vegan ingredients!

Ingredients:

- ¼ cup soft silken tofu
- 1/3 cup vegetable oil
- 1 cup unsweetened, plain soy milk
- 1 tsp. Salt
- 1 tbsp. Baking powder
- ¼ cup turbinado sugar
- 1 cup cornmeal
- 1 cup all-purpose flour

Directions:

1. Set your oven to 400°F (200°C) for preheating.
2. Prepare a 7" baking pan with grease.
3. In a mixing bowl, whisk your salt, baking powder, sugar, cornmeal and flour together. Set to the side.
4. Pour your oil, soy milk and tofu into a blender or food processor. Puree the mixture until it becomes smooth.
5. Form a well at the center of the dry cornmeal mixture and pour your puree into the well.
6. Begin to stir the cornmeal mixture until it has just moistened.
7. Pour the newly formed batter into your 7" baking pan.
8. Bake for 20 to 25 minutes at 400°F (200°C) or until a toothpick pushed into the center comes out clean.
9. Slice into 9 pieces and serve.

Spaghetti of Onion

Ready In: 40 minutes

Servings: 4   Calories: 471   Protein: 15.7g   Carbs: 81.5g   Fat: 10g

Here is a great onion-based spaghetti dish that will leave your whole family's taste buds asking for more! Enjoy fresh basil, crushed cloves of garlic, slices of onion and salt and pepper to taste in this low calorie, heart healthy spaghetti dinner.

Ingredients:

- 1 lb. Spaghetti
- ¼ cup water
- 1 tbsp. Chopped fresh basil
- 1/2 tsp. freshly ground black pepper
- 1 tsp. Salt
- 14.5 oz. Can of whole peeled tomatoes
- 1 tbsp. Tomato paste
- 2 cloves of garlic, crushed
- 4 large onions, sliced
- 2 tbsp. Olive oil

Directions:

1. Heat up your oil in a large skillet on medium heat. Allow your onions and garlic to cook in the oil until they become soft.
2. Mix in your water, basil, salt and pepper, tomatoes and tomato paste.
3. Cover the skillet and reduce the heat to a low simmer for 20 minutes.
4. While your sauce is simmering, prepare a pot of lightly salted water and set it on your stove. Bring it to a boil and cook your pasta for 10 minutes.
5. Toss the sauce with your pasta. Feel free to add garlic powder or extra salt and pepper to top it all off.

Mashed Potatoes

Ready In: 45 minutes

Servings: 3   Calories: 365   Protein: 5.6g   Carbs: 50.2g   Fat: 17.1g

Most mashed potato recipes rely on non-vegan products, but this one is of course completely vegan! Now you don't have to feel *completely* left out on Thanksgiving anymore. These creamy mashed potatoes are rich with the flavor of garlic, rosemary and fresh thyme!

Ingredients:

- 1 pinch salt
- 1 pinch black pepper
- ¼ cup olive oil
- 1 sprig fresh thyme
- 1 sprig fresh rosemary
- 8 cloves of garlic, peeled and smashed
- 2 lbs. Russet potatoes

Directions:

1. Prepare a large pot with your thyme, rosemary, garlic and potatoes. Cover contents of the pot with lightly salted water and bring it to a boil.
2. Allow contents to cook until the potatoes become easily pierced with a knife. This should last 30 minutes.
3. Drain the water from the pot, reserving 1 cup for later.
4. Place your garlic and boiled potatoes in a bowl. Throw out your rosemary and thyme.
5. Add pepper, salt and olive oil to your potatoes. Mash it all together with a potato masher and add however much of the leftover cooking water you spared to attain your desired consistency.
6. Top with your favorite vegan gravy!

Potatoes au Gratin

Ready In: 45 minutes

Servings: 6   Calories: 441   Protein: 19.6g   Carbs: 79.6g   Fat: 5.3g

Potatoes au Gratin literally translates to "potatoes sprinkled"! It is usually a non-vegan dish sprinkled with breadcrumbs or cheese or both. This particular recipe is seasoned extra well to make up for the lack of meat and, as a result, tastes even better than the original!

Ingredients:

- 3 tsp. Paprika
- 1 cup soft breadcrumbs
- 1 ½ cups shredded Cheddar-flavored soy cheese, divided
- 2 cups soy milk
- 1/8 tsp. Nutmeg
- ¼ tsp. Dry mustard
- ½ tsp. ground black pepper
- 1 tsp. Seasoning salt
- 2 tbsp. All-purpose flour
- 1 ¼ cups vegetable broth, divided
- 6 large potatoes, peeled and cubed

Directions:

1. Set your oven to 350°F (175°C) for preheating.
2. Prepare a large pot filled with lightly salted water and bring it to a boil.
3. Add potatoes into your pot and allow them to cook until they become tender, but still a bit firm. This should take 15 minutes.
4. Drain the water from the pot and place the potatoes in a 9" x 13" baking dish.
5. Place a saucepan over high heat and boil 2 tbsp. of vegetable broth.
6. Reduce the heat to a low simmer and stir in your nutmeg, mustard, pepper, seasoning salt and flour. Gradually begin to pour a bit of soy in and stir until the mixture has thickened.
7. Mix in half of your soy cheese and stir well. Continue stirring until the cheese has melted.
8. Pour the mixture over your potatoes into the baking dish. Stir together your bread crumbs with the remaining vegetable broth in a small bowl.
9. Evenly distribute the broth / breadcrumb mix over your potatoes and top with your remaining vegan cheese. Sprinkle the top with paprika.
10. Bake for 20 minutes at 350°F (175°C).

Greek Potato Salad

Ready In: 1 hour, 25 minutes

Servings: 6   Calories: 377   Protein: 8.2g   Carbs: 68.9g   Fat: 9.1g

This is one of the easiest dinner recipes you can prepare – even your kids could prepare it! Sweet, succulent potatoes flavored with garlic, onion, red wine vinegar, oregano, sugar, rosemary and red pepper will spice up your evening.

Ingredients:

- 1 pinch ground red pepper
- ¼ tsp. Dried rosemary, crumbled
- ¼ tsp. White sugar
- ¼ tsp. Dried oregano
- ½ tsp. Ground black pepper
- ½ tsp. Coarse salt
- ½ tsp. Onion powder
- ½ tsp. Garlic powder
- 1 ½ tsp. Fresh lemon juice
- ¼ cup red wine vinegar
- ¼ cup olive oil
- ¼ cup green onion, chopped
- 12 red potatoes

Directions:

1. Prepare a large pot of your red potatoes and cover them with lightly salted water.
2. Bring the contents of the pot to a boil and then reduce the heat to a medium-low simmer for 25 minutes. The potatoes should be tenderized before proceeding.
3. Drain the water and allow the pot of potatoes to chill in your freezer for 30 minutes.
4. Slice up your potatoes and dump them into a large salad bowl.
5. Toss green onion with your potatoes to mix them together.
6. In a separate bowl, whisk your red pepper, rosemary, sugar, oregano, black pepper, salt, onion powder, garlic powder, lemon juice, red wine vinegar and olive oil together to create a dressing.
7. Pour your dressing over the green onion / potato mixture and toss to blend.

Portobello Steak

Ready In: 1 hour, 20 minutes

Servings: 3   Calories: 195   Protein: 3.4g   Carbs: 5.4g   Fat: 18.2g

Don't be misled by the word steak in the title of this incredible meaty-flavored recipe! This vegan steak-replacement is composed primarily of Portobello mushroom. It is well-seasoned with balsamic vinegar, minced garlic, chopped onion and canola oil. If you're trying to convert a steak-lover to veganism, this is the recipe to prepare for them!

Ingredients:

- 4 tbsp. Balsamic vinegar
- 4 cloves garlic, minced
- 3 tbsp. Onion, chopped
- 1/4 cup canola oil
- 3 Portobello mushrooms

Directions:

1. Thoroughly cleanse your mushrooms under the faucet and remove their stems. Reserve their stems for other use.
2. Place mushroom caps on a plate with the gills upwards.
3. Stir the vinegar, garlic, onion and canola oil together in a small bowl.
4. Pour the mixture evenly over the gills of the mushroom caps and let sit for 1 hour.
5. Grill the marinated mushroom caps for 10 minutes and serve!

Popeye's Casserole

Ready In: 1 hour, 30 minutes

Servings: 6   Calories: 360   Protein: 15g   Carbs: 48.9g   Fat: 14g

Just like the other dishes named *Popeye's* in this cookbook, this delicious dinner recipe is packed full of muscle-building spinach! If you're sick of spinach, you can feel free to swap it out with green chard in this recipe and it will still taste just as good. This dish will deliver a lot of flavor and health!

Ingredients:

- 1 cube vegetable bouillon
- 1 tbsp. Vegan chicken flavored gravy mix
- 2 tsp. Nutritional yeast
- 1/8 cup whole wheat pastry flour
- 2 tbsp. Olive oil
- 1 cup spinach, chopped
- 1 cup fresh corn kernels
- 1 tbsp. Tamari
- 1 tsp. Paprika
- 1 tbsp. Vegetarian chicken flavored gravy mix
- 1 tbsp. Nutritional yeast
- 4 tbsp. Hickory flavored barbecue sauce
- 1 pound firm tofu, crumbled
- ½ lb. Fresh mushrooms, sliced
- 1 clove of garlic, minced
- ¾ cup red onion, diced
- 1 tbsp. Olive oil
- 1 tbsp. Olive oil
- 1 tbsp. Light miso paste
- 1 bay leaf
- 1 onion, chopped
- 8 whole black peppercorns
- 1 bunch fresh parsley, chopped
- 1 stalk celery, chopped
- 1 clove garlic, crushed
- 5 russet potatoes, peeled

Directions:

1. Set your oven to 400°F (200°C) for preheating.
2. Quarter and peel your potatoes.
3. Prepare a large pot with water and place your potatoes into it.
4. Add in bay leaf, onion, peppercorns, parsley, celery and garlic.
5. Bring the contents of the pot to a boil and then cover and allow to simmer on medium-low heat for 20 minutes.
6. In order to prepare your filling, prepare a skillet heated with 1 tbsp. of oil and sauté your garlic and onion within it for 1 minute.
7. Add your mushrooms into the skillet and sauté for an additional 2 minutes.
8. Crumble your tofu into chunk-like pieces and sauté them in the skillet for 2 minutes, while stirring well.
9. Pour your barbecue sauce, tamari, paprika, thyme, gravy mix and yeast into the skillet and mix well and stir frequently for 20 minutes on medium heat.
10. Drain the water from your potatoes and place them in a large bowl, but spare 3 ½ cups of the water to be used for later.
11. Add oil, miso and no more than 1 cup of your preserved potato water into the bowl of your potatoes. Be sure to add no more water than is needed to moisten your potatoes adequately. This potato mixture is supposed to be the crust covering of your casserole, so do not over moisten!
12. Add your corn and spinach mixture to the filling mixture and stir well to mix. Spoon the filling into a greased, but shallow oven-proof casserole dish. Use a spoon to pat it down evenly.
13. Spread your potato crust evenly over the top of the filling, while being sure to smooth the top. Dust the potato crust with paprika.
14. Bake for 35 to 40 minutes at 400°F (200°C). When finished, the crust should be a nice golden color.
15. As the casserole is baking, you will need to mix up your gravy. To do this, heat some oil up in a large skillet or frying pan.
16. Add yeast and flour into the frying pan and whisk together on medium heat to create a paste.
17. Slowly mix about ½ cup of your potato water into the frying pan and whisk as you stir to allow the gravy to thicken.
18. Pour in your instant gravy mix and continue to whisk until the gravy becomes smooth and thick. If needed, then add additional potato water.
19. When the casserole is done baking, serve it with the crust on the bottom and the filling on the top and top with gravy.

Vegan Enchiladas

Ready In: 1 hour, 50 minutes

Servings: 8   Calories: 438.2   Protein: 17.1g   Carbs: 61.5g   Fat: 16.6g

This enchilada recipe combines mashed potatoes and roasted veggies into a supreme Mexican dinner! This recipe relies heavily on vegan butter, Cheddar-flavored soy cheese and soy milk to create the same effect on your taste buds that the standard non-vegan enchiladas have. If you wish to use home-made mashed potatoes instead of the called-for instant mashed potato flakes, use the recipe found earlier in the dinner section of this cookbook!

Ingredients:

- 8 oz. Cheddar-flavor soy cheese
- 3 cups enchilada sauce
- 12 oz. Package of corn tortillas
- 7.6 oz. Package instant mashed potato flakes
- ¼ cup vegan butter alternative
- 1 cup soy milk
- 3 cups water
- Salt and pepper
- ¼ cup olive oil
- 2 cups chopped carrots
- 3 small zucchinis, chopped
- 8 oz. Whole button mushrooms
- 1 head broccoli, cut into florets

Directions:

1. Set your oven to 425°F (220°C) for preheating.
2. Prepare a large bowl mixed with your carrots, zucchini, mushrooms and broccoli.
3. Drizzle oil over the tops of your veggies in the bowl and season them with salt and pepper.
4. Layer your oiled and seasoned veggies into the bottom of a shallow baking dish to form a single layer.
5. Allow the veggies to roast in your oven for 20 minutes at 425°F (220°C).
6. Pull the veggies out and stir thoroughly before placing them back in your oven for an additional 20 minutes.
7. Remove baking dish of veggies from your oven and lower the heat to 350°F (175°C).
8. Prepare a large pot filled with your water, vegan butter alternative and soy milk and bring it to a boil.
9. Remove the pot from the heat source and mix your instant mashed potato flakes into its contents. Allow the pot to stand for 2 minutes and then stir the mashed potatoes until they become smooth.
10. Stir your roasted veggies into the pot.
11. Use a non-dry and non-stick skillet on medium heat to heat up each of your tortillas on both sides.
12. Dip your tortillas in your enchilada sauce and put a 1/3 cup of your potato / vegetable mixture into the center of each.
13. Top the mixture with 2 tbsp. of your Cheddar-flavored soy cheese and roll up your tortillas.
14. Place them seam-side down in a 9" x 13" baking dish.
15. Cover them with extra sauce and sprinkle with your remaining soy cheese.
16. Bake for 25 to 30 minutes at 350°F (175°C) or until the enchiladas have become heated through.

● ●

DID YOU KNOW?

The enchilada was a dish featured in the very first cookbook that originated from Mexico, in 1831.

● ●

Indian-Style Stuffed Eggplant

Ready In: 35 minutes

Servings: 8   Calories: 560   Protein: 3g   Carbs: 18.3g   Fat: 55.1g

This Indian-styled vegan recipe is very similar to potato boats, if you've ever tried them, but the difference is that what you're looking at here tastes spicy instead of cheesy! That said, if cheese is your thing, you can add some Cheddar-flavored vegan soy cheese as a sprinkle to the finished product.

Ingredients:

- 1 tsp. Salt
- 1 tsp. Chili powder
- 2 tsp. Vindaloo curry powder
- 2 tsp. Ground coriander
- 2 cloves garlic, minced
- 1 large onion, finely chopped
- ½ cup vegetable oil
- 4 small eggplants, halved lengthwise
- 1 quart vegetable oil for frying

Directions:

1. Hollow out the inside of your eggplant halves. Leave ¼" of flesh attached to the skin, on the inside.
2. Roughly chop your removed eggplant bits and set the shells aside.
3. Place a large skillet on medium heat and warm up your ½ cup of vegetable oil.
4. Stir your garlic and onion, as you cook it on the skillet, until the onion becomes translucent and soft. This should be about 5 minutes.
5. Stir in the vindaloo powder, salt, chili powder and coriander and continue to cook another 3 minutes until the herbs become fragrant.
6. Mix in your chopped eggplant bits and stir until they become very soft. Mash as you go.
7. Pour a bit of water into the skillet if you need to, in order to keep the eggplant from burning.
8. Heat up your oil in a large saucepan or in a deep fryer at 375°F (190°C).
9. Allow the eggplants to deep fry in hot oil until they become crisp. This may take up to 5 minutes.
10. Drain the eggplants upside-down on some paper towels. Once drained, scoop the reserved filling from the skillet into the center of your hollowed eggplants and serve!

Creamy Corn Chowder

Ready In: 1 hour, 15 minutes

Servings: 6   Calories: 645   Protein: 27.2g   Carbs: 106.4g   Fat: 17.2g

If you can't have clam chowder, cause you're a vegan, don't fret – you can enjoy a bowl of this creamy corn chowder! The thick and creamy texture of this chowder is all achieved without a single drop of milk. This is a perfect dinner choice that will be enjoyed by vegans and non-vegans alike!

Ingredients:

- Sea salt
- Black pepper
- 1/3 cup nutritional yeast
- 1 cup cashews
- 8 cups fresh corn kernels, divided
- 2 quarts vegetable broth
- ½ tsp. Dried oregano
- ½ tsp. Dried thyme
- 2 bay leaves
- 1 head cauliflower, cut into bite-size pieces
- 4 lbs. Russet potatoes, peeled and finely diced
- 3 carrots, finely chopped
- 3 ribs celery, finely chopped
- 1 onion, finely chopped
- 2 tsp. Extra-virgin olive oil

<u>Directions:</u>

1. Place a large soup pot on your stove at medium heat and heat up your oil in it.
2. Place your carrots, celery and onion in the pot and stir until they are softened for about 7 minutes.
3. Dump your potatoes, oregano, thyme, bay leaves and cauliflower into the pot and stir well while cooking for 5 more minutes.
4. Pour 6 cups of corn kernels and your vegetable broth into the veggie mixture in the pot and bring it to a boil.
5. Reduce the heat to a low simmer for 35 to 40 minutes or until the vegetables become tender. Throw away the bay leaves.
6. Prepare a blender and dump your nutritional yeast, cashews and 2 remaining cups of corn kernels into it. Add in a few large spoonfuls of your simmering broth from the stove top into your blender. Do not fill the blender more than half full per each batch to blend.
7. Pulse the blender a few times before finally just leaving it on to blend until completely smooth.
8. Stir your cashew mixture into the pot on the stove. Season well with your salt and pepper. Pour into bowls and serve!

Vegan Baguettes

Ready In: 1 hour, 50 minutes

Servings: 6   Calories: 209   Protein: 6.2g   Carbs: 42.2g   Fat: 1.3g

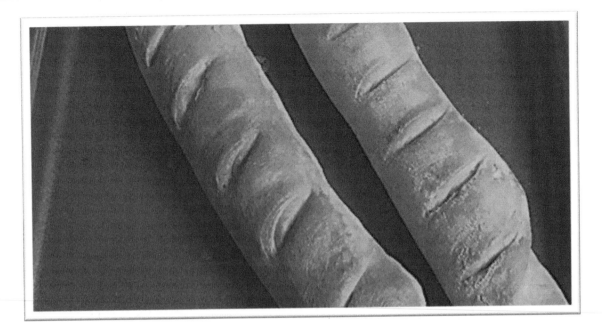

Baguettes are a popular dinner side in France. They usually are made with egg, but I've taken the liberty to create this vegan version of the original recipe using a vegan egg yolk replacer. To do this, I recommend using The Vegg brand Vegan Egg Yolk as a substitute. These mouthwatering, crispy pieces of bread make an excellent side dish to any of the dinners found in this cookbook!

Ingredients:

- 1 tbsp. Water
- 1 egg yolks equivalent of vegan egg replacer (The Vegg Vegan Egg Yolk recommended)
- 1 ½ tsp. Bread machine yeast
- 1 tsp. Salt
- 1 tbsp. White sugar
- 2 ½ cups bread flour
- 1 cup water

Directions:

1. Prepare a bread machine pan and put 1 cup of water and your salt, yeast and bread flour into it in the order recommended by the manufacturer. Select the option for "Dough Cycle" and press "Start".
2. Once the cycle has finished, place the dough into a bowl you have greased. Turn the dough about to coat all sides in the grease. Cover the dough and let it sit to rise for 30 minutes.
3. Punch down the dough like it's your least favorite president.
4. Prepare a floured surface to work your dough on. Roll the dough into a 16" x 12" rectangle, on the floured surface.
5. Cut the rectangle of dough into halves, creating two different 8" x 12" rectangles.
6. Tightly roll up each mini-rectangle of dough, starting with the 12-inch side and continually punching out any air bubbles, like they are your least favorite talk show hosts.
7. Roll the dough gently back and forth to taper end.
8. Place each roll of dough 3 inches apart on a greased baking sheet.
9. Cut deep diagonal slashes into the surface of each roll every 2 inches.
10. Cover the dough again and let it further rise for an addition 40 minutes in a moderately warm environment.
11. Set your oven to 375°F (190°C) for preheating.
12. Mix your vegan egg yolk replacer with 1 tbsp. of water and use a brush to coat the tops of your baguette dough.
13. Bake for 25 minutes or until the loaves become golden-browned.
14. Allow to cool a bit before cutting, but serve hot!

● ●

DID YOU KNOW?

Legend says that it was Napoleon who asked for the baguette to have a long shape. The long shape made it easier for his soldiers to carry their bread around tucked into their pants while navigating the battlefield.

● ●

General Tso's Tofu

Ready In: 1 hour, 40 minutes

Servings: 4   Calories: 550   Protein: 18.8g   Carbs: 91.7g   Fat: 13.1g

This General Tso's tofu recipe tastes so much like General Tso's chicken it's incredible! The best part is there is no deep frying which usually makes General Tso's a lot higher calorie and not so friendly for someone trying to watch their weight. Instead this recipe gets its flavor and texture by roasting and marinating a host of delicious ingredients that are going to satisfy any Chinese food lover!

Ingredients:

- 2 cups steamed brown rice
- 2 cups steamed broccoli
- 1/2 tsp. Grated fresh ginger
- 1 clove garlic, minced (1 tsp.)
- 4 green onions, green parts chopped (1/3 cup)
- 2 tsp. Vegetable oil
- ½ tsp. Sambal oelek chili paste
- 1 ½ tsp. Tomato paste
- 2 tsp. Cornstarch
- 2 tsp. Sesame oil
- 2 tsp. Rice vinegar
- 4 tsp. Mirin
- 1 ½ tbsp. Low-sodium soy sauce
- 2 tbsp. Sugar
- ½ cup low-sodium vegetable broth
- 1 tbsp. Cornstarch
- ½ tsp. Grated ginger
- ½ tsp. Minced garlic
- 1 tsp. Vegetable oil
- 1 tsp. Mirin
- 2 tsp. Rice vinegar
- 2 tsp. Low-sodium soy sauce
- 16 oz. Package of firm tofu, drained

Directions:

1. Start by slicing your block of tofu into two broad slabs. Use paper towel to wrap the tofu and place it between two cutting boards. Set many heavy soup cans on top of the uppermost cutting board to apply weight to tofu. Allow the tofu to sit under the weight for 30 minutes to drain the juice out of it.
2. Unwrap the tofu and discard the paper towels.
3. Slice the tofu into 1" cubes.
4. Prepare a sealable plastic container and fill it with your ½ tsp. of ginger, 1 tsp. of garlic, 1 tsp. of vegetable oil, 1 tsp. Mirin, 2 tsp. Rice vinegar and 2 tsp. Low-sodium soy sauce. Place your tofu in the newly created marinade and seal it in the container by placing the lid on it. Allow it to sit in your refrigerator to marinate for 30 minutes (to as long as overnight, if you have the time). The tofu should fully absorb all the marinade.
5. Set your oven to 350°F (175°C) for preheating.
6. Coat a cookie sheet with cooking spray. Sift 2 tsp. of cornstarch over your tofu and turn it over to coat it evenly.
7. Lay out your tofu on the cookie sheet and distribute it evenly across the surface.
8. Bake it in the oven for 35 to 40 minutes at 350°F (175°C). You'll know it's finished when the tofu becomes firm and crisp. Be sure to turn the tofu over several times throughout the course of baking to ensure all sides become browned.
9. While your tofu is baking, prepare your sauce. To do this, start by whisking together your ½ tsp. of sambal oelek, 1 ½ tsp. of tomato paste, 2 tsp. of cornstarch, 2 tsp. of sesame oil, 2 tsp. of rice vinegar, 4 tsp. of mirin, 1 ½ tbsp. of soy sauce, 2 tbsp. of sugar and ½ cup of broth in a small bowl. Set it to the side when finished.
10. Place a large skillet on medium-high heat and heat up some vegetable oil in it. Add in your 1 tsp. of garlic, 1/3 cup of green onions and ½ tsp. of ginger and stir-fry the mixture for 1 minute.
11. Add your broth mixture from step 9 to the skillet and cook for 1 additional minute or until it has thickened.
12. Combine with your tofu when it is finished baking and serve with 2 cups steamed brown rice and 2 cups of steamed broccoli.

Vegan Meatloaf

Ready In: 1 hour, 20 minutes

Servings: 6   Calories: 328   Protein: 13.5g   Carbs: 52.9g   Fat: 7.4g

Why not serve your family meatloaf without the meat for dinner? Prepare to be amazed at how good this vegan meatloaf tastes and how little you miss the meat! This delicious dinner loaf is composed of white rice, onion, lentils, mushrooms, vegetarian Worcestershire sauce, salt and pepper and a variety of other seasonings as well as vegan egg replacement. This stuff tastes fantastic!

Ingredients:

- ½ cup of ketchup
- 1 tbsp. dried parsley
- 1 tbsp. Italian seasoning
- 1 tbsp. Garlic powder
- 2 eggs equivalent of vegan egg replacement, beaten
- Salt and pepper
- 1 tbsp. Vegetarian Worcestershire sauce
- 1 cup chopped fresh mushrooms
- 1 cup cooked lentils
- 1 onion, finely chopped
- 2 tbsp. Vegetable oil
- 1 cup uncooked white rice

Directions:

1. Set your oven to 350°F (175°C) for preheating.
2. Bring a saucepan with 2 cups of water in it to a boil.
3. Add your rice into the saucepan and stir to cook. Reduce the heat and cover to let simmer for 20 minutes.
4. Place a small skillet on medium heat and warm your oil in it. Dump in your onions and allow to sauté. Set to the side.
5. Mix your cooked onions, parsley, Italian seasoning, garlic powder, vegan egg replacement, pepper, salt, vegetarian Worcestershire sauce, mushrooms, lentils and cooked rice together in a large bowl. Stir to blend the mixture.
6. Press the newly created mixture into a pan and spread ketchup over the top layer.
7. Bake for 45 minutes at 350°F (175°C).

Ramen

Ready In: 20 minutes

Servings: 4   Calories: 435   Protein: 12.8g   Carbs: 44.8g   Fat: 23.3g

Everyone needs a nice warm bowl of ramen for dinner every once in a while! This is probably some of the tastiest vegan ramen you will ever make. It has shiitake mushrooms, scallions and crunchy golden panko crumbs – not to mention the seasoning!

Ingredients:

- Panko
- 4 tbsp. Olive oil
- Sriracha
- 1 cup shredded carrots
- 2 cups chopped kale
- ½ cup chopped scallions
- 2 packages instant ramen (noodles only)
- 1 oz. Dried shiitake mushrooms
- 4 cups water
- 4 cups broth
- 4 tsp. Grated garlic
- 3 tsp. Grated ginger
- 1 tbsp. Sesame oil

Directions:

1. First and foremost, you need to make your crunchy golden panko crumbs. To do this, place a large skillet on medium heat and add 4 tbsp. of olive oil. Add in your panko and stir for 1 minute or however long it takes for the panko to turn golden-brown.
2. Remove the panko and place it on some paper towels to allow it to drain.
3. Now, using a second skillet (or thoroughly clearing out your old one first), heat your sesame oil in it on medium-low heat.
4. Add your garlic and ginger and stir fry for 2-3 minutes or until it becomes soft and fragrant.
5. Mix in your water and your broth. Bring the broth and water to a simmer.
6. Toss in your mushrooms and allow them to simmer for 10 minutes or until they have softened.
7. Add your instant noodles to the skillet and allow to simmer for another 5 minutes or until the noodles become soft.
8. Add your scallions and stir to mix in thoroughly.
9. Remove your skillet from the heat source and stir in the carrots and kale.
10. Top with crunchy panko crumbs and Sriracha.

Garlic Pasta & Tomatoes

Ready In: 30 minutes

Servings: 4   Calories: 439   Protein: 12g   Carbs: 67.7g   Fat: 14.3g

If you're hankering for an Italian dinner and you've already tried the lasagna, pizza and other similar recipes this cookbook has to offer, this is your next stop! This creamy and delicious garlic pasta is made with almond milk and whole wheat noodles. In just one cup of this delightful dinner, there's only 9 grams of fat. Not too shabby for a pasta!

Ingredients:

- 3 cups grape tomatoes, halved
- 2 ½ cups unsweetened plain *Almond Breeze*
- 4 tbsp. Unbleached all-purpose flour
- Sea salt and black pepper
- 8 large cloves of garlic, minced
- 2 medium shallots, diced
- Olive oil
- 10 oz. Whole wheat pasta

<u>Directions:</u>

1. Set your oven to 400°F (200°C) for preheating.
2. In a small bowl, toss together your sea salt, tomatoes and a little bit of olive oil.
3. Place your coated, halved grape tomatoes cut-side-up on a cookie sheet lined with parchment paper.
4. Bake for 20 minutes at 400°F (200°C).
5. While your tomatoes are cooking, prepare a pot of water and bring it to a boil on your stove. Cook your pasta in said pot, according to the packaging instructions. When the pasta is finished, drain it, cover it and set it to the side for now.
6. Prepare the sauce by placing a skillet on medium-low heat and coating it with 1 tbsp. of olive oil. Toss the garlic and shallot into the heating oil in the skillet. Add a little bit of sea salt and pepper and stir frequently while it cooks for 4 to 5 minutes. You'll know it's ready when it becomes soft and fragrant.
7. Add 4 tbsp. of flour to the skillet and mix it together with a whisk. Once it has combined, mix in your almond milk starting with just a little bit at a time.
8. Add a little more sea salt and pepper.
9. Bring the skillet to a simmer and allow to cook for 5 more minutes to thicken.
10. Leave the skillet running, but pour the sauce into your blender and blend until it becomes a creamy and smooth consistency and texture.
11. Place the contents of the blender back into the skillet and reduce heat for a low simmer. Allow to continue simmering until the desired consistency is achieved.
12. Add your finished pasta and roasted tomatoes to the skillet and stir.
13. Scoop into bowls and serve!

Spicy Chickpea Burgers

Ready In: 20 minutes

Servings: 7   Calories: 654   Protein: 29.6g   Carbs: 101.5g   Fat: 15.9g

Here is a solidly delicious hamburger alternative that will please any and every vegan who tries it! It's not just a burger, but it's a spicy burger. Use your imagination when it comes to topping this burger, but I recommend slices of avocado, salsa, crunchy pickles and lettuce!

Ingredients:

- 2 tbsp. Olive oil
- 1 cup quick oats
- ½ tsp. Sea salt
- 2 tsp. Black pepper
- 1 tsp. Garlic powder
- 1 tsp. Cumin
- 2 tbsp. Natural peanut butter
- 1 tbsp. Sriracha sauce
- 3 tbsp. Red wine vinegar
- 3 tbsp. Finely chopped cilantro
- 1 small zucchini, grated
- ½ red onion, finely diced
- 1 can chickpeas, drained, well-rinsed and mashed
- 7 whole wheat hamburger buns

Directions:

1. Drain and rinse your chickpeas and then place them in a bowl and mash them together with a fork.
2. Add all of your ingredients into the same bowl and use your hands to mix them together thoroughly and completely.
3. Form the mixture into 7 patties.
4. Cook on your barbecue at 400°F (200°C) for 10 minutes per side.
5. If you don't have a barbecue, fry them in a pan with some oil for 5 minutes or so.
6. Place your patties on whole wheat hamburger buns and top with your choice of toppings. I recommend starting with a layer of ketchup and mustard, then adding a few slices of lettuce. Layer with slices of avocado and red onion and then a couple crispy and crunchy pickles and finally a layer of salsa.

Green Chili & Mac

Ready In: 30 minutes

Servings: 4   Calories: 497   Protein: 16.2g   Carbs: 62.3g   Fat: 23.7g

What happens when you put a vegan macaroni and cheese dish together with a vegan green chili dish? Why this wonderful amalgamation, of course! You end up with a mouthful of cheesy, spicy, creamy and mouthwatering flavor that is going to no doubt have you coming back for seconds.

Ingredients:

- 1 cup tortilla chips and fresh cilantro
- 4 oz. Can of diced green chilies (scoop half into the sauce, reserve half for the finished macaroni and cheese)
- 2 tbsp. Nutritional yeast
- ¾ tsp. Chili powder
- ½ tsp. Cumin
- 1 tbsp. Cornstarch
- 1 ½ cups vegetable broth
- 1 cup raw cashews, soaked overnight
- 4 cloves garlic, minced
- ½ white onion, diced
- 10 oz. Large macaroni shells
- Sea salt and black pepper

Directions:

1. Set your oven to 350°F (175°C) for preheating.
2. Crush the tortilla chips into fine crumbs. Prepare a baking pan lined with parchment paper and add the crumbs to the baking pan. Spritz the tops of the crumbled chips with olive oil.
3. Sprinkle sea salt onto the top of your crunched chips and stir.
4. Bake for 10 minutes at 350°F (175°C).
5. Follow the package instructions to boil your macaroni.
6. Prepare a medium skillet on medium-low heat and sauté your garlic and onion in olive oil on it. Season well with sea salt and pepper. Stir while cooking for 7 minutes and allow the garlic and onion to become soft and fragrant. Set to the side when finished.
7. Place your garlic and onions into a blender with the remaining ingredients on the list (except for the tortilla chips, don't put those in the blender) and only use half of your green chilies.
8. Blend until the texture becomes smooth, using the "liquify" function, if your blender has one. Keep blending until it becomes completely smooth and creamy.
9. Drain your boiled noodles and set to the side, after covering them with a towel.
10. Using the same pot that you boiled the noodles in, add in your cashew cheese and cook at a low simmer. Constantly stir until the mixture begins to thicken.
11. Add your cooked noodles back into the pot with the cheese and also add your remaining green chilies into the mix. Stir well and pour into bowls.
12. Top each bowl with your crushed and toasted tortilla chips and cilantro.

Philly Cheese Seitan

Ready In: 30 minutes

Servings: 2   Calories: 225   Protein: 16.9g   Carbs: 13.4g   Fat: 11.6g

This is another vegan replacement for a traditionally non-vegan dish! To get the right texture and flavor of "cheese" for this cheese-less dish, it is recommended you use *Teese* vegan cheese. Feel free to use this as a filling for a sandwich or even a taco!

Ingredients:

- 2 tbsp. Hatch chilies, diced
- 1 small Anaheim chili, sliced
- 2 tsp. Extra virgin olive oil
- sea salt
- 2 tsp. Chipotle powder
- ¼ tsp. Black pepper
- 1 medium sweet onion, sliced
- 1 large red bell pepper, sliced into thin strips
- 5 tbsp. Teese brand vegan cheddar cheese
- 1 cup seitan strips
- Fresh cilantro
- Tomato, sliced
- Sliced jalapeno

186

<u>Directions:</u>

1. Prepare a large skillet and oil it on high heat.
2. Toss in your chilies, onions and peppers (not the jalapeno though, save that for later.) Cook until the edges start to turn black and your onions caramelize.
3. Season with your salt and pepper and other spices.
4. When the vegetables start to look about done, pour in your cheese and allow it to melt over the top of the vegetables.
5. Place the melted cheese and vegetable mixture on a plate.
6. Add more oil to the now empty skillet and lay in your seitan. Sauté the strips of seitan until edges begin to turn black. Season the seitan with spices, salt and pepper.
7. Add your melted vegan cheese and veggies to the skillet again and toss with your cooked seitan.
8. Remove the skillet from the heat source.
9. You can eat this mixture by itself on a plate or add it to a sandwich or a taco!

Sweet Potato Bakes

Ready In: 30 minutes

Servings: 4   Calories: 744   Protein: 29.2g   Carbs: 132.8g   Fat: 13.2g

These sweet, savory and smoky potato bakes are a great and healthy choice for a vegan dinner! They are topped with roasted garbanzo beans, a homemade herb and garlic sauce and fresh tomato salad. This is another one of my favorite *gluten-free* dishes that anyone with Celiac's disease or gluten intolerance can enjoy!

Ingredients:

- Chili garlic sauce
- 2 tbsp. Lemon juice
- ¼ cup chopped parsley, minced
- ¼ cup cherry tomatoes, diced
- Sea salt
- Unsweetened almond milk
- 3 cloves of garlic, minced
- ¾ tsp. Dried dill
- 1 tbsp. Lemon juice
- ¼ cup hummus
- ½ tsp. Cumin
- ½ tsp. Coriander
- ½ tsp. Cinnamon
- ½ tsp. Smoked paprika
- ½ tbsp. Olive oil
- 15 oz. Can of chickpeas, rinse and drained
- 4 medium sweet potatoes

Directions:

1. Set your oven to 400°F (204°C) for preheating.
2. Wash your potatoes thoroughly and then slice them in half length-wise.
3. Rinse and drain your chickpeas and then toss them together with olive oil and spices in a bowl. After you have tossed them, then lay them on a foil-lined baking sheet.
4. Rub some olive oil over each of the potato-halves and lay them face down on the same baking sheet.
5. Set your baking sheet in the oven to roast however long it needs to in order for the sweet potatoes to begin to become roasted. You will know they are finished when the sweet potatoes become fork-tender and the chickpeas become golden-browned. This should take about 25 minutes.
6. While baking, prepare your sauce. To do this, add your ¼ cup of hummus, 1 tbsp. of lemon juice, ¾ tsp. Dried dill, 3 cloves of garlic minced, some sea salt and a little bit of almond milk together in a bowl and whisk together. Add only enough almond milk for it to be a pour-able consistency. Adjust the seasonings as necessary. When thoroughly mixed, set the bowl aside.
7. In a second bowl, you need to prepare your parsley and tomato topping. To do this, place 2 tbsp. of your lemon juice in the bowl, followed by ¼ cup of diced cherry tomatoes, and ¼ cup of chopped parsley. Toss together and set to the side.
8. When the chickpeas have become golden-brown and the sweet potatoes are tender to a fork, remove them from the oven.
9. To serve the dish, flip the sweet potatoes right-side-up so their cut halves face the sky. Use a fork to smash down their insides to create a hollowing and top with first the chickpea mixture and then the sauce. Enjoy!

Butternut Squash Linguine

Ready In: 35 minutes

Servings: 4   Calories: 555   Protein: 26.2g   Carbs: 78.2g   Fat: 17.6g

This is the dinner you're looking for, if you're after something spicy, creamy and comforting! This delicious vegan dinner dish is fried with sage and is best served with roasted veggies for added flavor. If you love Italian food, then this is a recipe you have to try!

Ingredients:

- Vegan shaved parmesan
- 12 oz. Whole grain linguine
- 2 cups vegetable broth
- Black pepper
- Sea salt
- 1/8 tsp. Red pepper flakes
- 2 garlic cloves, chopped
- 1 medium yellow onion, chopped
- 2 lb. Butternut squash, peeled, seeded, cut into ½" pieces (3 cups)
- 1 tbsp. Finely chopped sage
- 2 tbsp. Olive oil

Directions:

1. Heat up a skillet on medium heat and fry some oil to cover the surface.
2. Add the sage to the skillet and toss well to coat. Once the sage becomes crispy, place it in a small bowl and sprinkle it with sea salt. Set the bowl aside.
3. Add the squash, red pepper flakes, garlic and onion to the skillet and season them with sea salt and black pepper.
4. Cook for 10 minutes while stirring frequently.
5. Pour in the vegetable broth and bring the mixture to a boil.
6. Reduce the heat and allow the skillet to simmer for 20 minutes or until the squash becomes soft and the liquid has reduced by 50% or so.
7. While the veggies are simmering, bring a pot of lightly salted water to a boil on your stove and cook your whole wheat linguine according to its packaging directions. Stir the pasta frequently. When draining, be sure to save 1 cup of the pasta's cooking water for later.
8. Once the squash on the skillet is done cooking, remove it from the heat source and allow it to sit to cool.
9. Save the skillet for later and dump its contents into a blender. Puree the squash and other veggies from the skillet until it all becomes a nice smooth texture. Then add more seasoning with salt and pepper.
10. Pour the puree and the set-aside pasta into the skillet as well as ¼ cup of cooking liquid.
11. Cook the contents of the skillet over medium heat, tossing together and adding more water and pasta as necessary. Continue to do this until the sauce completely coats the pasta. This should take 2 minutes.
12. Pour into bowls and top with your fried sage and parmesan.

Red Lentil Curry Soup

Ready In: 30 minutes

Servings: 4   Calories: 338   Protein: 14.4g   Carbs: 39.4g   Fat: 15g

This is an Indian soup that makes for a great dinner all on its own! It has a nice spicy zing to it that is complemented by the bold flavors of garlic and curry. It's incredibly healthy and is an ideal dinner for those with fewer calories to spend.

Ingredients:

- 3 tbsp. Finely chopped cilantro stems
- 1/3 cup chopped tart dried cherries
- 1 cup dried red lentils, rinsed
- 5 cups water
- ¾ cup unsweetened coconut milk, divided
- 2 tsp. Curry powder
- 1 ¼ tsp. Salt
- 2 large carrots, peeled and finely diced (1 cup)
- 1 large shallot, finely chopped (¼ cup)
- 6 garlic cloves, finely chopped (2 tbsp.)
- 1 piece (about 2 inches) fresh ginger, peeled and finely chopped
- 1 tbsp. Olive oil

Directions:

1. Place a saucepan on medium heat and heat up some oil in it.
2. Toss in your carrots, shallot, garlic and ginger. Season with a bit of salt and cook until it begins to become soft. This should take 7 minutes. Stir frequently.
3. Add your curry powder to the saucepan and stir continuously to cook it into the veggies. Stir and cook until the powder becomes fragrant, which should take 1 minute.
4. Add in the rest of your salt and ½ cup of your coconut milk. Add in the lentils and the water as well.
5. Bring the saucepan to a boil and immediately reduce the heat and cover to allow to simmer for 10 minutes or until the carrots become tender.
6. Pour the contents of the saucepan through a fine sieve to separate the solids from the liquids into a bowl. Save the solids for future use.
7. Allow the soup to cool and then puree in a blender until it becomes smooth. Work in batches, so that you don't clog up your blender jar. It should never be more than half-way full!
8. After blending, mix your saved solids back into it and stir well.
9. Save some of your cherries for a topping on the finished dish, but for now, stir some into it. Stir in your cilantro stems as well.
10. Scoop your soup out with a ladle into bowls and swirl in your leftover ¼ cup of coconut milk.
11. Top with your remaining cherries and cilantro leaves.

• •

DID YOU KNOW?

Red lentils contain all of the essential amino acids that our bodies need to produce the optimum amount of new muscle tissue.

• •

Three-Bean Chili

Ready In: 25 minutes

Servings: 10   Calories: 548   Protein: 29.9g   Carbs: 84.3g   Fat: 12.1g

This delicious vegan chili has a blend of three different beans! It is a mixture of garbanzo beans, cannellini beans, kidney beans and a wonderful blend of seasoning of chopped yellow onion, black pepper and garlic. If that's not enough flavor to subdue your cravings, add diced carrots and tomatoes and pine nuts.

Ingredients:

- 1 cup fresh flat-leaf parsley, chopped
- 3 tbsp. Pine nuts, chopped
- 1 clove garlic, finely chopped
- 15.5 oz. Can of kidney beans, rinse and drained
- 15.5 oz. Can of cannellini beans, rinse and drained
- 15.5 oz. Can of garbanzo beans, rinse and drained
- Sea salt
- Black pepper
- 15.5 oz. can of diced tomatoes, including liquid
- 2 carrots, diced
- 1 small yellow onion, chopped
- 1 tbsp. Plus ¼ cup extra virgin olive oil

Directions:

1. Place a large saucepan on medium-high heat and heat up 1 tbsp. of oil in it.
2. Add in your carrots and onion and cook for about 5 minutes.
3. Pour in 2 cups of water, 1 ½ tsp. Sea salt and ½ tsp. Pepper and the tomatoes with their liquid. Stir in well with the mixture on the saucepan.
4. Bring the contents of the saucepan to a boil.
5. Add in your garbanzo beans, kidney beans and cannellini beans and allow to cook for 3 minutes or until thoroughly heated through.
6. Prepare a small bowl with a mixture of your 1/8 tsp. Pepper, ¼ tsp. Salt, ¼ cup oil, parsley, pine nuts and garlic. Whisk together to mix well.
7. Evenly divide the chili among individual bowls and top with your pesto.

Vegan Campanelle

Ready In: 20 minutes

Servings: 4   Calories: 489   Protein: 13.5g   Carbs: 59.7g   Fat: 23.5g

This vegan campanelle dinner recipe is packed full of delicious Italian flavor! When you select this dinner option, you will enjoy the flavors of red bell peppers, Kalamata olives, roasted almonds and thyme leaves. It is a low-calorie option and a great source of fiber.

Ingredients:

- Sea salt
- Black pepper
- ¼ cup olive oil
- ½ cup roasted almonds, chopped
- ¾ cup pitted Kalamata olives
- 4 red bell peppers, seeded and sliced into quarters
- ¾ lb. campanelle pasta

Directions:

1. Follow the packaging instructions to prepare your pasta, but save ¼ cup of the cooking water when you drain the pasta.
2. Return the ¼ cup of reserved water to the pot of drained pasta.
3. Heat a broiler and place the peppers on a cookie sheet skin-side up. Broil them until they begin to turn black. This should take 10 minutes or so.
4. Use a knife to scrape off the charred skin from your peppers. Wipe them clean with a paper towel.
5. Cut the flesh of the peppers into 1" pieces.
6. Add the peppers, black pepper, sea salt, thyme, oil, almonds and olives to the pasta and toss together to mix.
7. Scoop into bowls and serve!

Winter Soup

Ready In: 1 hour

Servings: 4   Calories: 373   Protein: 15.1g   Carbs: 68.2g   Fat: 6.2g

This is one loaded soup! It packs more calories and is more filling than any of the lunch soups, which is why it's listed in the dinner section. When you prepare this hearty meal, expect a mouthful of kale, lentils, sweet potatoes and a hurricane of flavor!

Ingredients:

- ¼ cup grated vegan parmesan
- Sea salt and black pepper
- 1 tbsp. Fresh thyme
- ½ cup brown lentils
- 1 bunch kale, thick stems removed and leaves cut into ½" wide strips
- 2 sweet potatoes, peeled and cut into ½" pieces
- 28 oz. can of whole tomatoes, drained
- 4 leeks, cut into ¼" thick half-moons
- 1 tbsp. Olive oil

Directions:

1. Place a saucepan with your oil on medium heat.
2. Mix in the leeks and stir occasionally while cooking for 4 minutes. They should become soft.
3. Mix in your tomatoes and break them up with your spoon while they cook for 5 minutes.
4. Pour in 6 cups of water and bring the contents of the saucepan to a boil.
5. Mix in your pepper, sea salt, thyme, lentils, kale and sweet potatoes in a stirring fashion.
6. Lower the heat of the saucepan to bring it to a low simmer for 30 minutes.
7. When the lentils have become tender, ladle the soup into bowls and top with parmesan, if you wish.

Noodles of Coconut & Spice

Ready In: 20 minutes

Servings: 4   Calories: 344   Protein: 6.4g   Carbs: 27.5g   Fat: 25.7g

As the kids these days say, these noodles are lit! These creamy noodles are covered in chili paste, tomato paste, chili powder and kosher salt and cooked in unsweetened coconut milk. They are mixed with shredded coconut, bean sprouts and scallions. This is a nutritious and delicious choice to serve your family for dinner!

Ingredients:

- ¼ cup of shredded coconut, toasted
- 16 basil leaves
- 8 oz. Bean sprouts
- 3 scallions, thinly sliced
- 1 tbsp. Chili paste
- 1 tsp. Kosher salt
- 1 tsp. Chili powder
- 3 tbsp. Tomato paste
- 13.5 oz. Can of unsweetened coconut milk
- 8 oz. Rice noodles

Directions:

1. Follow the packaging instructions that came with your rice noodles to prepare them. Drain and set to the side.
2. Place a large saucepan on medium heat and stir the chili paste, chili powder, salt and coconut milk together in it.
3. Bring the contents of the saucepan to a boil and then immediately lower to a simmer for 3 minutes.
4. Stir your drained noodles into the mixture of sauce prepared in the saucepan.
5. Dish out into individual bowls and top with your shredded and roasted coconut, basil, sprouts and scallions.

Artichoke & Olive Baked Taters

Ready In: 1 hour, 25 minutes

Servings: 4   Calories: 197   Protein: 5.8g   Carbs: 40.9g   Fat: 2.4g

Why settle for your average run-of-the-mill baked potato when you can sink your taste buds into one of these? What you're looking at is a baked potato stuffed with tender artichoke hearts, Kalamata olives and grated lemon zest! If you're feeling adventurous, try swapping out the russet potatoes with sweet potatoes instead.

Ingredients:

- 1 ½ tsp. Grated lemon zest
- ¼ cup Kalamata olives
- 1 cup oil packed artichoke hearts, quartered, plus ¼ cup of the packaging oil
- 1 tsp. Olive oil
- 4 medium russet potatoes (8 to 10 oz. each)

Directions:

1. Set your oven to 400°F (204°C) for preheating.
2. Rub your potatoes thoroughly with your olive oil.
3. Prepare a rimmed baking sheet and spread your potatoes out evenly on it.
4. Bake the potatoes for 70 minutes and turn them over a few times throughout the baking process. You'll know they are finished when they are easily pierced with a knife or a fork.
5. While baking, prepare a small bowl in which you whisk your lemon zest, olives, artichokes and their oil together.
6. When your potatoes are done baking, split them open and divide your artichoke mixture evenly across all four potatoes. Allow to cool and serve!

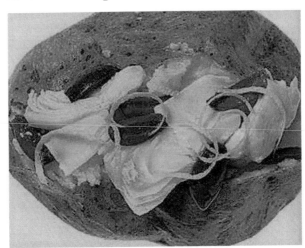

Vegan Stir-Fried Noodles & Tofu

Ready In: 25 minutes

Servings: 4   Calories: 315   Protein: 16.9g   Carbs: 39.2g   Fat: 12.9g

Every now and then, most of us find ourselves craving a good stir-fry. This is possibly the best vegan stir-fry recipe out there! It contains tofu with the best sauce and seasoning you've ever tasted on tofu, fried rice noodles and a healthy host of vegetables to boot. Give this recipe a shot and I guarantee you that it won't be your last time making it!

Ingredients:

- ½ cup fresh cilantro
- ¼ cup roasted peanuts, roughly chopped
- 4 scallions, thinly sliced
- 2 cups bean sprouts
- 1 tbsp. Grated fresh ginger
- 1 red bell pepper, thinly sliced
- 2 carrots, cut into thin strips
- 1 tbsp. canola oil
- 14 oz. Package of firm tofu, cut into ½"-thick slices.
- 2 tbsp. Fresh lime juice
- ¼ cup low-sodium soy sauce
- ¼ cup vegan brown sugar replacement
- 8 oz. Package of rice noodles

Directions:

1. Follow the packaging instructions that came with your rice noodles to prepare them. Drain them thoroughly and return them to the pot.
2. While your noodles are preparing, whisk your lime juice, soy sauce and sugar together in a small bowl.
3. Press your tofu slices between thick layers of paper towels to remove the excess juices from them. After they are sufficiently dried, cut them into ½-inch thick slices.
4. Heat your oil in a large skillet set on medium-high heat.
5. Add your ginger, bell pepper and carrots to the skillet and stir while it cooks for 2 minutes.
6. Toss in your tofu and your bean sprouts. Continue to cook and stir for 4 more minutes, so that the vegetables become slightly tender.
7. Toss your cooked rice noodles with half of the soy sauce mixture from your small bowl and cook together over medium heat until it becomes heated through. This should take 2 minutes.
8. Transfer your skillet's contents to a platter and top them with the cooked veggies and your left-over soy sauce mixture.
9. Top with cilantro, peanuts and scallions.

Squash & Peanut Stew

Ready In: 2 hours

Servings: 6   Calories: 492   Protein: 18.9g   Carbs: 66.5g   Fat: 19.7g

This recipe creates a chunky, delicious stew filled with squash and roasted peanuts! Also enjoy the flavor of vegan brown sugar alternative, black-eyed peas, fresh ginger, green serrano chili, garlic, kosher salt, tomato and even peanut butter! The thick, sweet and creamy taste almost makes this feel like a dessert that you're eating.

Ingredients:

- 2 tbsp. Chopped roasted peanuts
- 2 x 16 oz. Cans of black-eyed peas, rinsed
- 2 tbsp. Vegan brown sugar alternative
- 1 medium acorn squash, peeled, seeded and cut into 1" thick crescents
- ½ cup smooth peanut butter
- 28 oz. Can tomato puree (2 ½ cups)
- 4 cups vegetable broth
- 1 tsp. Ground cumin
- 2 tsp. Kosher salt
- 3 cloves garlic, finely chopped
- Small green serrano chili, finely chopped
- 1 tbsp. Grated fresh ginger
- 2 yellow onions, finely chopped (2 cups)
- 2 tbsp. Peanut oil
- 1 cup brown rice

Directions:

1. Heat your peanut oil in a skillet set on medium heat.
2. Stir in your onions and cook for 15 minutes.
3. Stir in the cumin, salt, garlic, chili and the ginger. Cook for 5 more minutes and stir frequently.
4. Pour in your tomato puree and your broth. Stir in the vegan brown sugar alternative, acorn squash and the peanut butter.
5. Cover your skillet and allow to cook for 30 minutes or until the squash has tenderized.
6. Stir the black-eyed peas into the mix and allow them to heat through.
7. Transfer your stew into a large bowl and sprinkle with peanuts. Serve with the rice.

Red Cabbage Slaw Tacos

Ready In: 50 minutes

Servings: 4   Calories: 400   Protein: 3.1g   Carbs: 27.5g   Fat: 31.8g

These vegan tacos are loaded with red cabbage slaw and a number of winter vegetables. The best part about these tacos is the ridiculously low-calorie count.

Ingredients:

- ½ head cabbage, finely shredded
- Salt and pepper
- ½ cup canola oil
- 1 tbsp. agave
- 2 tbsp. chopped cilantro leaves
- ¼ cup fresh basil leaves
- 2 cloves garlic, coarsely chopped
- ½ small red onion, coarsely chopped
- ¼ cup freshly squeezed lime juice
- ½ cup freshly squeezed orange juice
- 4 Taco shells

Directions:

1. Blend all your ingredients, except for the red cabbage, together in a food processor or a blender. Blend until smooth completely. Add salt and pepper.
2. Toss together with your cabbage and let it sit for 30 minutes in your refrigerator to marinate before you serve. Scoop filling out into tacos and serve!

● ● ● ● ● ● ● ● ● ● ● ● ● ● ● ● ● ● ●

DID YOU KNOW?

The flavonoid anthocyanin in red cabbage can be used as a natural dye for clothing or food.

● ● ● ● ● ● ● ● ● ● ● ● ● ● ● ● ● ● ●

Vegan Grilled Cheese

Ready In: 15 minutes

Servings: 1   Calories: 627   Protein: 44.1g   Carbs: 44.3g   Fat: 34.1g

Maybe you don't have a lot of time to prepare an elaborate dinner. Perhaps you are cooking for your picky children or grandchildren. If either of those cases describe your situation, this is the dinner recipe for you! The taste of vegan cheese and tempeh bacon come together in this delightful grilled cheese sandwich that takes just 15 minutes to make!

Ingredients:

- 4 slices tempeh, fried until crisp
- 1 tbsp. Vegan butter, divided
- 1/3 cup vegan cheese shreds (mozzarella and cheddar blend), plus extra
- 2 slices sandwich bread (½" thick)

Directions:

1. Place a bit of your vegan cheese shreds on one of your slices of bread.
2. Layer on your sliced tempeh bacon and then follow it by another layer of vegan cheese.
3. Top with the second slice of bread.
4. Prepare a non-stick skillet over medium heat and coat it with ½ tbsp. of your vegan butter.
5. Set your sandwich in the skillet and toast until it becomes golden-brown and crispy. Use a spatula to flip it over to cook the other side too. Add another ½ tbsp. of vegan butter when you flip it over.
6. After you flip it over, sprinkle the cooked side with a very light bit of the shredded vegan cheese.
7. When the bottom side is golden-brown, use your spatula to remove the sandwich from the skillet and slice it diagonally. Let it sit to cool for a few minutes and enjoy!

Vegan Crab Salad Sandwich

Ready In: 15 minutes

Servings: 4   Calories: 347   Protein: 7.1g   Carbs: 63.5g   Fat: 9.1g

Due to the sheer volume of calories and preparation involved, this sandwich qualifies as a dinner sandwich rather than being put with its cousins in the lunch section of the cookbook. Using the power of jackfruit, this sandwich in every way looks, tastes and feels like a real crab sandwich! The creamy texture will melt in your mouth, while the veggies and seasonings offer a rainbow spectrum of various flavors to be enjoyed.

Ingredients:

- Salt and pepper
- ½ tsp. Kelp granules
- 2 tsp. Pickled relish
- 1 ½ tsp. Dijon mustard
- 1/3 cup egg-free mayonnaise
- 1 tsp. Lemon juice
- ¼ tsp. Paprika
- ¾ tsp. Tarragon
- 2 tbsp. Red onion
- 1 tbsp. Fresh chives, minced
- 1 stalk celery (½ cup), chopped
- 20 oz. can of jackfruit (packed in brine, not syrup), rinse and drained
- 1 large fresh tomato, sliced
- Lettuce
- 4 Sub sandwich buns

Directions:

1. Squeeze as much water as possible out of each piece of your jackfruit.
2. Pull each piece of jackfruit apart into shreds. Use a knife, if needed.
3. Mix your kelp granules, salt, pepper, pickled relish, mustard, egg-free mayo, lemon juice, paprika, tarragon, red onion, chives, celery and shredded jackfruit together in a large bowl. Stir together until perfectly combined.
4. Spread mixture into your sub sandwich buns.
5. Top with a layer of lettuce and then with a few slices of fresh tomato.

Scaloppini Cordon Bleu

Ready In: 50 minutes

Servings: 4   Calories: 406   Protein: 32g   Carbs: 30.6g   Fat: 16.4g

You've heard of chicken cordon bleu, but you probably never expected such a meaty recipe could ever be perfectly recreated completely vegan! Prepare to be wowed by the incredible deep flavor of the chicken scaloppini replacement in this crispy, breaded and mesmerizingly flavored dinner.

Ingredients:

- Squeeze of lemon juice
- Non-stick spray
- 1 cup ice cold water
- 4 tbsp. Follow Your Heart VeganEgg powder
- 1 clove garlic, minced
- 2 tsp. Fresh thyme, chopped
- 2 tbsp. Vegan margarine, melted
- Salt and pepper
- 1 cup panko bread crumbs
- ¼ cup all-purpose flour
- 2 slices Tofurky Smoked Ham, cut in half
- 3.5 oz. Follow Your Heart Provolone Block, shredded
- 4 pieces Gardein Chick'n Scaloppini

Directions:

1. Set your oven to 350°F (175°C) for preheating.
2. Allow your Scaloppini to partially thaw.
3. Once thawed, slice the cutlet almost all the way, leaving just a little bit intact.
4. Layer the Tofurkey inside each sliced cutlet as well as the shredded vegan cheese.
5. Place the Tofurkey and vegan cheese-stuffed cutlets into your refrigerator and allow them to chill for the time being.
6. Stir your melted margarine, salt and pepper, breadcrumbs and flour together in a large bowl.
7. In a second bowl, whisk your ice-cold water and VeganEgg powder together.
8. Pull your chilled cutlets from the refrigerator and soak each of them in the VeganEgg mixture.
9. Sprinkle both sides of each in your breadcrumb mixture and place in the oven.
10. Bake for 35 minutes at 350°F (175°C). They are done when the breading has become golden and the cheese is fully melted.

Pizza Pull Apart

Ready In: 2 hours, 50 minutes

Servings: 6   Calories: 315   Protein: 35.9g   Carbs: 16.9g   Fat: 12.3g

This pizza pull-apart recipe is better than pizza itself! Imagine pieces of bread, almost like breadsticks, but when you pull them apart from the main loaf, you find yourself eating cheesy-tasting, delicious pizza. This is one of the most delicious recipes in the entire cookbook and, if you've stumbled across it, then try it!

Ingredients:

- 1/3 cup plain, unsweetened soy milk, warmed to 100°F(35°C)
- 1 tbsp. Maple syrup
- 1 tbsp. Active dry yeast
- 2 cups spelt flour
- 1 tbsp. Vital wheat gluten flour
- 1 tbsp. Salt
- 3 tbsp. Melted refined coconut oil
- ¼ cup + 1 tbsp. Unsweetened applesauce
- ¼ cup plain, unsweetened soy milk
- ¼ cup pureed silken tofu
- Extra flour for kneading
- Cashew mozzarella
- 1/3 cup tomato sauce
- 1 large clove of garlic, minced
- 2 tbsp. Plain unsweetened soy milk
- 1 tbsp. Olive oil
- Dried oregano
- Red pepper flakes

Directions:

1. The first step is to proof your yeast. In order to do this, stir 1/3 cup of soy milk, 1 tbsp. Maple syrup and 1 tbsp. Active dry yeast together. Set to the side for 10 minutes.
2. Now it's time to make your dough! Sift your different flours and salt together in a mixing bowl.
3. Once sifted, form a well in the center of the flour mixture and pour in the yeast mixture, tofu, applesauce, coconut oil and ¼ cup soy milk.
4. Stir well with a fork until your mixture begins to form together into a smooth texture and, when it does, switch to mixing with your hands.
5. Add as much extra flour as is necessary while you knead the dough into a ball. Try to minimize the amount of flour you use, if possible. Knead for 10 minutes on a floured surface or until smooth. The desired texture is so that it is moist and sticks to your hands, but easily comes off.
6. Shape the dough into a bowl and place it in a bowl. Cover the bowl with a damp towel and let it rest in a warm place for an hour or until it has doubled in size.
7. You need to make your filling. Simply mix together your shredded cashew cheese, 1 clove of garlic minced and 1/3 cup of tomato sauce in a small bowl, blending well. Set the bowl to the side for now.
8. Back to the pizza pull-apart itself! Poke your prepared dough a bit to deflate it and then gently roll it onto a flour surface. Try and flatten it out to the point it is somewhere between 1/8" to ¼" thick. Use a rolling pin to shape it into a rectangle as much as is possible.
9. Spoon and spread your filling that consists of tomato sauce, minced garlic and shredded cashew cheese all over the surface of your doughy rectangle. Evenly cover the entire surface.
10. Use a pizza cutter to cut the dough into 12 equal-sized squares.
11. Prepare a lightly greased loaf pan in which you stack your squares together and arrange them next to each other sideways. Cover the pan with a lightly dampened towel and let it rise for at least another hour in the refrigerator. If you have two or three hours, then that would work better, but one hour is fine. It should get a lot larger while sitting in there.
12. Place the loaf pan on a baking sheet to catch the drips and bake for 15 minutes at 350°F (175°C).
13. While it is baking, whisk together your red pepper flakes, dried oregano, 1 tsp. Olive oil and 2 tbsp. Soy milk to prepare the topping.
14. After you remove the pizza pull apart from the oven, quickly brush it down with your topping mixture using a baking brush.
15. Bake for 20 more minutes at the same heat. If the bread becomes too browned before the insides are done cooking, cover the top with aluminum foil.
16. When done baking, allow it to sit for 10 minutes to cool before eating.

Parm & Pesto Breadsticks

Ready In: 1 hour, 35 minutes

Servings: 12   Calories: 267   Protein: 7.4g   Carbs: 25.5g   Fat: 15.6g

These delicious parmesan and pesto breadsticks are an absolute *must* to go along with any of the Italian recipes that this cookbook has to offer! The pesto itself consists of fresh basil, walnut, olive oil, garlic, sea salt and pepper, vegan parmesan cheese and an ever-so-small bit of lemon juice. These crispy yet tender flavorful breadsticks will add a bit of pizzazz to any vegan Italian dinner!

<u>Ingredients:</u>

- 1 tbsp. Lemon juice
- 3 tbsp. Vegan parmesan cheese
- healthy pinch of sea salt and black pepper
- 4 large cloves of garlic, chopped
- ½ cup extra virgin olive oil
- 1/3 cup raw walnuts
- 2 cups fresh basil, rinsed and dried
- 4 tbsp. Vegan parmesan cheese
- 3 tbsp. Vegan-friendly basil pesto
- 3 cups unbleached all-purpose flour
- 1 tsp. Sea salt
- 2 tbsp. olive oil
- 1 tbsp. Cane sugar
- 1 packet active dry yeast

Directions:

1. Prepare your pesto! To do this, mix 2 cups of fresh basil, 1/3 cup raw walnuts, ½ cup olive oil, 4 chopped up cloves of garlic, sea salt and black pepper, 3 tbsp. Vegan parmesan cheese and 1 tbsp. Lemon juice together in a blender or food processor and process until combined. Leave a little bit of texture. Place in the refrigerator for now.

2. To prepare your breadsticks, add a cup of warm water to a large mixing bowl. If it's too hot, it will kill the yeast! Make sure it's just moderately warm. Add in your packet of yeast and let it stand on its own until it becomes foamy. This should only take 5 minutes.

3. Stir in your salt, oil and sugar.

4. Use a spoon to slowly mix in the flour until a ball of dough begins to come into form. You probably won't need all 3 cups of the flour right now, so be sure to save some in case you need more while kneading later.

5. Place the dough on a lightly floured surface and use your hands to knead it for about a minute. The ball should become smooth when it comes together.

6. Clean out your mixing bowl and add 1 tbsp. of olive oil to it. Put your dough back into the mixing bowl and flip it over a few times to make sure it's completely covered in the oil. Cover the bowl with plastic wrap and set it in a warm place for an hour. The dough should become twice the volume.

7. Cut the dough in half and save one of the halves for future use. It can store in the freezer for up to 3 months!

8. Set your oven to 400°F (205°C) for preheating.

9. Take whichever half of the dough you have chosen and roll it into a rectangle about ¼" thick on a floured surface.

10. Line a baking sheet with parchment paper and place the rectangle of dough onto it, reforming it into a perfect rectangle.

11. Brush with your vegan pesto mixture from step 1, while leaving the edges of the rectangle bare.

12. Top with an evenly distributed layer of vegan parmesan cheese.

13. Bake for 13 minutes at 400°F (205°C) or until the crust and cheese have become golden-brown. Slice and serve.

Lasagna Rolls

Ready In: 2 hours, 50 minutes

Servings: 10   Calories: 580   Protein: 23.2g   Carbs: 76.5g   Fat: 21.4g

If you like lasagna and also appreciate creativity, you'll love this amazing caprese lasagna roll dinner! The trick to this vegan alternative is using soy milk, a vegan mozzarella cheese replacement of your choice and the power of Flegg instead of eggs!

Ingredients:

- Balsamic glaze
- 18 cooked lasagna noodles
- 1/3 cup basil
- Black pepper
- 1 egg's equivalent of Flegg (1 tbsp. flax meal mixed with 3 tbsp. water)
- ¾ cup vegan parmesan cheese
- 2 cups vegan mozzarella flavored cheese, shredded
- 2 ½ cups soy milk
- 3 tbsp. All-purpose flour
- 3 tbsp. Unsalted vegan butter replacement
- 3 cloves garlic, minced and diced
- Kosher salt
- 2 tbsp. Balsamic vinegar
- 2 pt. Cherry tomatoes, halved
- 2 tbsp. Extra virgin olive oil
- 1 ½ cups raw cashews, soaked
- ½ cup water
- Juice of 1 large lemon
- 2 tbsp. Nutritional yeast
- 1 clove of garlic
- Dash of onion pepper
- Himalayan sea salt

<u>Directions:</u>

1. The first step is to prepare the cashew-based ricotta cheese replacement. To do this, soak the cashews in enough water to cover them for 2 hours. Be sure to have an extra 3 inches of water than is needed to cover them, because they will swell up.

2. Drain the cashews and place them as well as the extra ½ cup of water, juice of a large lemon, 2 tbsp. Nutritional yeast, clove of garlic, dash of onion pepper and a bit of Himalayan sea salt into a blender. Blend until it becomes a nice creamy texture.

3. Now it's time to start preparing the actual lasagna. Set your oven to 350°F (190°C) for preheating.

4. Place a skillet on medium heat and heat your oil.

5. Add in 2 tbsp. of balsamic vinegar and your cherry tomatoes. Cook for 5 minutes or until the tomatoes start to break down.

6. Season with salt and stir in your garlic until it becomes fragrant. Pour the contents of the skillet into a bowl and wipe the skillet clean.

7. To prepare your sauce, coat the same skillet on medium heat with your vegan butter alternative of choice.

8. When the vegan butter has melted, toss in your remaining garlic and cook until it becomes fragrant. This shouldn't take more than 1 minute.

9. Pour in your flour and cook until it becomes golden. This should take 2 more minutes.

10. Stir in your soy milk with a whisk and allow it to simmer for 3 minutes.

11. Mix in your 1 cup of shredded vegan mozzarella cheese replacement and all of the vegan parmesan replacement.

12. Prepare an 8" x 8" baking dish and coat the bottom with a thin layer of the newly resulting sauce from the skillet.

13. In a small bowl, whisk together your cashew-based ricotta cheese replacement with 1 egg's equivalent of Flegg. Season well with sea salt and black pepper.

14. Lay your cooked lasagna noodles into a single layer within the baking sheet.

15. Add an even layer of your tomato mixture on top of the noodles followed by another even layer of the cashew-ricotta cheese and Flegg mixture on top of it.

16. Sprinkle the top-most layer with basil and drizzle with sauce.

17. Roll it up in the lasagna noodles. Pack the roll ups tightly and position them upright in the baking dish.

18. Cover the tops of the roll ups with the remaining sauce and sprinkle them lightly with the vegan mozzarella replacement.

19. Bake for 30 minutes at 350°F (190°C).

20. When the lasagna rolls are finished baking, drizzle them in balsamic glaze and sprinkle with a touch of more basil.

Lime & Avocado Chilaquiles

Ready In: 40 minutes

Servings: 4   Calories: 471   Protein: 13.1g   Carbs: 78.9g   Fat: 16.1g

Imagine a bowl lined with toasted tortilla chips and topped with corn, salsa, chipotle peppers, roasted zucchini, onion, garlic and more and topped with fresh tender slices of avocado and flavored with lime. That's what you're about to sink your teeth into when you prepare this delicious authentic Mexican recipe!

Ingredients:

- Lime wedges, for garnish
- ½ avocado, thinly sliced
- ½ bunch fresh cilantro leaves, chopped
- Freshly ground black pepper
- Kosher salt
- Juice and zest of 2 limes
- 14 oz. Thick tortilla chips
- 1 ½ cup low-sodium vegan chicken-flavored broth
- 2 tbsp. Minced chipotle peppers in adobo sauce
- 2 ½ cup store-bought red salsa
- 1 medium zucchini, halved lengthwise and thinly sliced
- 2 cloves garlic, minced
- ½ sweet onion, diced
- 2 tbsp. Extra virgin olive oil
- 2 ears sweet corn

Directions:

1. Set your oven to 375°F (190°C) for preheating.
2. Place a large skillet on medium-high heat and lay the corn in it.
3. Turn the cobs over every 2 minutes to make sure it is charred evenly.
4. When the corn has gained a nice char, but is still edible, remove the corn from the skillet and use a knife to slice the kernels from the cobs. Throw away the cobs.
5. Put your 2 tbsp. of extra virgin olive oil into the skillet and cook your garlic and onion for 3 minutes.
6. Reduce the heat of the skillet to medium and cook for 2 minutes more.
7. Mix in your zucchini and cook an additional 5 minutes.
8. Add your corn kernels back into the skillet and blend together with the zucchini, garlic and onion.
9. Remove half of your mixture from the skillet and set to the side for later.
10. Pour your broth, adobo and salsa into the skillet and stir together.
11. Bring the mixture to a boil and start adding your tortilla chips to the skillet in handfuls. Make sure every chip gets coated thoroughly. Continue to do this until all the chips have been coated evenly.
12. Add in your lime juice and zest. Season the mixture with salt and pepper and fold together.
13. Transfer the contents of the skillet into a baking dish and cook for 12 minutes at 375°F (190°C) or until all the liquid has been absorbed.
14. When done baking, top with your remaining zucchini and corn mixture, sliced avocados and cilantro. Serve with your lime wedges for garnish.

Stuffed Spinach Pockets

Ready In: 2 hours, 10 minutes

Servings: 4   Calories: 729   Protein: 21.2g   Carbs: 91g   Fat: 31g

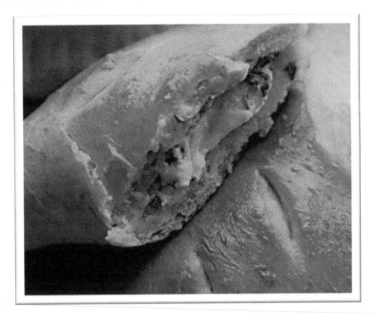

When you decide you're adventurous enough to test out this dinner recipe, you'll find that you're essentially eating a vegan cheesy hot pocket, stuffed with spinach! This recipe relies heavily on GO VEGGIE brand Vegan Classic Plain Cream Cheese and Flegg egg replacement. You're also going to need a vegan mozzarella-flavor cheese replacement. Bring all of these ingredients together with fresh spinach and you're in for a family-pleasing dinner!

Ingredients:

- 2 cups shredded vegan mozzarella-flavored cheese replacement
- ¼ tsp. Kosher salt
- 3 cloves of garlic, minced
- 1 ½ cups chopped fresh spinach
- 8 oz. GO VEGGIE brand Vegan Classic Plain Cream Cheese
- 1 large egg's equivalent of Flegg (1 tbsp. flax meal mixed with 3 tbsp. water), beaten together with 1 tbsp. Soy milk
- ¾ tsp. Kosher salt
- 2 tbsp. Extra-virgin olive oil, plus extra for greasing
- 1 tbsp. Granulated sugar
- 3 ½ cups all-purpose flour, plus more for work surface
- 1 1/3 cups warm (NOT HOT) water
- 2 ¼ tsp. Active dry yeast (1 standard packet)

Directions:

1. Stir together your yeast and warm (NOT HOT) water in a large mixing bowl. Hot water will kill the yeast, so use slightly warmer than lukewarm. Let sit until the mixture becomes foamy. This shouldn't take more than 5 minutes.
2. Add ¾ tsp. salt, 2 tbsp. olive oil, 1 tbsp. granulated sugar and 3 ½ cups all-purpose flour. Mix together with your hands for 1 minute.
3. Continue to knead with your hand until the dough becomes smooth and elastic. If you need to, feel free to add just a tiny bit more water. If it becomes too wet add increments of ¼ cup of flour. Use your index finger to poke the dough. If it slowly bounces back, it's ready to rise. If it doesn't, continue to knead it.
4. Use your hands to shape the dough into a spherical ball shape and place it in a lightly greased, large enough mixing bowl. Turn the dough to coat all sides of it.
5. Cover the bowl of greased dough in plastic wrap and allow it to rise in a warm environment for about an hour or until it is 50% larger.
6. To prepare your filling, beat the GO VEGGIE vegan cream cheese, garlic, salt and spinach together in a medium bowl. Cover this mixture and set it in the refrigerator for now.
7. Set your oven to 400°F (205°C) for preheating.
8. Line two large baking sheets with parchment paper.
9. Once the dough is risen, punch it down as hard as you would punch down people who torture dogs, in order to release the air.
10. Prepare a lightly floured surface and turn the dough out onto it.
11. Use a sharp knife to slice the dough in half and then slice the halves into quarters. This should result in you having 8 pieces.
12. Use a rolling pin to flatten each piece to a shape that is 6" long and 4" wide.
13. Lay out your flattened dough pieces on your two baking sheets.
14. Remove your filling from the refrigerator and spread 2 tbsp. of it on the ends of each piece of dough. Top the filling with ¼ cup of shredded vegan mozzarella cheese replacement.
15. Fold the un-topped ends of each piece of dough over the top of the topped ends and pinch with your fingers to seal shut, around the perimeters. Use a fork to crimp the edges.
16. Brush the tops of each pocket with the Flegg and soy milk mixture and slice 3 slits in the tops of each pocket to function as air vents.
17. Bake the pockets for 25 minutes at 400°F (205°C) or until golden-brown.

Vegan Cheese-Stuffed Artichoke

Ready In: 45 minutes

Servings: 4   Calories: 550   Protein: 22.2g   Carbs: 61.3g   Fat: 26.8g

These vegan cheese-stuffed artichokes deliver incredible flavor and texture! They use a vegan mozzarella cheese replacement of your choice, vegan parmesan replacement and a ton of other great ingredients. They taste the absolute best when you dip them in marinara sauce!

Ingredients:

- Warm marina, for dipping
- Kosher salt and black ground pepper
- 2 cloves of garlic, minced
- 1/3 cup extra virgin olive oil
- ¼ cup fresh parsley, chopped
- 1 cup vegan parmesan replacement
- 1 cup vegan mozzarella-flavored cheese replacement, plus more for sprinkling
- 2 cups panko bread crumbs
- 4 large artichokes, trimmed
- 1 lemon, thinly sliced

Directions:

1. Preheat a broiler.
2. Prepare a large pot with ½ inch of water and your lemon slices.
3. Add in your four trimmed artichokes and bring the pot to a simmer. Steam for 25 minutes or until the artichokes have become tender.
4. Remove the pot from the heat source and allow to cool.
5. Stir together your panko bread crumbs, garlic, olive oil, parsley, vegan parmesan replacement, and shredded vegan mozzarella-flavored cheese replacement in a large bowl. Mix well. Season with salt and pepper.
6. Pack the breadcrumb mixture into the artichoke leaves.
7. Prepare a lightly greased baking dish and lay the artichokes into it.
8. Sprinkle the tops of each artichoke with more vegan mozzarella-flavored cheese replacement.
9. Bake in the broiler for 5 minutes or until the bread crumbs have turned golden and the cheese replacement has melted. Serve with the marina to dip in.

Mac & Cheese-It Inferno

Ready In: 30 minutes

Servings: 8   Calories: 666   Protein: 32.5g   Carbs: 60.8g   Fat: 32.1g

No, regular Cheeze-Its are sadly not vegan, but this recipe relies on Earth Balance Vegan Cheddar Flavor Squares, which you can purchase on Amazon! Imagine vegan macaroni and cheese topped with crushed cheese it crackers and you're looking at a mac and cheese inferno. This is a kid's-favorite dinner dish!

Ingredients:

- ¼ cup Earth Balance Vegan Cheddar Flavor Squares (looks and tastes like Cheeze-Its)
- ¼ cup panko breadcrumbs
- 3 tbsp. Vegan butter replacement
- 2 cups vegan pepper jack-flavored cheese replacement, shredded
- 4 cups vegan sharp white cheddar-flavored cheese replacement, divided into 3 ½ cups and ½ cup
- 4 cups soy milk
- ½ tbsp. Black pepper
- 1 tbsp. Salt
- 1 tsp. Cayenne pepper
- ½ cup flour
- ½ cup vegan butter replacement
- 1 lb. Cavatappi pasta

Directions:

1. Set your oven to 350°F (175°C) for preheating.
2. Prepare a large pot of lightly salted water and bring it to a boil.
3. Prepare your pasta in the boiling water, according to the packaging instructions.
4. Drain the pasta noodles and set to the side for now.
5. Place a large saucepan over medium heat and melt your ½ cup. of vegan butter replacement in it.
6. Sprinkle the flour into the saucepan and whisk it to create a roux.
7. Mix in your pepper, salt and cayenne.
8. Slowly pour in the soy milk and continue to whisk as you go.
9. Whisk while simmering for 5 to 6 minutes to thicken.
10. Add in your vegan pepper jack and cheddar replacements, stirring until they have melted and combined.
11. Remove the saucepan from the heat source.
12. Add cooked pasta noodles into a 9" x 13" baking dish and pour the vegan cheese replacement sauce you have just created on top, stirring gently to mix and combine.
13. Melt 3 tbsp. of vegan butter replacement in the same saucepan on medium heat.
14. Add in your panko breadcrumbs and crushed Earth Balance Vegan Cheese Flavored Squares. Stir non-stop for 4 minutes or until it all has become lightly goldened.
15. Sprinkle the panko / cracker combination over your macaroni and bake for 14 minutes at 350°F (175°C) or until the cheese has melted.

● ● ● ● ● ● ● ● ● ● ● ● ● ● ● ● ● ●

DID YOU KNOW?

Earth Balance's cheddar squares are not only vegan, but they are free from GMO's and have no trans fat either!

● ● ● ● ● ● ● ● ● ● ● ● ● ● ● ● ● ●

Chapter 7: Desserts, Smoothies & Treats

This final section of the cookbook is your collection of desserts, smoothies and other treats. You can expect to find a massive supply of smoothie varieties, ice cream, cakes, puddings and other delicious treats that do not fit into the categories of breakfast, lunch or dinner.

You will notice that the calories as well as the grams of protein, fat and carbohydrates per each recipe are listed right beneath the name. The macronutrients listed correspond with the designated serving size. For example, if a recipe has servings listed as 4, then the total yield should be divided into fourths. If a recipe has servings listed as 6, then divide the total yield of the recipe into six different portions.

Tropical Blast Smoothie

Ready In: 5 minutes

Servings: 1   Calories: 435   Protein: 7.2g   Carbs: 79.9g   Fat: 12.5g

A delicious smoothie consisting of: mixed frozen berries, banana, frozen strawberries, shredded coconut, chia seeds and orange juice.

Ingredients:

- ¾ cups orange juice
- 1 tbsp. Chia seeds
- ¼ cup shredded coconut
- ½ cup frozen strawberries
- 1 banana
- 1 cup mixed frozen berries

Directions:

1. Combine your chia seeds, coconut, strawberries, banana and frozen berries in a blender.
2. Pulse briefly to mix.
3. Add in your orange juice and blend until smooth.

Popeye's Green Smoothie

Ready In: 10 minutes

Servings: 1   Calories: 296   Protein: 13.9g   Carbs: 46.1g   Fat: 7.4g

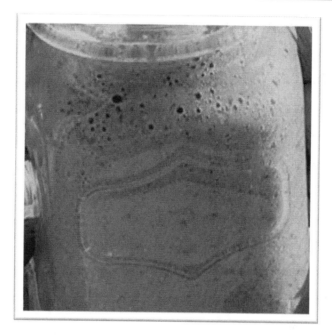

A delicious smoothie consisting of: banana, spinach, frozen mixed fruit, flax seed meal, vegan protein powder, chia seeds, Matcha green tea powder and water.

Ingredients:

- Water to cover
- ½ tsp. Matcha green tea powder
- 1 tbsp. Chia seeds
- ½ scoop vegan protein powder
- 1 tbsp. Flax seed meal
- ½ cup frozen mixed fruit
- 1/3 cup frozen chopped spinach
- 1 banana

Directions:

1. Dump your Matcha powder, chia seeds, protein powder, flax meal, mixed fruit, spinach and banana together in your blender.
2. Add just enough water to cover.
3. Blend until it becomes smooth in texture.

Vegan Pina Colada Smoothie

Ready In: 10 minutes

Servings: 1   Calories: 638   Protein: 10.2g   Carbs: 81.5g   Fat: 33.5g

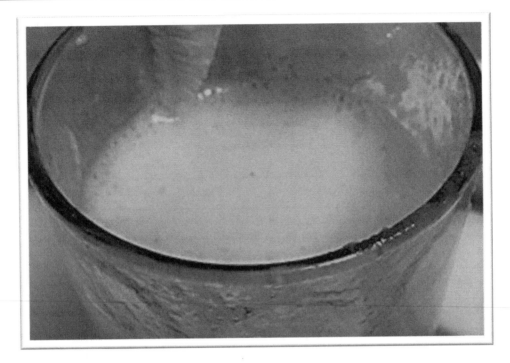

A delicious smoothie consisting of: crushed ice, banana, pineapple, coconut milk, soy milk, agave nectar, ground flax seed and pure vanilla extract.

Ingredients:

- 1 tsp. Pure vanilla extract
- 1 tbsp. Ground flax seed
- 1 tbsp. Agave nectar
- ½ cup soy milk
- ½ cup coconut milk
- 1 cup fresh pineapple chunks
- 1 banana
- 3 ice cubes

Directions:

1. Blend all your ingredients together in a blender.
2. Pour the resulting smoothie into a glass and enjoy!

Green Hulk Smoothie

Ready In: 5 minutes

Servings: 1   Calories: 343   Protein: 7.1g   Carbs: 82.5g   Fat: 1.9g

A delicious smoothie consisting of: coconut water, baby spinach, banana, fresh strawberries and dates.

Ingredients:

- 5 dates, pitted
- 6 sliced fresh strawberries
- 1 banana
- 1 cup baby spinach
- 2 cups coconut water

Directions:

1. Blend all your ingredients together in a blender.
2. Pour the resulting smoothie into a glass and enjoy!

Sweet Avocado Smoothie

Ready In: 5 minutes

Servings: 4   Calories: 314   Protein: 2.9g   Carbs: 13.4g   Fat: 30.1g

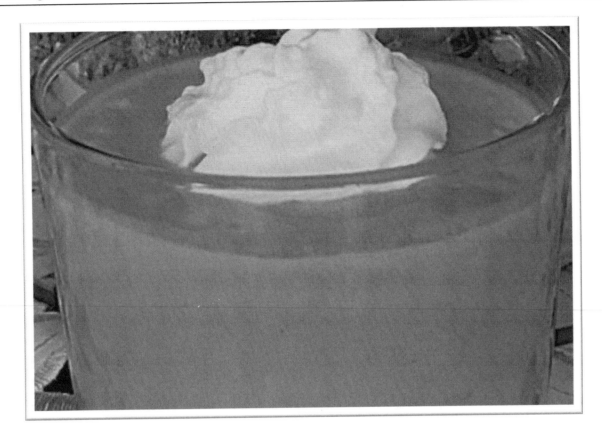

A delicious smoothie consisting of: almond milk, avocado and agave.

Ingredients:

- 1 tbsp. Agave
- 1 avocado, peeled and pitted
- 12 fluid oz. Unsweetened almond milk

Directions:

1. Blend all your ingredients together in a blender.
2. Pour the resulting smoothie into a glass and enjoy!

Oats & Strawberry Smoothie

Ready In: 10 minutes

Servings: 2   Calories: 481   Protein: 6.6g   Carbs: 52.6g   Fat: 30.4g

A delicious smoothie consisting of: almond milk, oats, strawberries, banana, agave nectar and vanilla extract.

Ingredients:

- ½ tsp. Vanilla extract
- 1 ½ tsp. Agave nectar
- 1 banana, broken into chunks
- 14 frozen strawberries
- ½ cup rolled oats
- 1 cup almond milk

Directions:

1. Blend all your ingredients together in a blender.
2. Pour the resulting smoothie into a glass and enjoy!

Mango & Chia Smoothie

Ready In: 15 minutes

Servings: 1   Calories: 388   Protein: 8.1g   Carbs: 84.3g   Fat: 5.6g

A delicious smoothie consisting of: mango, banana, romaine lettuce, crushed ice, flax seeds, chia seeds and water.

Ingredients:

- 1 tbsp. chia seeds
- 1 tsp. flax seeds
- 2 ice cubes
- ½ cup chopped romaine lettuce
- ¾ cup cold water, or as needed
- 1 banana, sliced
- 1 mango, chopped

Directions:

1. Blend all your ingredients, except for the chia seeds, together in a blender.
2. Pour the resulting smoothie into a glass. Allow to sit for 2 minutes to thicken.
3. Sprinkle in your chia seeds and stir well. Enjoy!

Coconut & Berry Smoothie

Ready In: 10 minutes

Servings: 1   Calories: 528   Protein: 8g   Carbs: 52.6g   Fat: 36.4g

A delicious smoothie consisting of: banana, blueberries, almond butter, flaked coconut and water.

Ingredients:

- ½ cup of water, or as needed
- 1 tbsp. Unsweetened coconut flakes
- 1 tbsp. Almond butter
- ½ cup frozen blueberries
- 1 banana

Directions:

1. Blend all your ingredients together in a blender.
2. Pour the resulting smoothie into a glass and enjoy!

Hemp & Chocolate Smoothie

Ready In: 10 minutes

Servings: 1   Calories: 336   Protein: 21.8g   Carbs: 55.6g   Fat: 6g

A delicious smoothie consisting of: banana, crushed ice, hemp protein powder, cocoa powder and coconut water.

Ingredients:

- 1 tbsp. Cocoa powder
- 3 tbsp. Hemp protein powder
- ½ cup ice cubes
- 1 sliced frozen banana
- 8 fluid oz. Coconut water

Directions:

1. Blend all your ingredients together in a blender.
2. Pour the resulting smoothie into a glass and enjoy!

Cocoa Banana Nut Smoothie

Ready In: 10 minutes

Servings: 1   Calories: 574   Protein: 25.5g   Carbs: 68.1g   Fat: 25.1g

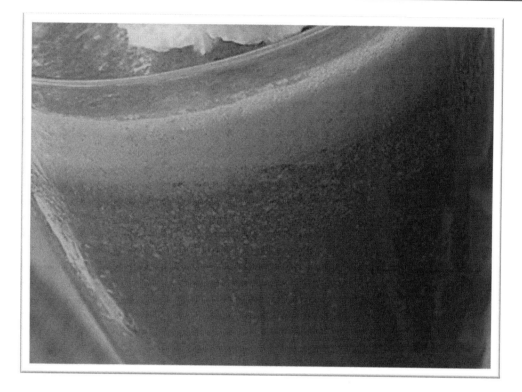

A delicious smoothie consisting of: chocolate soy milk, crushed ice, banana and peanut butter.

Ingredients:

- 2 tbsp. Creamy peanut butter
- 1 large banana
- 2 cups chocolate soy milk
- 2 cups ice

Directions:

1. Blend all your ingredients together in a blender.
2. Pour the resulting smoothie into a glass and enjoy!

White Bean & Coconut Smoothie

Ready In: 10 minutes

Servings: 2   Calories: 342   Protein: 8.2g   Carbs: 54.8g   Fat: 12g

A delicious smoothie consisting of: banana, mango, kale, white beans, shredded coconut, Matcha green tea and water.

Ingredients:

- 1 cup water
- ½ tsp. Matcha green tea powder
- 2 tbsp. Unsweetened shredded coconut
- 3 tbsp. White beans, drained
- 2 leaves of kale, torn into several pieces
- 1 cup frozen mango chunks
- 1 banana

Directions:

1. Blend all your ingredients together in a blender.
2. Pour the resulting smoothie into a glass and enjoy!

Blueberry & Mint Smoothie

Ready In: 10 minutes

Servings: 2   Calories: 337   Protein: 5g   Carbs: 40g   Fat: 20.6g

A delicious smoothie consisting of: blueberries, fresh mint leaves, avocado, orange juice, lemon juice and water.

Ingredients:

- 2 tsp. Lemon juice
- 1/2 cup orange juice
- 1 avocado, peeled and pitted
- 1 cup fresh mint leaves
- 1 cup water
- 2 cups frozen blueberries

Directions:

1. Blend all your ingredients together in a blender.
2. Pour the resulting smoothie into a glass and enjoy!

Almond & Blueberry Smoothie

Ready In: 10 minutes

Servings: 2   Calories: 281   Protein: 4.3g   Carbs: 28.8g   Fat: 19.2g

A delicious smoothie consisting of: blueberries, banana, almond milk, almond butter and water.

Ingredients:

- Water as needed
- 1 tbsp. Almond butter
- ½ cup almond milk
- 1 banana
- 1 cup frozen blueberries

Directions:

1. Blend all your ingredients together in a blender.
2. Pour the resulting smoothie into a glass and enjoy!

Walnut & Banana Smoothie

Ready In: 10 minutes

Servings: 2   Calories: 353   Protein: 6.5g   Carbs: 59.3g   Fat: 13g

A delicious smoothie consisting of: banana, pineapple, cashew butter, walnuts and water.

Ingredients:

- 2 cups water or as needed
- 2 tbsp. Chopped walnuts
- 2 tbsp. Cashew butter
- 1 cup frozen pineapple chunks
- 2 bananas

Directions:

1. Blend all your ingredients together in a blender.
2. Pour the resulting smoothie into a glass and enjoy!

Sesame Seed & Mango Smoothie

Ready In: 10 minutes

Servings: 2   Calories: 285   Protein: 7g   Carbs: 49.8g   Fat: 9.8g

A delicious smoothie consisting of: banana, mango, cucumber, spinach, cashew butter, sesame seeds and water.

Ingredients:

- 1 cup water or as needed
- 1 tsp. Toasted sesame seeds
- 2 tbsp. Cashew butter
- 2 cups fresh spinach
- 1 small cucumber, chopped
- 1 cup frozen mango chunks
- 1 banana

Directions:

1. Blend all your ingredients together in a blender.
2. Pour the resulting smoothie into a glass and enjoy!

Maca & Flax Seed Smoothie

Ready In: 10 minutes

Servings: 1   Calories: 341   Protein: 5.3g   Carbs: 71.2g   Fat: 6.5g

A delicious smoothie consisting of: rice milk, banana, blueberries, raspberries, moringa powder, ground flax seed, maca and tahini.

Ingredients:

- 1 heaped tsp. Tahini
- 1 heaped tsp. Maca
- 1 heaped tsp. Ground flax seed
- 1 heaped tsp. Moringa powder
- ½ cup fresh raspberries
- ½ cup frozen blueberries
- 1 large banana
- ¾ cup rice milk

Directions:

1. Blend all your ingredients together in a blender.
2. Pour the resulting smoothie into a glass and enjoy!

Pumpkin Smoothie

Ready In: 10 minutes

Servings: 2   Calories: 289   Protein: 6.4g   Carbs: 60.6g   Fat: 3.7g

A delicious smoothie consisting of: almond milk, chai tea, pumpkin puree, vanilla, pumpkin pie spice and bananas.

Ingredients:

- 2 frozen bananas
- ½ tsp. Pumpkin pie spice
- 1 tsp. Vanilla
- 3 tbsp. Pumpkin puree
- 1 tsp. Chai tea (leaves from teabag)
- 2/3 cup unsweetened almond milk

Directions:

1. Blend all your ingredients, except for the banana, together in a blender. Blend until the tea leaves have completely broken down.
2. Add in chunks of the frozen bananas and blend together till completely broken down.
3. Pour the resulting smoothie into a glass and enjoy!

Beet & Raspberry Smoothie

Ready In: 10 minutes

Servings: 4   Calories: 428   Protein: 4.9g   Carbs: 43.6g   Fat: 29.4g

A delicious smoothie consisting of: bananas, raspberries, peeled beetroot, almond milk, dates and flax seeds.

Ingredients:

- 2 tsp. Flax seeds
- 2 Medjool dates, pitted
- 2 cups almond milk
- 100 gr. raw peeled beetroot
- 1 cup raspberries
- 2 ripe bananas

Directions:

1. Blend all your ingredients together in a blender.
2. Pour the resulting smoothie into a glass and enjoy!

Apple Pie Smoothie

Ready In: 10 minutes

Servings: 2   Calories: 467   Protein: 6.1g   Carbs: 40.7g   Fat: 35.1g

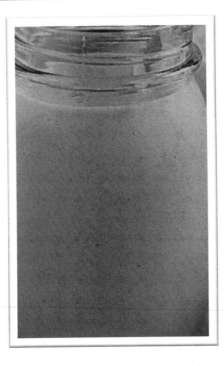

A delicious smoothie consisting of: apples, almond milk, walnuts, flax meal, vanilla extract, cinnamon, nutmeg and crushed ice.

Ingredients:

- 4 ice cubes
- ½ tsp. Ground nutmeg
- 1 tsp. Ground cinnamon
- 1 tsp. Pure vanilla extract
- 1 tbsp. Flax meal (ground flax seeds)
- 2 tbsp. Raw walnuts, chopped
- 1 cup almond milk
- 2 medium apples, cored and roughly chopped

Directions:

1. Blend all your ingredients together in a blender.
2. Pour the resulting smoothie into a glass and enjoy!

Pear & Apple Smoothie

Ready In: 10 minutes

Servings: 1   Calories: 355   Protein: 8.2g   Carbs: 82g   Fat: 2.8g

A delicious smoothie consisting of: cilantro, romaine lettuce, spinach, celery, gala apple, pear, banana, freshly squeezed lemon juice, turmeric, spirulina and water.

Ingredients:

- 1 tsp. Spirulina
- 1 tsp. Turmeric
- Juice from ½ a lemon
- 1 ripe banana
- 1 ripe pear
- 1 gala apple
- 4 stalks of celery
- 3 big handfuls of spinach
- 1 head of romaine lettuce, base cut off
- 1 handful of cilantro
- 2 cups of unfiltered water

Directions:

1. Pour your 2 cups of water into a blender, followed by your spinach, lettuce and cilantro. Blend from medium to high until it is perfectly blended. Add more water if it looks too thick and more spinach if it looks too thin.
2. Add your apple (with the seeds removed), celery, pear, banana, lemon juice, spirulina and turmeric. Blend from medium to high speed until smooth.
3. Pour the resulting smoothie into a glass and enjoy!

Peanut Butter & Jelly Oatmeal Smoothie

Ready In: 8 hours, 10 minutes

Servings: 4   Calories: 299   Protein: 8.3g   Carbs: 33g   Fat: 16.6g

A delicious smoothie consisting of: overnight oats, peanut butter, almond milk, chia seeds, sea salt, frozen banana, raspberries, blackberries, blueberries and maca powder.

Ingredients:

- 1 tbsp. Maca powder
- ¼ cup blueberries
- ¼ cup blackberries
- ¼ cup raspberries
- 1 frozen banana
- 1 pinch of sea salt
- 2 tbsp. Chia seeds
- ½ cup almond milk
- 2 tbsp. Peanut butter
- 1 cup raw oats

Directions:

1. To prepare the overnight oats for the smoothie, mix together the oats with your 2 tbsp. Peanut butter, 1/2 cup almond milk, 2 tbsp. Chia seeds and a pinch of sea salt in a mason jar. Stir it a bit into a very thick texture and mixture. Blend together well by stirring with a spoon.
2. Let the mason jar of ingredients sit in the refrigerator overnight.
3. The following morning, it's time to prepare the topping! To do this, blend your frozen banana (in chunks), ¼ cup raspberries, ¼ cup blackberries, ¼ cup blueberries and 1 tbsp. Maca powder together in a high-powered blender for 40 seconds. Tamper with it a bit to make sure you get all the pieces grinded up.
4. Scoop out the topping onto your overnight oats and enjoy!

Cacao & Kale Smoothie

Ready In: 10 minutes

Servings: 2   Calories: 504   Protein: 18g   Carbs: 98g   Fat: 19g

A delicious smoothie consisting of: bananas, almond milk, cacao powder, flax seeds, kale, blueberries and blackberries.

Ingredients:

- 1.5 handfuls of blueberries
- 1.5 handfuls of blackberries
- 5 tbsp. Flax seeds, ground
- 5 tbsp. raw cacao powder
- 3 cups almond milk
- 3 bananas

Directions:

1. Blend all your ingredients together in a blender.
2. Pour the resulting smoothie into a glass and enjoy!

Green Smoothie-Sicles

Ready In: 20 minutes

Servings: 4   Calories: 212   Protein: 4.9g   Carbs: 38.6g   Fat: 6.1g

This is more than another smoothie! This is what is called a smoothie-sicle. It's essentially a smoothie frozen into a popsicle and boy does it make for a fine treat on a hot summer day! This particular smoothie-sicle is headed with raspberries, red currants and chia seeds, while the body contains banana, apple, orange, kiwi, pineapple, spinach, dried dates, passion fruit, more chia seeds, flax seeds and sesame seeds. Your kids are going to love this!

Ingredients:

- ¾ cup of water
- 1 tbsp. Sesame seeds
- 1 tbsp. Flax seeds
- 1 tbsp. chia seeds
- 1 passion fruit
- 2 dried dates
- 2-3 handfuls of fresh spinach
- ¼ pineapple, peeled and roughly chopped
- 1 kiwi, peeled
- 1 orange, peeled and chopped
- 1 apple, peeled and chopped
- 1 banana peeled and chopped
- 1 cup frozen raspberries and red currants
- ¼ cup of water
- 1 tbsp. Chia seeds
- Popsicle molds

Directions:

1. The first step is to prepare the red tip of the smoothie-sicle. To do this, put the red currants and raspberries together with 1 tbsp. chia seeds and ¼ cup of water in the blender. Blend until smooth.
2. Pour the raspberry and currant mixture into the tip of your popsicle molds and let them sit in the freezer for a few hours to freeze, while you are preparing your green smoothie. Set them in an upright position so they freeze properly.
3. Prepare your green smoothie by putting the banana, apple, orange, kiwi, ¼ pineapple, 2-3 handfuls of fresh spinach, 2 dried dates, 1 passion fruit, 1 tbsp. chia seeds, 1 tbsp. flax seeds, 1 tbsp. sesame seeds and 3/4 cup of water together in the blender and blending to a nice smooth consistency.
4. If the red part of the smoothie-sicle has frozen completely, pour the green part on top of it into your molds. If not, wait until the red tip of the popsicle has frozen first.
5. After you have poured in the green section of the smoothie-sicle, put your molds back into the freezer and allow them to freeze for 3 hours. When they're done freezing, enjoy!

● ●

DID YOU KNOW?

The Popsicle was accidentally invented by an 11 year old boy when he was mixing powdered soda pop on his doorstep and mistakenly left it outside to freeze overnight.

● ●

Vanilla-Nut Smoothie

Ready In: 2 hours, 10 minutes

Servings: 2   Calories: 367   Protein: 7.7g   Carbs: 48.7g   Fat: 23g

A delicious smoothie consisting of: hazelnuts, almonds, Medjool dates, vanilla bean, cinnamon, sea salt and water.

Ingredients:

- 1 pinch of sea salt
- ½ tsp. Cinnamon
- 1 vanilla bean, chopped
- 2 ½ pitted Medjool dates
- 3 ½ cups of water
- ¼ cup raw almonds
- ¾ cup raw hazelnuts

Directions:

1. Soak your almonds and hazelnuts in a small bowl of water, so that they are completely covered for 2 hours.
2. Drain the soaked nuts and rinse them well.
3. Place the soaked nuts into a blender with your cinnamon, salt, vanilla bean, pitted dates and water.
4. Blend on the highest speed for 1 minute.
5. Position a nut milk bag over a large bowl and pour the milk mixture into the bag slowly. Squeeze the bottom of the milk bag to release the milk. This may take up to 5 minutes and you should be left with 1 cup of pulp in the bag.
6. Thoroughly clean out your blender and pour the milk back into it, without the pulp. Blend again for 30 seconds to 1 minute.
7. Pour the blended milk into a mason jar and tightly fasten a lid on it. Let sit in the fridge for 1 hour at least, before drinking.

Butternut Date Smoothie

Ready In: 35 minutes

Servings: 2   Calories: 409   Protein: 7.3g   Carbs: 103.7g   Fat: 8.3g

A delicious smoothie consisting of: almond milk, roasted butternut squash, Medjool dates, chia seeds, cinnamon, pure vanilla extract, ground ginger, ground cloves and crushed ice.

Ingredients:

- 6 large ice cubes, or as needed
- 1 sprinkle of ground cloves
- ½ tsp. Ground ginger
- 1.5 tsp. Pure vanilla extract
- 2 tsp. Cinnamon
- 1 tbsp. Chia seeds
- 4 large Medjool dates
- 1 cup + ¼ cup (packed) roasted butternut squash
- 1 cup + ½ cup almond milk

Directions:

1. Set your oven to 400°F (200°C) for preheating and line a baking sheet with parchment paper.
2. Remove the stem from the squash and slice the squash in half length-wise.
3. Use a spoon to scoop out the seeds of the squash.
4. Brush the squash with a little bit of oil and sprinkle a pinch of salt onto it.
5. Place the squash on the baking sheet with the cut side up.
6. Roast the squash for 40 to 45 minutes at 400°F (200°C) or until it has become tender to a fork and browned on the bottom. Allow it to cool when finished.
7. Once it has cooled, add it and the rest of the smoothie ingredients to a blender and blend at high speed until the consistency has become perfectly smooth. Enjoy!

Tahini Granola Smoothie Bowl

Ready In: 20 minutes

Servings: 4   Calories: 539   Protein: 15.5g   Carbs: 66.8g   Fat: 26g

A delicious smoothie bowl consisting of: tahini, maple syrup, vanilla extract, cinnamon, sea salt, oats, pistachio, dried rose petals, vegan yogurt, frozen berries, banana and soy milk.

Ingredients:

- ½ cup tahini
- ½ cup maple syrup
- 1 tsp. Vanilla extract
- ½ tsp. Cinnamon
- ¼ tsp. Sea salt
- 2 cups old fashioned rolled oats
- 1 cup pistachios
- ½ cup dried rose petals
- 8 oz. Container of vegan yogurt
- ½ cup frozen berries (blueberries, raspberries or strawberries or mixed)
- ½ cup fresh berries (as topping)
- ½ cup soy milk
- 1 banana

Directions:

1. Set your oven to 350°F (175°C) for preheating and line a baking sheet with parchment paper.
2. Stir your sea salt, cinnamon, vanilla extract, maple syrup and tahini together in a large bowl to combine.
3. Mix in the pistachios and the oats.
4. Spread the mixture onto your baking sheet, forming a thin and even layer. It should be a very sticky mixture.
5. Bake for 10 minutes at 350°F (175°C).
6. Remove the baking dish from the oven and flip the mixture over and stir it well.
7. Bake for another 5 minutes at the same heat.
8. When it is finished baking, allow it to sit to cool for 20 minutes.
9. When cool, toss it together with dried rose petals.
10. Now pour the vegan yogurt, banana, berries and soy milk into a blender and blend until smooth completely.
11. Pour the mixture into a bowl and top it with fresh berries and your granola.

Pitaya Smoothie Bowl

Ready In: 10 minutes

Servings: 4   Calories: 494   Protein: 26.1g   Carbs: 108.2g   Fat: 47.5g

A delicious smoothie bowl consisting of: pitaya, frozen berries, almond milk, chia seeds, hemp seeds, granola, berries, banana slices and kiwi chunks.

Ingredients:

- 1 kiwi, broken into chunks
- 1 banana, cut into slices
- 1 cup mixed berries
- 1 cup granola
- 1 tbsp. Hemp seeds
- 1 tbsp. Chia seeds
- 1/3 cup almond milk
- 3.5 oz. Package frozen pitaya

Directions:

1. Break apart your frozen pitaya into large chunks. Place chunks of pitaya into a blender or food processor.
2. Add your other fruit and your almond milk and blend to a nice smooth texture.
3. Pour the mixture into a bowl and top it with your granola, hemp seeds, chia seeds and any other toppings you wish.

Cherry Nut Smoothie Bowl

Ready In: 5 minutes

Servings: 4   Calories: 668   Protein: 17.7g   Carbs: 56.2g   Fat: 53.6g

A delicious smoothie bowl consisting of: rolled oats, frozen cherries, bananas, almond butter, hemp hearts, cacao nibs, raw cacao powder, chia seeds, toasted coconut, homemade granola and any fresh seasonal fruit of your choice.

Ingredients:

- Fresh seasonal fruit of your choice
- Homemade granola
- Toasted coconut
- Hemp seeds
- Chia seeds
- raw cacao powder
- cacao nibs
- 2 tbsp. Hemp hearts
- 2 tbsp. Almond butter
- 2 frozen bananas
- 1 cup frozen cherries
- ¼ cup rolled oats (soaked overnight in 1/3 cup water)

Directions:

1. Dump the 2 tbsp. of hemp hearts, 2 tbsp. almond butter, 2 bananas, 1 cup of cherries, ¼ cup rolled oats and their soaking water into a blender or food processor.
2. Begin on the lowest powered setting and slowly begin to increase the speed to high speed.
3. Add water as needed to keep it from getting too thick. Continue to process until the texture becomes smooth. This shouldn't take more than a minute.
4. Pour the smoothie into bowls and top with the toppings of fresh seasonal fruit, granola, hemp seeds, chia seeds, cacao powder and cacao nibs.

Kiwi-Cado Smoothie Bowl

Ready In: 5 minutes

Servings: 4   Calories: 367   Protein: 5.6g   Carbs: 41.4g   Fat: 23.3g

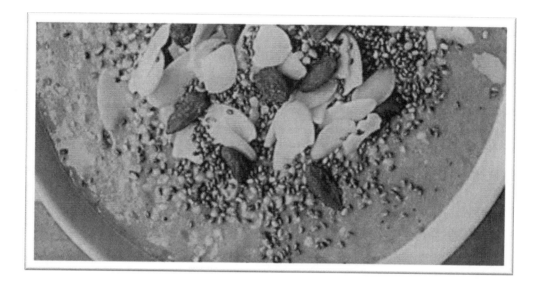

A delicious smoothie bowl consisting of: spinach, mango, kiwi, avocado, almond milk, maca and your choice of toppings, but I recommend goji berries and sliced almonds.

Ingredients:

- Goji berries
- Sliced almonds
- 1 tsp. Maca
- 1 cup almond milk
- ½ avocado
- 2 small kiwis
- 2 cups mango
- 2 cups spinach

Directions:

1. Pour all of your ingredients (except for the almonds and goji berries) into a blender or food processor and blend until smooth.
2. Pour into a bowl and top with the goji berries and sliced almonds. Enjoy!

Coco & Hazelnut Smoothie Bowl

Ready In: 5 minutes

Servings: 2   Calories: 482   Protein: 16.5g   Carbs: 58.7g   Fat: 23g

A delicious smoothie bowl consisting of: chocolate hemp protein powder, raw cacao, toasted hazelnuts, bananas, almond milk and sea salt.

Ingredients:

- ¼ tsp. Sea salt
- 1 cup unsweetened almond milk
- 2 bananas, peeled
- ½ cup toasted hazelnuts
- 1 tbsp. Raw cacao
- 2 tbsp. Hemp chocolate protein powder
- Toasted hazelnuts for topping

Directions:

1. Combine every ingredient (excepted for the toasted hazelnuts) together in a blender and blend until it all becomes a smooth texture.
2. Pour into a bowl and top with toasted hazelnuts and any other topping you wish, such as additional banana slices.

Vegan Chocolate Pudding

Ready In: 3 hours, 30 minutes

Servings: 2   Calories: 317   Protein: 3.3g   Carbs: 50.7g   Fat: 12.1g

A dessert pudding consisting of: vanilla extract, semisweet chocolate, Flegg egg replacement, white sugar, soy creamer, soy milk and cornstarch.

Ingredients:

- 2 tsp. Vanilla extract
- 3 oz. Semisweet chocolate, chopped
- 3 tbsp. Flegg (1 tbsp. flax meal mixed with 3 tbsp. water)
- ½ cup white sugar
- 1 cup soy creamer
- 1 cup soy milk
- 2 tbsp. cornstarch

Directions:

1. Stir your soy creamer, soy milk and cornstarch together in a medium-sized saucepan and place it on medium heat.
2. Stir your sugar into the saucepan. Whisk frequently until the contents of the saucepan come to a low boil, then remove the saucepan from the heat source.
3. Whisk your Flegg together with ¼ cup of the heated soy milk / creamer / cornstarch mixture in a small bowl.
4. Return the mixture, now with the addition of Flegg, back to the saucepan and cook on medium heat for 4 minutes or until it has become thick, but isn't boiling.
5. Dump your chopped semisweet chocolate into a medium-sized bowl and pour the hot soy milk mixture over it. Let it sit for 30 seconds and then stir until the chocolate has melted and the texture has become smooth.
6. Allow bowl to cool for 15 minutes and then whisk in the vanilla extract.
7. Pour the mixture into custard cups and cover the tops with plastic wrap and refrigerate for 3 hours.

Quinoa Pudding

Ready In: 40 minutes

Servings: 4   Calories: 331   Protein: 7.3g   Carbs: 70.9g   Fat: 3g

A dessert pudding consisting of: quinoa, apple juice, raisins, lemon juice, ground cinnamon, salt, vanilla extract and water.

Ingredients:

- 2 tsp. vanilla extract
- Salt
- 1 tsp. Ground cinnamon
- 2 tbsp. Lemon juice
- 1 cup raisins
- 2 cups apple juice
- 2 cups water
- 1 cup quinoa

Directions:

1. Rinse your quinoa thoroughly, using a fine mesh strainer under running tap water. Rinse thoroughly for at least 5 minutes. If you don't successfully rinse *all* of the saponins off the quinoa, they will make you nauseous.
2. Pour the rinsed quinoa into a medium saucepan with water.
3. Bring the saucepan to a boil on high heat.
4. Cover the pan with a lid and lower the heat to a low simmer for 15 minutes. All of the water should be absorbed.
5. Mix in your raisins, cinnamon and salt and pour your apple juice and lemon juice into the saucepan as well.
6. Put the lid back on the saucepan and allow to simmer for another 15 minutes.
7. Stir in your vanilla extract and serve while still warm.

Raspberry Chia Pudding

Ready In: 8 hours, 20 minutes

Servings: 4   Calories: 330   Protein: 8.4g   Carbs: 30g   Fat: 21.2g

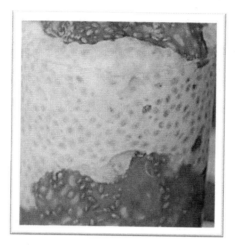

A dessert pudding consisting of: coconut milk, rice milk, chia seeds, maple syrup, vanilla extract and, of course, fresh raspberries.

Ingredients:

- 1 cup coconut milk
- 1 cup unsweetened rice milk
- 6 tbsp. Chia seeds
- 2 tbsp. Maple syrup
- 2 cups fresh raspberries
- 2 tbsp. Chia seeds
- ¾ tsp. Vanilla extract

Directions:

1. Whisk your rice milk, coconut milk, maple syrup and 6 tbsp. chia seeds together in a bowl and let it sit for 10 minutes. Whisk until smooth. Cover the bowl up with plastic wrap and put it in the refrigerator overnight or for 8 hours.
2. In a separate bowl, mash your raspberries together and whisk in 2 tbsp. of chia seeds and vanilla extract. Cover with plastic wrap and place it in your refrigerator, also overnight.
3. To prepare your puddings to serve, prepare 4 serving glasses. In the bottom of each pudding glass, scoop some of the raspberry mixture.
4. Stir the refrigerated chia seed pudding with a spoon until it becomes smooth. Divide it evenly among the serving glasses.
5. Scoop the remaining raspberry mixture to the top of each pudding glass.

Coconut Milk & Rice Pudding

Ready In: 1 hour

Servings: 10   Calories: 577   Protein: 7.4g   Carbs: 91.2g   Fat: 23.6g

A dessert pudding consisting of: raisins, peaches, nutmeg, cinnamon, vanilla, vegan butter alternative, soy milk, sea salt, sugar, coconut milk, Flegg, basmati rice and water.

Ingredients:

- 1 cup raisins
- 15 oz. Can sliced peaches
- 1 tsp. Ground nutmeg
- 2 tsp. Ground cinnamon
- 1 tbsp. Vanilla extract
- ¼ cup vegan butter alternative of your choice
- 2 eggs equivalent of Flegg (2 tbsp. flax meal mixed with 6 tbsp. water)
- 1 cup soy milk
- ½ tsp. Sea salt
- 1 ½ cups raw sugar
- 3 cups coconut milk
- 1 ½ cups basmati rice
- 3 cups water

Directions:

1. Pour your dry rice and water into a saucepan and bring it to a boil.
2. Reduce the heat of the saucepan to medium-low and cover it with a lid. Allow it to simmer for 20 minutes or until the rice becomes tender and all the liquid is absorbed.
3. Whisk your salt, sugar, coconut milk and cooked rice together in the saucepan and, once again, bring it to a boil.
4. Reduce the heat and allow it to simmer for 18 minutes or until it becomes a thick and creamy pudding.
5. Whisk in your Flegg and soy milk and stir constantly to keep it from sticking to the sides of the saucepan for 2 minutes.
6. Remove the saucepan from the heat and stir in the vegan butter substitute, cinnamon, vanilla and nutmeg until it is well mixed. Add your peaches and raisins in and serve!

Tapioca Pudding

Ready In: 25 minutes

Servings: 4   Calories: 345   Protein: 2.3g   Carbs: 34.5g   Fat: 23.7g

A dessert pudding consisting of: small pearl tapioca, coconut milk, sea salt, vanilla extract, almonds, banana, blueberries, kiwi and water.

Ingredients:

- 14 oz. can full-fat coconut milk
- 1 tsp. Pure vanilla extract
- 1 pinch sea salt
- 1/3 cup maple syrup
- ¾ cup water
- 1/3 cup Bob's Red Mill Small Pearl Tapioca

Directions:

1. Prepare a saucepan with your water and pearl tapioca and allow it to soak for 30 minutes. Do not drain after soaking.
2. Place the saucepan on medium heat and add in your sea salt and coconut milk. Stir it occasionally until it comes to a low boil. Allow it to simmer without a lid on very low heat for 15 minutes. Stir frequently until the mixture thickens.
3. Remove the saucepan from the heat and allow it to cool for 15 minutes.
4. Stir in the maple syrup and vanilla. Top with almonds, berries or whatever sounds good to you and its ready to serve!

Chocolate Chip Mint Ice Cream

Ready In: 1 hour

Servings: 10   Calories: 498   Protein: 6.8g   Carbs: 49g   Fat: 35.1g

A creamy vegan ice cream featuring: fresh mint, cashews, coconut milk, peppermint, sugar, maple syrup, coconut oil, dates, vanilla, walnuts and cocoa powder.

Ingredients:

- 1/3 cup cocoa powder
- 1 ¼ cups raw walnuts
- 1 cup packed dates, pitted
- 3 tbsp. Coconut oil, melted
- ¼ cup agave nectar or maple syrup
- ¼ cup cane sugar
- ½ tsp. peppermint extract
- 14 oz. Can of full fat coconut milk
- 1.5 cups raw cashews
- ½ cup fresh mint, divided
- 2 cups coconut milk

Directions:

1. Put your churning bowl in your freezer to chill overnight, the night before you intend to prepare this recipe.
2. Put your cashews in a small bowl and cover them up with water. Allow them to soak overnight.
3. Steep ¼ cup (out of your total ½ cup) of fresh mint leaves in your coconut milk in a saucepan. Bring the saucepan to a low simmer and use a wooden spoon to poke the mint leaves to leaks its flavor into the coconut milk. Simmer for 15 minutes and then remove the saucepan from the heat source. Allow to sit to cool for 5 minutes.
4. Pour the mixture into a fine mesh strainer to separate the infused coconut milk from the leaves. Discard the leaves.
5. Pour the coconut milk as well as well as your soaked and drained cashews, 14 oz. Can of full fat coconut milk, remaining ¼ cup of fresh mint, ½ tsp. Peppermint extract, ¼ cup cane sugar, ¼ cup agave nectar and 3 tbsp. Melted coconut oil into a blender.
6. Blend the mixture together until it becomes smooth and creamy with the "liquify" option. This should take 4 minutes.

7. Pour the mixture into your chilled ice cream maker bowl and churn it according to the manufacturer's included instructions. Continue churching until it has become thoroughly chilled and resembles thick soft serve ice cream. This shouldn't take more than 45 minutes.

8. As the ice cream is churning, you may begin preparing the brownie portion of this recipe from which it derives its chocolatey flavor. To do this, start by running your pitted dates through a food processor until it becomes a ton of small bits. Put the dates in a small bowl and set them to the side for now.

9. Put your raw walnuts into the food processor and process until small bits are all that's left.

10. Add the date bits back into the processor and the 1/3 cup of cocoa powder as well. Process until the mixture is well combined.

11. Transfer the mixture to a sheet of plastic wrap and use your hands to form into a brick shape. Set the brick in the freezer to chill for now.

12. When the churning of the ice cream is finished, break chunks off your brownie brick and stir it into the ice cream. Use as much or as little of the brownie as suits your needs.

13. Put your newly created ice cream into a freezer-safe container and cover it up with a sheet of plastic wrap. Place it in the freezer for a minimum of 6 hours. This ice cream will keep up to a whole week before going bad.

14. Allow it to thaw for 15 minutes before serving.

● ● ● ● ● ● ● ● ● ● ● ● ● ● ● ● ● ● ● ●

DID YOU KNOW?

Each 1 cup serving of coconut milk gives you a whopping 3.9 milligrams of iron, making it a healthier choice than regular milk when preparing ice cream.

● ● ● ● ● ● ● ● ● ● ● ● ● ● ● ● ● ● ● ●

Cherry Pie Ice Cream

Ready In: 2 hours, 50 minutes

Servings: 10   Calories: 568   Protein: 7g   Carbs: 74.2g   Fat: 30.1g

A creamy vegan ice cream featuring: cashews, full-fat coconut milk, olive oil, agave nectar, cane sugar, vanilla extract, sea salt, red cherries, orange juice, maple syrup, flour, vegan butter and water.

Ingredients:

- 3 tbsp. Ice cold water
- 6 tbsp. Vegan butter alternative of your choice
- ¼ tsp. sea salt
- 1 ¼ cups all-purpose flour
- 1 tbsp. flour
- 2 tbsp. Maple syrup
- 2 tbsp. Orange juice
- 3 cups sweet red cherries, pitted and halved
- 1 pinch sea salt
- 1 tsp. Pure vanilla extract
- ¼ cup organic cane sugar
- ¼ cup agave nectar
- 3 tbsp. Melted coconut oil or olive oil
- 13.5 oz. Can of full-fat coconut milk
- 1 ½ cup raw cashews, soaked in cool water for 6 hours or overnight.

Directions:

1. The day before you plan to prepare this recipe, allow your cashews to soak in water over night and put your ice cream maker bowl in your freezer to chill sufficiently.
2. Drain your cashews and put them in a blender, along with your pinch of sea salt, 1 tsp. Vanilla, ¼ cup sugar, ¼ cup agave nectar, 3 tbsp. Olive oil and 13.5 oz. Coconut milk.
3. Blend until it becomes smooth and creamy. Scrape down the sides as necessary.
4. Pour into a bowl and cover with a sheet of plastic wrap. Allow to freeze in freezer for 1 ½ hours.
5. The next step is to prepare your cherry compote. To do this, add your 2 tbsp. Orange juice, 3 cups of cherries, 2 tbsp. of maple syrup and 1 tbsp. of flour to a small-sized saucepan. Bring the contents of the saucepan to a simmer on medium heat and use a spoon to smash apart the cherries and stir them well. Be

sure to break them down well now so they are an easy-to-scoop size in the ice cream at the end.

6. Turn the heat to low and allow it to simmer until it begins to look like a cherry pie filling. This shouldn't take more than 5 minutes.

7. Remove the saucepan from the heat and set to the side for now.

8. Set your oven to 350°F (175°C) for preheating.

9. Pour your ¼ tsp. sea salt and 1 ¼ cup of all-purpose flour into a blender together to begin making your crust. Pulse the blender to emulate whisking.

10. Add in your vegan butter alternative and pulse the blender until it becomes the texture of wet sand.

11. Add cold water just a single tablespoon at a time and pulse frequently until a loose dough begins to form. Lightly cover a work surface in flour, for your dough.

12. Place the dough on the floured work surface and form it into a 1" thick disc with your hands. Do this while minimizing handling it as much as possible.

13. Dust the top of your dough with flour and use a rolling pin to flatten it into a large and thin circle that is the shape of your pie pan. Add however much more flour you need to.

14. Place the dough into a pie pan.

15. Form it into the shape of the pie pan and crimple up the edges.

16. Pour your cherry filling into the shaped pie dough.

17. Bake on the center rack for 46 minutes at 350°F (175°C). The crust should turn a golden-brown color and the cherry filling should become bubbly. Allow to sit and cool when finished.

18. Put your chilled ice cream maker together and pour your chilled ice cream batter into it. Add in the equivalent of one slice of your pie, including the crust and crumbling a bit.

19. Churn your ice cream batter and pie together until it becomes thick and creamy and the same texture as soft serve. This should take around 20 minutes.

20. During the last 30 seconds, add in as much more pie as you would like for flavor, but take into consideration the fact that the more you add, the more difficult it will be to scoop.

21. Save at least ¼ of the pie crust to serve with your ice cream. Churn until it has just incorporated and power off your ice cream maker.

22. If you like soft serve, you can eat it immediately. Otherwise, put it in a freezer safe container and store it in the freezer for 5 hours. You may need to use a hot spoon to scoop!

Chocolate Ice Cream

Ready In: 30 minutes

Servings: 10   Calories: 343   Protein: 4.5g   Carbs: 43.6g   Fat: 20.7g

A creamy vegan ice cream featuring: coconut cream, cocoa powder, pitted dates, vanilla extract, almond milk, espresso, cinnamon and cacao nibs.

Ingredients:

- Cacao nibs
- ½ tsp. Cinnamon
- 1 oz. Espresso, cooled
- ½ cup unsweetened almond milk
- 1 tbsp. Pure vanilla extract
- 16 oz. Pitted dates
- 2/3 cup unsweetened cocoa powder
- 2 x 14 oz. Cans of coconut cream, chilled overnight in the refrigerator.

Directions:

1. Chill a large mixing bowl in the freezer for 12 minutes.
2. Add your dates to a food processor and process until they become small bits. Add a little bit of hot water at a time and continue processing until they form into a paste. Save paste for later.
3. Without tilting your coconut cream cans, scoop out the cream into your large mixing bowl from the freezer.
4. Use a mixer to whip the coconut cream until it becomes smooth.
5. Add cocoa powder, almond milk, vanilla and half of your date paste to the coconut cream. Continue to whip these ingredients together until it has become fully formed.
6. Line a freezer-safe container with parchment and fill it with the concoction you just whipped together. Cover it with a sheet of plastic wrap, followed by a sheet of tin foil to help it freeze better.
7. Allow it to freeze in your freezer overnight.
8. Thaw for 20 minutes before eating and scoop with a spoon that has been warmed under warm water.

Vanilla Cake

Ready In: 45 minutes

Servings: 6   Calories: 378   Protein: 4.6g   Carbs: 60.5g   Fat: 13.2g

This is a spongy textured and basic vegan cake. This recipe is just for the cake itself. Feel free to decorated with toppings like frosting and candies for whatever your occasion requires.

Ingredients:

- ¼ tsp. Almond extract
- 1 tbsp. Vanilla extract
- 1 tbsp. Lemon juice
- ¼ cup water
- 1/3 cup canola oil
- ½ tsp. Salt
- 1 tsp. Baking powder
- 1 tsp. Baking soda
- 1 cup white sugar
- 1 ½ cups unbleached all-purpose flour
- 1 tbsp. apple cider vinegar
- 1 cup plain soy milk

Directions:

1. Grease an 8" x 8" baking dish and coat it with flour.
2. Set your oven to 350°F (175°C) for preheating.
3. Pour your vinegar and soy milk together into a large glass measuring cup and stir them well.
4. Prepare a bowl of your salt, baking powder, baking soda, sugar and flour and whisk them together in it.
5. Pour almond extract, vanilla extract, lemon juice, water and canola oil into the large glass measuring cup containing your vinegar and soy milk and mix them all together.
6. Stir the liquid mixture into the baking soda / flour mixture and continue stirring until the resulting batter doesn't have any more lumps.
7. Pour this batter into the 8" x 8" baking dish.
8. Bake for 35 minutes at 350°F (175°C). You'll know it's finished when a tooth pick inserted to the center comes out clean.

Chocolate Cake

Ready In: 40 minutes

Servings: 6   Calories: 657   Protein: 7.9g   Carbs: 118.3g   Fat: 19.8g

This is a moist, creamy and completely vegan chocolate cake. This delicious recipe is so unbelievably simple that it doesn't even require a mixer! This recipe is just for the base chocolate cake. It's up to you to top it with whatever frosting and candies you would like to.

Ingredients:

- ¼ cup cider vinegar
- ½ cup canola oil
- 2 cups water
- 2 tsp. baking soda
- ½ cup unsweetened cocoa powder
- 2 cups white sugar
- 3 cups all-purpose flour

Directions:

1. Set your oven to 350°F (175°C) for preheating.
2. Grease a 9" x 13" baking dish.
3. Pour your baking soda, cocoa powder, sugar and flour together in a bowl and whisk them all together.
4. Add in your water, vinegar and canola oil. Continue whisking until the batter is smooth.
5. Pour the batter into the baking dish and place it in the oven.
6. Bake for 30 minutes at 350°F (175°C) or until a toothpick inserted at the center comes out clean.

Fudge Cookies

Ready In: 30 minutes

Servings: 6   Calories: 309.3   Protein: 3.4g   Carbs: 51.3g   Fat: 12.6g

These soft and moist cookies are packed with richly favored fudge, delivering a chocolatey flavor and texture that are hard to find elsewhere! You'll need a vegan brown sugar substitute to get the flavor exactly as its intended to be, but, other than that, the other ingredients are probably already in your pantry!

Ingredients:

- 5 tbsp. coconut oil
- 1/3 cup mashed banana
- 1/3 cup vegan brown sugar substitute
- 7 tbsp. unsweetened cocoa powder
- 2/3 cup white sugar
- 1/8 tbsp. salt
- ¼ tsp. baking soda
- 1 cup whole wheat flour

Directions:

1. Set your oven to 350°F (175°C) for preheating.
2. Pour your salt, baking soda and flour together in a large bowl and stir together.
3. Put a saucepan on low heat and mix your mashed banana, coconut oil, vegan brown sugar substitute, cocoa powder and white sugar in it. Cook and stir constantly until it becomes smooth. This should take no more than 5 minutes.
4. Pour your flour / baking soda mixture into the saucepan and stir it until it becomes a smooth-textured dough.
5. Prepare a couple of baking sheets and scoop out spoonfuls of the dough onto them. Space them 2 to 3 inches apart from one another on the baking sheets.
6. Bake for 8 minutes at 350°F (175°C) or until the edges turn golden-brown.

Chocolate Chip & Peanut Butter Cookies

Ready In: 35 minutes

Servings: 12   Calories: 263.3   Protein: 5.7g   Carbs: 41g   Fat: 11.7g

Combining the smooth nutty flavor of peanut butter with chunks of crunchy chocolate chips and walnuts, these oatmeal cookies sure are a crowd-pleaser! If you're looking for a dessert that combines crunch with rich flavor, look no further.

Ingredients:

- ½ cup walnut pieces
- ½ cup vegan semi-sweet chocolate chips
- ½ tsp. baking soda
- 1 cup rolled oats
- 1 cup whole wheat flour
- 1 tsp. pure vanilla extract
- 2 tbsp. canola oil
- 1/3 cup peanut butter
- 1/3 cup soy milk
- 1 cup white sugar

Directions:

1. Set your oven to 425°F (220°C) for preheating.
2. Whisk your sugar, soy milk, peanut butter, vanilla extract and canola oil together in a fair-sized bowl and blend until smooth.
3. In a separate bowl, stir your salt, baking soda and oats together.
4. Pour this dry mixture into the peanut butter mixture and stir it together well.
5. Slowly begin to fold your walnut chunks and pieces of chocolate chips into the mix.
6. Prepare a baking sheet with oil.
7. Take large spoonfuls of the resulting batter from step 5 and drop them onto your baking sheet.
8. Bake for 10 minutes at 425°F (220°C) or until the edges turn golden-brown.
9. Allow to cool for 10 minutes before eating.

Tickerdoodles

Ready In: 20 minutes

Servings: 14   Calories: 202   Protein: 1.4g   Carbs: 28.7g   Fat: 7.9g

These vegan variety of snickerdoodles are names after my pet hedgehog, Ticker! These quick and easy sugar cookies are *not* the result of any animal cruelty or suffering, so you can enjoy their rich, sweet cinnamon-sugar taste 100% free of guilt.

Ingredients:

- ½ cup cinnamon-sugar
- 1 tbsp. vanilla extract
- 1 tbsp. vanilla-flavored almond milk
- 4 oz. container of applesauce
- ½ cup vegetable oil
- ½ tsp. salt
- ½ tsp. baking soda
- ½ cup white sugar
- 1 ½ cups whole wheat flour

Directions:

1. Set your oven to 375°F (190°C) for preheating.
2. Stir your salt, baking soda, sugar and flour together in a medium-sized bowl, blending thoroughly.
3. In a second bowl, whisk your vanilla extract, almond milk, applesauce and vegetable oil together.
4. Add the flour mixture into the wet mixture and stir to combine well.
5. Split the resulting dough up into 14 even-sized portions and roll them each into individual balls.
6. Spread your cinnamon-sugar into a wide and shallow dish.
7. Roll the dough balls in the cinnamon-sugar. Make sure they are completely covered.
8. Place the covered cinnamon-sugar dough balls onto a baking sheet and bake for 10 minutes at to 375°F (190°C).

Brownies

Ready In: 50 minutes

Servings: 12   Calories: 375   Protein: 3.2g   Carbs: 52.4g   Fat: 19.1g

This vegan cookbook really *does* have everything – even vegan brownies! When you bake these delicious brownies of chocolatey goodness, expect a mouthful of gooey and rich sweet flavor. These brownies are so moist and flavorful that you will find yourself making them again and again and again!

Ingredients:

- 1 tsp. vanilla extract
- 1 cup vegetable oil
- 1 cup water
- 1 tsp. salt
- 1 tsp. baking powder
- ¾ cup unsweetened cocoa powder
- 2 cups white sugar
- 2 cups unbleached all-purpose flour

Directions:

1. Set your oven to 350°F (175°C) for preheating.
2. Stir your flour, baking powder, salt, cocoa powder and sugar together in a bowl.
3. Pour the water, vegetable oil and vanilla extract into the dry powder mixture and stir well until blended.
4. Spread the mixture out in a 9" x 13" baking pan.
5. Bake for 28 minutes at 350°F (175°C) or until the top of the brownies are no longer shiny.
6. Allow to cool for 15 minutes and cut into squares.

Almond Cookies

Ready In: 1 hour, 45 minutes

Servings: 6   Calories: 222   Protein: 5.4g   Carbs: 31.6g   Fat: 9g

Enjoy oven roasted almond cookies, made with real maple syrup! If you're looking for a simple dessert recipe, this is it – there are only four ingredients. It couldn't get much easier than this.

Ingredients:

- 1 tsp. almond extract
- ½ cup real maple syrup
- 1 cup oat flour
- 1 cup raw whole almonds

Directions:

1. Set your oven to 275°F (135°C) for preheating.
2. Spread out your almonds onto a greased baking sheet.
3. Toast them in your oven for 45 minutes. They should turn golden and become fragrant. Keep a close eye on them, because they do easily burn. Set them aside once roasted.
4. Increase the temperature of your oven to 350°F(175°C).
5. Grease a baking sheet with vegetable oil.
6. Mix your almond extract, maple syrup and oat flour in a bowl.
7. Grind up your roasted almonds in a food processor and add them to the bowl with the syrup and almond extract. Stir together.
8. Divide the mixture into 6 balls and flatten them into cookies about ¼" thick.
9. Place your cookie dough pieces on the baking sheet.
10. Bake for 12 to 15 minutes at 350°F(175°C) or until the edges become golden and crisp.
11. Allow to cool before eating.

Dawn's Protein Bars

Ready In: 45 minutes

Servings: 8   Calories: 229.2   Protein: 6.3g   Carbs: 35.9g   Fat: 7.2g

This recipe was provided by a vegan Facebook friend of mine, Dawn Delea, whose *beautiful* testimony of how veganism changed her life can be found listed as testimony number 65 in Chapter 8 of this cookbook!

Ingredients:

- 1 ½ cups quinoa
- Almond milk
- 1 tbsp. cinnamon
- ¼ cup raw coconut, shredded
- 2 tsp. vanilla extract
- 1/8 cup maple syrup
- Stevia
- Medjool dates, chopped
- Almond butter
- ¼ cup mini dark chocolate chips
- ¼ cup finely chopped almonds
- 2 tsp. palm sugar

Directions:

1. Cook 1 ½ cups of quinoa with the correct amount of almond milk and 1 tbsp. of cinnamon, ¼ cup of raw shredded coconut and 2 tsp. of vanilla extract, 1/8 cup of maple syrup and some stevia to taste.
2. When the quinoa is about ¾ of the way done cooking, add some chopped up Medjool dates.
3. Allow the mixture to finish cooking.
4. Add in enough almond butter to help it all stick together (like a protein bar), ¼ cup mini dark chocolate chips and ¼ cup finely chopped almonds.
5. Roll the bar into your desired shape.
6. Roll in some extra chopped nuts, shredded coconut and 2 tsp. palm sugar.
7. Put in the freezer or fridge to harden. Enjoy!

Davy Crockett Bars

Ready In: 35 minutes

Servings: 12   Calories: 384.4   Protein: 4.2g   Carbs: 57.2g   Fat: 16g

The same great taste you'd expect from a regular Davy Crockett bar, if you've ever had one, but these ones are completely vegan! They're just as gooey and chocolatey as you remember, packed with chocolate chips, oats, white sugar and a vegan brown sugar substitute.

Ingredients:

- ¾ cup vegetable oil
- 1 tsp. vanilla extract
- 1 cup vegan chocolate chips
- 2 cups quick cooking oats
- 1 cup vegan brown sugar substitute
- 1 tsp. baking soda
- 1 tsp. baking powder
- 1 tsp. salt
- 1 cup white sugar
- 2 cups all-purpose flour

Directions:

1. Set your oven to 350°F (175°C) for preheating.
2. Stir your baking soda, baking powder, salt, white sugar and flour together in a large bowl.
3. Mix in the chocolate chips, oats and vegan brown sugar substitute.
4. Combine your vanilla extract and oil in a second bowl and then stir it into the flour mixture to create a dough.
5. Prepare a 15" x 10" jelly roll pan and press the dough into the bottom of it, fitting its shape perfectly.
6. Bake for 15 minutes at 350°F (175°C).
7. Allow the bars to cool before cutting them out.

Coconut Oatmeal Bars

Ready In: 55 minutes

Servings: 8   Calories: 206.1   Protein: 4.5g   Carbs: 37.3g   Fat: 5.5g

These delicious bars are great for a snack, dessert or even breakfast! Due to the sheer volume of coconut and oatmeal that these treats are composed of, they are an excellent source of fiber. They also taste great, being made from agave, mashed bananas, pitted dates, chopped walnuts and – of course – oatmeal and shredded coconut!

Ingredients:

- 1 pinch salt
- 1 pinch ground nutmeg
- 1 tsp. vanilla extract
- 3 tbsp. agave
- ¼ cup chopped walnuts
- ¼ cup chopped pitted dates
- ½ cup shredded coconut
- 3 large bananas, mashed
- 2 cups quick-cooking rolled oats

Directions:

1. Set your oven to 350°F (175°C) for preheating.
2. Stir your salt, nutmeg, vanilla extract, agave, walnuts, dates, coconut, bananas and oats together in a large bowl with your hand.
3. Press the mixture into a 9" baking dish.
4. Bake for 30 minutes at 350°F (175°C).
5. Allow to cool on a wire rack before cutting the bars.

Granola Bars

Ready In: 1 hour

Servings: 10   Calories: 251.2   Protein: 5.4g   Carbs: 41.4g   Fat: 7.5g

A chewy and delicious granola bar recipe that contains sliced almonds, shredded coconut, vegan brown sugar, applesauce, dried cherries, agave nectar, chocolate chips, oats and even sunflower seeds!

Ingredients:

- ½ tsp. vanilla extract
- ½ tsp. baking soda
- 2 tbsp. packed vegan brown sugar alternative
- ¼ cup sunflower seeds
- ¼ cup shredded coconut
- ¼ cup sliced almonds
- 1/3 cup applesauce
- ½ cup chopped dried cherries
- ½ cup agave nectar
- ½ cup all-purpose flour
- ¾ cup vegan dark chocolate chips
- 2 ½ cups rolled oats

Directions:

1. Set your oven to 325°F (165°C) for preheating.
2. Grease a 7" x 11 ½" pan.
3. In a large mixing bowl, stir your vanilla extract, baking soda, vegan brown sugar substitute, sunflower seeds, coconut, almonds, applesauce, cherries, agave nectar, flour, chocolate chips and oats together.
4. Press this mixture into your prepared pan.
5. Bake for 20 minutes at to 325°F (165°C), or until they become golden-browned.
6. Let the bars cool before cutting them out and removing them from the pan.

Blueberry Bars

Ready In: 2 hours, 15 minutes

Servings: 12   Calories: 352.6   Protein: 8.3g   Carbs: 57.8g   Fat: 10.9g

These blueberry bars are surprisingly delicious, considering how healthy they are! Imagine two layers composed of oats, cornstarch, flour, vegan brown sugar and mashed chickpeas with a fine layer of gooey blueberry in the center. It almost ends up tasting a bit like a Pop-Tart!

Ingredients:

- ½ tsp. baking soda
- 1 tsp. vanilla extract
- ¼ cup olive oil
- ½ cup vegan brown sugar substitute
- 1 cup all-purpose flour
- 1 ½ cups rolled oats
- ¼ cup cold water
- 2 tbsp. cornstarch
- 1 tbsp. lemon juice
- 2 tbsp. white sugar
- 3 cups blueberries
- ¼ tsp. salt
- ¼ tsp. baking soda
- 1 tsp. baking powder
- 2 tsp. vanilla extract
- ¼ cup olive oil
- ½ cup vegan brown sugar substitute
- ½ cup rolled oats
- 14 oz. can of chickpeas, drained and rinsed

Directions:

1. Set your oven to 350°F (175°C) for preheating.
2. Dump your chickpeas, salt, ¼ tsp. baking soda, baking powder, 2 tsp. vanilla extract, ¼ cup olive oil and ½ cup rolled oats into a blender or food processor.
3. Blend it together until it becomes the consistency of dough.
4. Press the mixture into an 8" x 11" baking pan.
5. Bake for 20 minutes at 350°F (175°C), or until it becomes lightly browned and crisp.
6. Put a saucepan on medium-low heat and add your white sugar, lemon juice and blueberries into it. Cook until the blueberries have reduced. This should take no longer than 15 minutes.
7. Whisk your water and cornstarch together in a glass or small bowl, then stir it into the blueberry mixture on the saucepan.
8. Continue to cook in the saucepan until the mixture begins to thicken. This should take about 3 minutes.
9. Pour the blueberry mixture over the cooked crust from the oven.
10. In a large bowl, stir your ½ tsp. baking soda, 1 tsp. vanilla extract, ¼ cup olive oil, ½ cup brown sugar, flour and 1 ½ cup rolled oats together. Continue to stir until it becomes the consistency of bread crumbs. Sprinkle it over the top of the blueberry mixture.
11. Put it back into the oven to bake for another 20 minutes at 350°F (175°C). You'll know it's finished when the blueberry filling has become bubbly and the crumble topping has turned light golden-brown.
12. Allow to cool thoroughly, then cut into 12 bars and store it in your refrigerator.

Chapter 8: Testimonials

In this chapter of the book, you will see how eating a vegan diet has helped and healed hundreds of people. If you have someone you love who you are trying to convince to make the switch to a plant-based diet, this is the chapter to have them read. Take careful note of the variety of mental disorders and physical ailments that the people in this chapter have successfully remedied with a vegan diet. Do you know anyone who suffers from any of these issues? If you do, then you have just found their cure!

TESTIMONIALS

1. "I've noticed a lot of benefits from veganism. The main positives are primarily a clear conscience about the commodities I consume causing far less cruelty and pollution than consuming animals. Secondly, I've seen drastic drops in my weight and cholesterol levels. The third benefit has been meeting/networking with other compassionate and health-conscious folks."

-- Jake G.

2. "It has been 10 years that I have been a vegan. Before I became a vegan, I easily and frequently would fall sick. Many times, I felt weak and always became tired quickly. I saw a man teaching about veganism and I went to challenge him. I accused him of telling lies and I told him that we needed meat for protein. He gave me some books to read and that's how I became vegan. In the beginning, it was tough. I changed my diet all in one day. My body became weak and I got some pain in my legs. Sometimes I didn't feel my leg when I was walking. I was told that the body will fight me if I changed my food too quickly. I did not give up. In about three weeks everything was fine."

-- Selassie A.

3. "I truly believe God loves his animals as he loves us. I'm sure he wants us to love and take care of them. It helps me to sleep at night knowing I'm helping in some small way to get people to stop eating meat. I try not to preach. Rather, I just say little things about the animals and people's health."

-- Joyce L.

4. "I see people loving their pets like they were part of their family. Their dogs, cats, guinea pigs, whichever it is. When you ask someone if they would be fine eating

their pet, they look at you in disgust and utter distaste. I then ask what the difference is with other animals. Most of the time, I don't get an answer."

-- Melanie C.

5. "I was a big meat-eater, eating mindlessly whatever "I" wanted. I had been interested in self-development for a few years, which made me more self-aware and conscious about my decisions in life. I remember thinking one day 'do I really enjoy meat enough to justify taking another's life, if it's not necessary...' but then I thought a little deeper, 'should my enjoyment of something be more important than a living being's life?' I concluded no, morally. I started to research and watch documentaries, to gain the knowledge I'd need to make the changes and ensure I'd stick with it. It was all about perspective for me, considering the affect my choices had on others. I wasn't making conscious decisions when I was consuming these "products"... A sentient beings body, secretions and by-products are considered products, how morally wrong is that? Ask anyone (almost anyone) in the world, what is the perfect world? They will mostly say 'peaceful' and 'happy'... Well it's about time we stop saying these things and actually act on it."

-- Jason S.

6. "A lot of great things resulted from my switch to veganism. The first was being welcomed into the vegan community and having such compassionate and loving people around me. Another was no longer having stomach aches, because I would get them all the time when I ate meat and dairy, but once I stopped they went away (this is just a personal experience, not saying it happens for everyone). I also found myself making such a genuine connection to animals. Before becoming vegan, you may like animals, but once you are vegan the connection is so deep and you see all animals as a life form and something you'd never want to consume. You see them as friends or family and even animals like cows or goats are something you'd want to pet and play with when before you may not have even cared about them. It has been a neat experience finding out all the amazing dishes you can make with vegan ingredients! There are such a vast world of vegan foods and now you can start experimenting and making a ton of foods and getting creative. It doesn't take animal ingredients to make something taste good."

-- Mariah D.

7. "Here are five positive benefits I've experienced since I've switched to veganism... 1. I'm focusing on the dharmic virtue of nonviolence, and the suffering of other beings every time I eat. Selflessness. 2. I am reading the menu and studying the food packaging labels more and more. Awareness. 3. I eat more vegetables and fruit. Healthy. 4. I am less entertained by violent entertainment and news, and more

concerned for the welfare of animals and people around me. Peaceful. 5. Eating vegan feels natural and full of nutrients and I appreciate my food more. Before, I saw veggies as a side dish. Alignment."

-- Michael S.

8. "I've seen benefits in my health. The environment and the animals all benefit so much! We can live without harming others."

-- Madison G.

9. "Going vegan has given me a mission in life and the benefits have been the vanishing of disease, no more flues or colds, etc."

-- Casper H.

10. "I went vegan for my health. I was diagnosed with gastroparesis which is a condition where my stomach doesn't empty when it's supposed to, so when I was eating meat, eggs, and dairy I was always bring back up what I ate. I went from being 120 lbs. down to 105 lbs. in a short amount of time. Since going vegan I haven't brought my food back up and I have more energy and my quality of life is a whole lot better."

-- Ashley M.

11. "Because of going vegan, I now have a clear conscience! Additionally, I have no heart issues and I'm not overweight like most friends my age. I have also "converted" several people!"

-- Larry J.

12. "I made the switch at the beginning of the year. I used to suffer from terrible migraines, but since switching, I don't anymore. I have a lot more energy and feel better than I did in my 20s! I dropped from 205 lbs. down to 145 lbs. and I continuously see better results from exercise. My sexual health has seen notable improvements also. The most important thing is that no creature had to be sacrificed for any of these benefits."

-- Manuel L.

13. "Personally, the positive benefits are for me: living in alignment with my ethics, better energy, better digestion, better skin, better hair, better nails, more delicious foods, etc."

-- Austin M.

14. "I've been vegan since the 1st of December in 2015, and I was vegetarian for about eight months before that. That said, I always tried to eat healthy so I didn't notice any significant difference other than the fact that now I always feel lighter after finishing a meal."

-- Kalman T.

15. "I didn't want to put this out there publicly. I was diagnosed with Multiple Sclerosis 2 years ago and decided to go plant based since. There's no cure for it, but it has helped to keep me stable and I haven't relapsed for a while. *Fingers crossed* At the end of the day we all react differently to medicines, diets and what not. I just go with what works for me and it's a bonus that I love animals and believe in equality for all sentient beings."

-- Anonymous

16. "Going vegan helped with my dairy, pollen, and pet allergies and migraines. Going raw-vegan relieved endometriosis and hypoglycemia. Fruitarian relieved depression and PTSD. I'm 58 and enjoy super wellness. Thank you."

-- Mara M.

17. "The positive benefits have been many. Physically, I'm slimmer, have more energy, recover faster from runs (I'm a trail runner), my skin has cleared up, I sleep better, my migraines have almost disappeared, my allergies have gotten better. Mentally, I have a feeling of wellbeing and happiness that I didn't before going vegan that comes from knowing that my eating habits contribute much less to the suffering of other beings."

-- Ian R.

18. "I've lost 40 pounds in 5 months, I've reversed my acute pancreatitis, and my blood work has never been better!"

-- Amber R.

19. " I don't have the guilt of animals suffering and dying for me anymore. I don't feel bloated and disgusting after my meals anymore either. I'm a way happier person now!"

-- Courtney C.

20. "I'm still in the early process of transitioning to veganism. I used to have oily skin on my face and it caused acne. During my transition, so far, it's cleared up and my face isn't so oily. My hair used to be dry all the time and I had to moisturize 4-6 times a day. I only must do it 3-4 times now. I'm not bloated as much and I have very little menstrual pain. I also have much less blood loss. Sorry if that was too much information! I can easily run off very little sleep and I won't be tired. Most days I get only 6-7 hours of sleep. I'm never tired and it's easy to get up at 3:45 a.m. to get ready for work! I'm always happy now. I used to have these horrible dreams but those stopped since I've started transitioning. I have a bad knee... I had reconstructive surgery a few years ago and currently need another surgery. I used to have so much knee pain and had to take lots of pain medication. I barely take it now and it hardly ever hurts."

-- Jessica C.

21. "The main reason I enjoy being vegan is feeling better about not hurting animals. I'm eating better and learning to cook with different spices and sauces. My health is better. My annual wellness blood work came back very good. I can model to others that you can live and feel well without animal products. A person only needs 0.8 grams of protein per kg of body weight for good protein levels. I probably pay less at the grocery store weekly not buying animal products. I like to point out the fact that we love domestic animals and eat farm animals to people... most of whom have never made that connection... I read the book Why We Love Dogs, Eat Pigs & Wear Cows. I LOVE TO MAKE PEOPLE THINK ABOUT WHAT THEY ARE DOING! I know the penny dropped for me after seeing the video If Slaughterhouses Had Glass Walls. It was very eye-opening! Many people are conditioned not to see these things."

-- Mary J.

22. "For starters, going vegan has helped me lose 150 lbs. I lost enough weight that I could become a more active person. Now I train MMA, as well as run marathons and at least once a year, I go on a nine-day bicycle ride across the state! Of course, that's just personal health. There's also the smaller Eco footprint and knowledge that I'm helping to dismantle a system that exploits animals and people."

-- Ryan L.

23. "I've seen differences in my skin as well as my body. I feel much better overall. I have more energy and less digestion issues."

-- Traci B.

24. "Once I opened my eyes to the truth of the animal agriculture industry, there was no turning back for me. That was 7 1/2 years ago. I then started learning about all the health benefits of a vegan diet and there was no denying that humans are herbivores. I feel great and I rarely get sick. The worst illness I had was a ruptured appendix, which some ignorant people tried to blame on my vegan diet!"

-- Patti C.

25. "Since going vegan, I've experienced lots of positive changes! I feel better and have more energy. I know this is going to sound insane but I feel more relaxed... I've also lost 33 pounds since becoming vegan and I have also been able to stop taking 2 of the 3 blood pressure meds I've been on for years (and the doctor cut the dose of the third one in half!"

-- Wally T.

26. "Since becoming a vegan, I've lost a stone and a half. I have more energy and my general health is improving but it's more than that... I'm a different person. Veganism has changed the way I see the world and people around me. I cannot believe I was so ignorant for so many years, I always assumed that these animals had happy lives in fields and had humane deaths! I assumed that we had the surplus milk, etc.! Now I know the truth and I cannot un-see all that I've seen. I try to educate the uneducated, guide them to the correct info and then it's their choice! The only negative to being a vegan is other people and their daft questions, but I must remind myself that I used to be like them too. No one hated a vegan more than I did! I am not religious at all and it may sound stupid, but veganism has given me something to feel passionate about! I've warned my family that I will be getting into activism (they sighed). Some of us have to step up and speak up for the voiceless. Vegans together can make serious changes, we are changing the world one person at a time"

-- Jan D.

27. "I guess the biggest change for me is that I feel much healthier. I used to suffer with IBS even during the time I was vegetarian. Now it's all gone! I also found that, from the time I became a vegan, there is much more variety of different foods and I started to really enjoy cooking."

-- Zuzana P.

28. "Ever since I became a vegan, my blood sugar has been going back to normal. I'm losing weight (even though I am plateauing right now) and I have more energy."

-- Ashley K.

29. "I've noticed a number of things happen when you go vegan:

1. I do not mean this in a bragging way: becoming more intelligent (politically, spiritually/intuitive wise, logical thinking, etc.), just because you're not living under the burden to subconsciously have to rationalize the unthinkable all the time.

2. Independence of the mind/ humility: quite the opposite of being arrogant: because I was wrong way into adulthood about something so simple and obvious, I'm maybe having to question a lot of other things I believe as a result.

3. Corny, but: Compassion. As Kafka said once, after he became vegetarian: "Now that I don't eat you anymore, I can look at you". When you feel caught up in human problems, with others or your own mind, just watching an animal and just being feels healing.

4. Also corny, but for me to an extent which had surprised me: A closer sense to nature.

5. You know the truth about climate change (from documentaries like Cowspiracy, for example), so, in a way, you don't know at which point in history you're living right now, without getting out of denial about what we do to animals.

6. You learn A LOT about denial itself.

7. You soften up emotionally."

-- Arjuna T.

30. "Since becoming a vegan, I've experienced increased peace, health, compassion, and many other positive benefits."

-- Greg W.

31. "I'm never sick. My allergies went away and I've noticed less weight fluctuation. Even my athletic recovery is faster since becoming a vegan. I find myself feeling more compassionate in every area of my life. I have noticed that I now have even more of a special connection to animals."

-- Christopher W.

32. "I've noticed many improvements. The main ones have been better feeling about my food (cruelty free as far as possible), health benefits such as easier loss of weight, increase in muscle strength, CV ability, etc."

-- Joe S.

33. "I've benefited considerably by going vegan! Physically: I have more energy, better skin and hair, better digestion, feeling lighter and more energized after eating. Emotionally/spiritually: I feel more positive and happier, more peaceful, guilt-free and loving."

-- Julia P.

34. "My strength in weight training went through the roof after I converted to veganism! I now sleep better than I ever have and my skin is the clearest it's ever been and everyone comments on it. Even my digestion is better and I don't get bloated like I used to. I have more energy overall and I get less headaches. I also don't catch coughs or colds anymore."

-- Mel K.

35. "When I switch to vegetarianism 28 years ago, it was all about health. However, when I went vegan it was for the animals and the planet (number 1 reason). Having said that, the side benefits on my health have been great! I have more energy, I'm maintaining a healthy weight, I've noticed better running performance and a renewed love of food... real food!"

-- Janik L.

36. "There are a lot of reasons I and others have decided to go vegan. I think for me it's that I've always cared about being cruelty-free (I love animals so much!), but also I just feel better health wise!"

-- Collier L.

282

37. "The main positive benefits I've seen, not only for myself, but for all beings, is more empathy and understanding! I've found that I have a spiritual connection with the world and I realize how ignorant I used to be regarding the food industry and regarding welfare. Becoming vegan makes you see the world in a more open and positive way."

-- Elaine B.

38. "I am a raw vegan, so my diet saves me plenty of time to do whatever I want to. Besides that, my hair grows much longer and my hazel eyes are turning grey. Let's talk about the energy level too - It's so high!"

-- "Vomit Heart"

39. "I've been vegan a year nearly. The benefits are spiritual, mental and physical! Spiritually and mentally, because once I knew, I just knew and it opened my mind and soul up to further seek the beauty on earth and within it and with God and all nature. Physically, I'm healthier. My skin is better and my energy is better. I had acute iron deficiency and it was critical. There was not enough iron going through my body to support my heart, but becoming vegan and eating right helped a lot. I got my iron back up to where it should be.

Once you know, man you know and it is gut wrenching and heart breaking every single day knowing the atrocities that go on even more than I had imagined - especially in the dairy industry! The peace of mind I focus on is that I don't contribute to it at all - any of it! So, there you go. That's my little vegan life so far."

-- Kate A.

40. "When I was a meat eater, I ate a lot of junk food like McDonald's, ice cream, etc. I went vegan for the animals and as a vegan, I find it's not as easy finding vegan junk food (at least in Sweden, where I live). I've been eating a lot healthier as a result, which has made me lose weight and it has cleared my skin up a lot! I have more energy and I don't have to feel guilty when I'm eating, because I know no animals were harmed. It has been nothing but positive things for me."

-- Emma M.

41. "I personally don't spend as much on groceries since converting to veganism and I have learned so much more about human anatomy. I am learning more about myself as a human and, although I didn't start this for the animals, I love how my mind has been broadened to being more compassionate toward other beings. I guess I never thought of packaging as something that was once living with feelings. More

importantly, my energy levels are high and, although there are some vegans that can be rough around the edges, I get more help, support and understanding as to why I feel the way I do. For example, lacking Vitamin B12, Vitamin K2, etc. People never hesitate to help me figure out how to "fix" it. I taste more when I eat food. My food is colorful and beautiful. I'm not in the bathroom for hours at a time. I'm happier, more energetic and feel quite a bit more enlightened! Also, as of yesterday, I need to check back my judgments, but I do feel more educated after being approached by non-vegans asking for money to help save the environment (lmao)."

-- Kay-Kay S.

42. "I feel a greater connection to all that is nature. I have more energy. Health wise, my blood pressure is completely normal!"

-- Kristi J.

43. "I lost 200 pounds to begin with and I have felt benefits of a sharper mind, improved memory, energy, improved mental focus, less anxiety and no more depression! A few other benefits which probably have more to do with the weight loss is that I no longer have feet and back issues. I also feel that my quality of life in general has improved. I changed only the ingredients in my food. I still eat about the same volume that I used to eat.

I also would like to mention that I was diagnosed with hay fever and was allergic to many fruits and vegetables and, now that I'm vegan, I am no longer allergic to any fruit or vegetable that I know of."

-- Sean D.

Sean included the following image to show his weight loss transformation through veganism:

44. "I've been vegan since December 2014 and some of the biggest benefits have been physical, even though I went vegan purely for the animals: Being able to eat until satisfied at every meal and maintaining a healthy weight super easily by eating vegan and primarily whole foods. I have lost 22 kg. since going vegan - though it didn't come off that easily in the beginning as I was eating a lot of vegan junk like fried falafels and samosas, as I used to be quite busy and never really had time to cook at home. I now have way more energy than I used to and I don't NEED those 3-4 cups of coffee every day anymore. I just drink a cup every now and then, if I feel like for taste, but not for the caffeine boost. I also haven't been ill once since I went vegan. Before that - even though I was eating quite varied and healthy I would get ill like every month with something and I would have a lot of different infections. A common cold back then would last me at least 3-4 weeks. Mentally, I don't know how I have changed. I mean, besides learning more and more about the horrors of animal agriculture, I still have just as many mental struggles as in the past, so I can't say that veganism is some magic potion but it has improved various of aspects of my life.

Besides that, it's super awesome to see how many people are turning to veganism these days. Being around people that see the things you see, and being able to support each other while trying to end this animal holocaust is quite rewarding. It's always great to share beliefs with likeminded people."

-- Skaði N.

45. "I've noticed less skin problems, weight loss, more energy, I get full faster, I don't always feel like I'm starving anymore, I have this "light" feeling about me. Almost euphoric. I don't mean like lightheaded, but almost a natural high. I just feel so much better in these two months of being vegan than I've ever felt in my life. I feel whole and at peace. I also feel it's positively affecting my mental health. I am bipolar and feel as though I don't have as much depression or mood swings, if any."

-- Lisbeth S.

46. "I have experienced the following positive changes since converting to veganism:

1. It helps my tummy and internal scar tissue after having a tumor removed.

2. I feel 'lighter' physically.

3. I go to bed at night and I don't get a yucky feeling through my esophagus that I used to get when I ate cheese, eggs, drank milk, etc.

4. I feel so much better knowing that I'm contributing to the sustainability of the earth, not contributing to the inhumane treatment of animals and being healthier myself."

-- Heather C.

47. "I feel physically better, my skin has gotten clearer, super light periods now, instead of being heavy. I also feel better morally. Like I can now actually call myself an environmentalist and an animal lover. Also, interesting to point out, I went from eating meat straight to vegan in November. I'd previously been ovo-lacto vegetarian from 2006-2013 and didn't have pretty much any of those benefits."

-- Evey M.

48. "There are a lot of benefits of being vegan: my life is so much better. For my beliefs, I think that animals and humans have a soul and we can't discriminate against them. I respect other's lives and my mind is so much more peaceful. For me, it was very hard control my weight and not feel guilty about what I used to eat, but since I started

this lifestyle I can eat without guilt and I can eat more food and actually enjoy what I eat. I feel happy because I'm doing a good behavior for the planet, because I care about the life of the other living things (humans, animals, plants). I'm following the Buddha's teachings, so I'm grateful to the universe for giving me this path."

-- Alejandra M.

49. "I was vegetarian since I was just a child (from a family of meat eaters). I eat very little dairy and, to be honest, the dairy I did eat was in things like cake and chocolate. So, I wanted to go vegan for quite a while and was unsure about how to achieve it, until one day I just decided I'm doing it and I'll figure it out as I go. That's what I did. My initial reason for doing it was for the animals and the fact that, since I was a child, eating flesh was always disgusting to me. I honestly saw it as a kind of cannibalism. I was also aware of the health benefits, but not to the extent that I am now. I also knew about the environmental effects but again not to the extent that I do now. The impact it has on everything is huge. On top of all of that, I'm Jewish and I don't believe that it was part of God's plan for us to destroy the earth for our appetites. So, even if I didn't feel so strongly on all of these things combined, any one of them separately would be motivation enough for me not to eat animals!"

-- Abbie R.

50. "I feel more healthy and peaceful since I have taken the plunge and converted to veganism."

-- Contreras C.

51. "6 years ago I was diagnosed with Arthritis. 2 years ago, I was on my deathbed, twice. The poison meds they gave me almost killed me. So, I changed the way I ate to the Starch Solution and I lost weight, stopped all my meds, and got my life back."

-- Mike C.

52. "Some positive effects I've experienced from living a vegan lifestyle are:

1) Increased energy and a boosted mood.

2) Reduced cholesterol, triglycerides and blood pressure, as well as weight loss.

3) No more guilt about animal suffering with relation to what I eat, wear or do (aside from driving).

4) Expanded meal menus, more creative dishes and variety.

5) I feel a lot less inflammation overall. I feel great waking up in the morning.

6) My skin is much smoother and healthier. My eyes are brighter.

7) I've become more involved in animal welfare. Volunteering at project wildlife to rehabilitate injured or sick wildlife; I routinely offer my services in Graphic Design and website design & production pro-bono for animal charities. I'm also involved in beach, riverbed and canyon cleanup in San Diego."

-- Michael G.

53. "For any personal benefits, I consider them a side effect that plays a small role, a very small role, in why I have chosen to live vegan. For personal benefits, one can always become a vegetarian, take up a *mostly* plant-based diet, or even a carnist who follows a strict diet. I see veganism as a liberation movement on behalf of victims that cannot and never would be able to liberate themselves from human exploitation. It's ALL about THEIR benefit and happiness however they're able to conceive it."

-- Oscar I.

54. "For my health, I have more energy. My dermatitis and acne on my skin has cleared up altogether too. Mentally, my depression has gone as I feel better in myself to be living my truth and with kindness and respect for the earth and all living upon her. My self-esteem is much better as I am kinder toward myself since becoming a vegan.

I use my produce that I grow in my garden too so I am organic and living semi-self-sufficiently as well."

-- Tania H.

55. "I have been vegan for four years and a while back, like a month ago, I started drinking kale, avocado, banana, blueberries, blackberries, strawberries, pineapple, mango and kiwi smoothies daily and it has helped my severe chronic pain that I have dealt with for 19 years. I drank this drink back in 2013, but I quit after a while. I restarted it in an attempt to get rid of my pain.

My blood work has been perfect ever since I became a vegan and I helped saved animals lives."

-- Eddie S.

56. "I no longer feel guilty when I eat. That is the biggest plus! I also used to have severe gastric distress every day (I literally lived with Pepto on hand at all times). The gastric distress went away after going vegan. I used to be anemic and I no longer have issues with that either. I also lost some weight. I just physically feel better all around!"

-- Victoria C.

57. "I have lost 12 kg, without any exercise! My cholesterol went from high to normal, my hair now does not stop growing whereas it used to only grow to a certain length (most ladies will get this). I've learned more about humanity in just the two years I've been vegan than I had in my whole life before that! I am now by default very conscious of what goes into my body. My blood tests are all perfect and I am much, *much* happier! I've had zero negative effects."

-- Nicole T.

Nicole included the following image to show her weight loss transformation through veganism:

58. "I reduced my blood pressure medication in half since becoming a vegan. My lab work is all normal. I feel physically better. My skin has cleared up. I feel better knowing that nothing is being harmed for me to make a meal."

-- Ryan O.

59. "I think the most important benefit veganism has had for me is the huge change in my belief system. That we are not victims of what society does to us; we have the power to choose compassion over violence. That we can stand alone and say: *'no, this is wrong, I'm not going to do this.'* The second benefit is a clearer conscience and

as a result a LOT less anxiety and depression that were hidden in my subconscious, because of the pain that I knew I was unnecessarily causing to both animals and the planet. The third benefit is of course health and getting better results in the gym."

-- Feshe D.

60. "I've become healthier overall from veganism. My mental clarity increases each day, my natural energy increased, I'm stronger and leaner than ever (served USMC and sports my entire life), I'm more compassionate and fearless. The positive vibes flow easier with the vibrant mindset."

-- Brenden F.

61. "The first thing veganism did to help me was about my health. I was constantly worried about getting sickly when I would grow older and then I realized it was all about what you put into your body. I have been vegan for over four years now and I have never looked back and have no regrets -- I'm loving it! Secondly, I went vegan for the sake of being fair to all living beings: both humans and animals. Veganism is self-realization that we can be better than we were yesterday and promote love all the time, because LOVE is the answer."

-- Joe V.

62. "Since I went vegan, the absolute biggest benefit for me has to be me mental health. My conscience is much clearer as I am now living out my beliefs. Before I went vegan, I experienced a lot of guilt, shame and anxiety. The anxiety still lingers but overall, I feel so much better. Physically, I lost a lot of weight when I went vegan. My blood pressure got a lot lower and my digestion improved a lot. Before I went vegan, I had a lot of trouble with stomach aches, acid reflux and indigestion. All of that is gone now! My allergies have also cleared up, but not all the way. The best thing about going vegan has to be all the amazing compassionate, kind and caring people I get to connect with."

-- Freya L.

63. "Since I've become a vegan, other sentient beings no longer die because of my choices. This alone is the only reason I need to stay vegan."

-- Evy S.

64. "As a vegan, I have experienced better health, better sleep and found out so many facts that I did not know about the environment! I feel more confident as a person now and I've even stopped wearing makeup. I'm much happier and less anxious. I feel more connected to nature and more caring about the world. I just started to see the bigger picture and I feel like I'm truly experiencing a spiritual awakening."

-- Roberta Z.

65. "I was dying in a wheelchair from lupus. I was diagnosed terminal in 2000. My liver was attacked and failing and I was given 6 months on February 14th of 2011. Going vegan gave me the energy and the strength to get out of the chair after surviving a severe beating and starvation -- which took a year to recover from. I said a simple prayer, "Lord, give me the strength to leave!" I was determined to die free. I would either die or *really* live. I dumped all my meds, got out of the chair, only for a few minutes at first, and walked on a treadmill. I was praying unceasingly and went vegetarian at first, then shortly after that I went full vegan. At Christmas that year, I received a miracle and was told the day after Christmas by my doctor, who was shocked to see me walk in, that my liver was healed and lupus was not just in remission, but it was *completely* gone! My desire for freedom, God and veganism all played a role. The miracle was the icing on top. I am a princess warrior!"

-- Dawn D.

66. "I've had a couple benefits since going vegan. To begin, I have had a lot more energy, which a lack thereof was my main issue – I never had energy. The second, and my favorite benefit from veganism, has been that I've been losing weight! I think those two are the major ones. Other than that, I get to sleep better every night."

-- Diana C.

67. "Personally, I went raw at the same time as I went vegan. I became more intelligent and clear-headed than I'd even imagined possible! I also felt more ease and peace in my day to day life. I suppose this peace and clarity came from being able to digest the foods I ate far more efficiently! On top of this, I got to the point of seeing the aura of plants and humans. Words can't fully describe the many changes I've experienced. To summarize, I clearly felt better than I had ever before as a meat-eater or than I did as a vegetarian."

-- Bach G.

68. "The following items are what I enjoy about being a vegan:

1. Tastier food. 2. Cheaper food. 3. Feeling better about not contributing to animal deaths and suffering. 4. Believing I am eating healthier. 5. Believing that I am not contributing to climate change, loss of wildlife and GMO foods and wildlife habitat destruction that is due to loss of habitat and climate changes as well as depriving poor people starving in this world due to their land being used to grow farm animal crops."

-- Noelle O.

69. "Some of the benefits I have experienced are: 1. Improved digestion. I was already vegetarian and was still having problems digesting my food. I cut out the dairy and it IMMEDIATELY improved permanently 2. I lost 13 pounds within the first 6 days and I have kept the weight off! 3. I am far more energetic in the gym, on the running trail and in my day-to-day life. 4. I am stronger than I have ever been."

-- Corey B.

70. "I have been a vegan for 23 years now. I don't really remember much from before, since I was just 17 when I converted, but, for me, I unfortunately did not lose weight as most of the people say they do. However, what I definitely can say is that I feel my soul is clearer since I don't kill animals to eat. This is the important thing for me."

-- Sundy G.

71. "My benefits from eating on a vegan diet are an end to binge eating, spiritual benefits for meditation, lower blood pressure and cholesterol, I feel happier and more authentic and I have clearer thinking."

-- Jobie B.

72. "I'd say the spiritual aspect has been the biggest surprise. I have felt happier and less stressed out in day to day life since I stopped consuming the energy of horribly mistreated souls."

-- Tom H.

73. "Chef Mary serves vegetable patties, cause she knows they don't have any daddies! She, the vegan Queen of San Fran scene, for no meat does her store front carry!"

-- Chef Mary

74. "I just overall feel a lot better about myself. I'm proud to be who I am now, and totally brag that I'm a vegan. It's opened up a whole new world for me, and been the most informative learning experience I have ever had."

-- Kara L.

75. "I was always a vegetarian, but was quite ignorant of the condition for cows for milk, as it was on my shadowy side. As soon I got awakened, I switched to veganism! It's been 3 years now and it makes me feel more truthful to myself and hopeful of my view of utopia."

-- Himanshu M.

76. "I don't even know where to begin! I've seen mental, physical and emotional improvements. I also got my mind back. I'm no longer under hypnosis thinking humans are omnivores and other absurdities that we're taught. Anyway, the first thing I noticed was my mucus and inflammation decreased and then my energy levels started to improve. I've become calmer too and I just feel better than ever in general. I started to enjoy meals a lot more too."

-- Joaquim O.

77. "My health is better! I was suffering from acid reflux disease and now I have been healed and I lost a lot of fat. Finally, the most important thing I am really happy about is that now I can say I love animals without hypocrisy or duplicity."

-- Mahmoud E.

78. "Since I went vegan, I felt that all of the bad fat in my body started to melt and my smell got better. I rarely feel lazy anymore. All what vegan food gives you is pure energy and total satisfaction! My muscles are growing faster with the same workout plan that I used to follow, not mentioning the spiritual inner peace and the empowering energy of love and harmony I feel with every soul and in every place. When you become vegan, you feel like you have finally got back to where you truly belong: the sweet warm

heart of our mother earth. You start to see the beauty that every creature holds inside of them. That's what veganism is truly all about -- love and peace! It's only our true nature to be vegans. I hope that you achieve your goal and make some humans change their minds about veganism."

-- Nour H.

79. "Feeling much happier living in alignment with my morals. Also, much healthier (I have an autoimmune disease and was following the Autoimmune Protocol, which said you had to eat meat to heal as you couldn't do the protocol vegetarian/vegan). I decided that I just had to try vegan for the animals, because I felt miserable contributing to their suffering. I feel much lighter and brighter and happier and more energetic! Though I must say I try and follow the 80/10/10 raw vegan style of eating. This make me feel fantastic."

-- Rachael V.

80. "I've had a few benefits from my conversion to veganism. First, I would say more energy and power. I now have better skin and I also look way younger than women who are my age. I don't get sick like I used to. On the social aspect, I have met amazing people!"

-- Sophia A.

81. "It is nice knowing that I'm not contributing to the murder of innocent beings. Other benefits are that I have lower cholesterol, almost no stomach aches or diarrhea, I cleared up my acne/zits and I never get sick or gets colds to the point where I need bed rest. Before going vegan, I'd get a flu shot every year and an annual cold that forced me into bed. I don't have to get the flu shot anymore. On top of this, there are so many more benefits that I can't even think of right now."

-- Jennifer P.

82. "All my life, I have had really bad asthma and had to use my two inhalers daily - sometimes my third inhaler, which is actually a steroid. It costed me over $100 every three months to renew my prescription and fill up on inhalers. I was literally living on them all the time. When I switched to veganism, I haven't had to use my inhalers at all -- not a single time! My breathing is fine and I'm convinced that it was the dairy that caused such health issues. All I know is that I save way more money now and I don't have to visit the doctor's office every three months.

Another positive thing about being vegan is the VARIETY OF FOOD YOU CAN EAT! Before I went vegan, I didn't even know what an eggplant was or what it looked or tasted like! I have really broadened my food intake nowadays and find myself trying a wider variety of foods too, instead of eating my normal old "eggs, meat, sausage and mince." When I was an omnivore, I was eating a much more limited variety of foods as opposed to now. ALSO, being a vegan is great because vegetables are cheap in my country. I never realized how expensive eggs and meat really are."

-- Maioha K.

83. "Becoming vegan has had so many benefits for me:

1. Feeling more positive that I'm doing something to help animals.

2. It has made me more environmentally aware, so I try not buy food with a lot of packaging and I try and use reusable products, i.e. I carry a reusable coffee cup and metal straws, etc. I also use environmentally friendly cleaning and washing products.

3. I've made lots of interesting friends from all over the world, which makes me realize I'm not alone in this and I get to see so much great work being done to help animals.

4. Feeling more awake and connected to the planet we live on.

5. My cholesterol has gone down, even though I've not lost weight as I can't eat fresh fruit and salad, because my stomach won't digest it. I never became vegan for diet reasons anyway. It was never about me and it was always for the animals."

-- Sarah T.

84. "I have more energy, I'm happier and feel more at peace. A sense of guilt has left my life since switching to veganism, my heart health has improved drastically, my erections are fuller and easier to attain and my shoulder and back acne have finally cleared away! I have a feeling of ethical superiority compared to non-vegans, instant camaraderie with fellow vegans that I've never met and my brain has become sharper and can learn and remember things much easier."

-- Tanner H.

85. "I'm 50 years old and have been a vegan since I was 25 years of age. I can't see myself ever living any other lifestyle than the vegan lifestyle!"

-- Caroline G.

86. "Well, I didn't go vegan for myself or for any 'positive benefits', but I did it for the animals and because it was the right thing to do. I'm a vegan activist now, so it's only created more stress and sadness and, with more knowledge and awareness of the cruelty of animal exploitation, it becomes more of a burden. You deal with all kinds of criticism and ridicule from others and your heart is always sad and broken. It's also allowed me to become a part of a community that is filled with compassion and empathy, and I share a common bond with people from all around the world.

Health-wise, my food digests better and I know I'm going to live longer and have less diseases. It's actually easier to grocery shop and prepare meals now (I eat a lot of whole foods). Yeah, I can't really think of anything else. Like I said, I didn't do it for myself or for any positive rewards, but I did it for the sake of the animals; to minimize their suffering and because I want to make a statement to all those around me, so that they will hopefully educate themselves and go vegan as well.

After thousands of years of domination and oppression and torture and violence toward our fellow Earthlings, I think being vegan is the very LEAST we can do. Yeah, I'm probably not the best person to talk to about this... I'm driven and motivated by my love for animals and for the Earth. It has nothing to do with myself or other people; I seek justice, equality and animal liberation. I care about the victims and all the innocent souls condemned to a lifetime of misery and slavery and torture and pain. That's why I've chosen this cruelty-free lifestyle... for them. They don't have voices, they can't protest in a language that people readily understand, so WE must be their advocates and I will defend them, and all sentient beings, until the day that I die."

-- Poffo O.

87. "I started eating vegan because of health reasons. I lost a lot of weight and got my blood pressure to a healthy level. I got more energy and am much better at handling stress. My skin now glows. It used to be a bit pasty and had dry skin. I'm much calmer even though it can be an issue dealing with meat-eaters at times and I have become more compassionate to other earthlings. I'm also a lot more aware of how people are conditioned to think that animal exploitation is ok."

-- Mladen K.

88. "Since switching over to a vegan diet, my ability to recover after strenuous exercise has increased and my recovery time decreased. I was able to run a little bit

faster. My cholesterol has finally dropped to under 150. By incorporating live Foods into my diet, I believe I've been able to keep the hair on my head -- at least its natural color -- and I think that that's just from getting all the gunk out of my system. I don't get sick all that often. In fact, I rarely get sick. I've met some of the best people."

-- Dean D.

89. "I've noticed the following benefits as a result of following a vegan diet: You can eat without feeling guilty. Your body becomes healthier with less toxins in the system - but the vegetables and fruit should be organic! Your mind expands more easily during meditation. You know a lot of nice vegans from all parts of the world. The animals can feel that you are a friend and not an enemy. It's an amazing experience. If you believe in karma, your consciousness will be at ease because you are not destroying the planet. You'll feel better in every aspect of your life. Learn how to cook delicious vegan food and GO VEGAN!"

-- Lia M.

90. "Because of following a vegan diet, I've experienced weight loss, lower blood pressure, a rush of creativity (in the form of poetry), clarity of thinking, peaceful attitude, better understanding of life's injustices, no more bleeding gums, drier skin, reductions in body aches and a stronger immune system (only 1 cold in 15 months). I cannot comment on energy levels as I'm disabled, but I'm sure I would have experienced an increase there, just based on my weight loss. I've seen a massive reduction in irritable bowel syndrome without even taking medication each day. Basically, veganism will change your life. That's some claim for anyone!"

-- Anthony R.

91. "I have been vegan for 9 years. Since going vegan, I have had more energy and my iron levels have been in the normal range (before going vegan, I had low iron). I am more happy and positive in general. Just knowing that I am walking lighter on this earth makes me feel happy!"

-- Maree J.

92. "The first thing that's benefited from going vegan: my general mood, which is probably due to low blood pressure. I'm living aligned with my ethics, secondly. After that: energy! My aches and pains are gone. The best way I can describe it is feeling like a superhero most of the time! I catch myself saying that daily. I've also noticed

increased testosterone. It just seems like everything is better! It's hard to quantify in a sound bite. A two-day seminar seems more appropriate!"

-- Rod G.

93. "I've only been vegan for 3 months. I've lost 20 pounds, experienced less depression, and have clearer and less oily skin. Other than that, I've enjoyed learning to cook with whole foods and taste all the great flavors the earth has to offer! I still love what I eat, and surprisingly so, because I thought I'd never enjoy eating without cheese and such."

-- Krystan N.

94. "I feel more energetic and healthy than before. Being vegan also helps me feel a lot better about myself and my lifestyle."

-- Vivek V.

95. "I feel more active and have a sensation of being fully awake. My digestive system has become more efficient also and I feel like I absorb more nutrients. I've gained control of my body weight. I'm also more sensitive to taste and notice new flavors from the same old fruits!"

-- Mike H.

96. " I'll share some benefits, there are many. The biggest personal benefit for me was curing Hashimoto's thyroiditis after being told that it is incurable. Treatment would have consisted of synthetic thyroid hormone, which I found out I would have had to take the hormone for the rest of my life if I had started taking it.

I also had a terrible problem with muscle spasms. While exercising, I'd always end up taking 20 to 30 minutes out of my routine to wait for random muscles to relax before I could continue. It was bad enough that I couldn't work my muscles to exhaustion, because they would spasm before they got there. That's not an issue anymore either!

Some other benefits are: clear skin, no more constipation, no brain fog, when I'm out of shape the soreness after exercise is noticeably less than what it used to be, better stamina, and it's also made me a much better person toward animals.

My mom and my cousin went vegan along with me and they have lost a huge amount of weight. My mom was on 13 medications and after going vegan is now taking zero. My cousin almost died from a bleeding ulcer and has since cured that through eating a vegan diet."

-- Mike H.

97. "I think the biggest benefit is that my actions and lifestyle align with my moral values. I definitely think that going vegan had made me a more compassionate and kind person. I think maybe that's because veganism had allowed me to fully embrace that part of myself. Other benefits I've experienced are increase in energy and productivity, feeling lighter and more comfortable in my own skin, and less brain fog."

-- Katherine L.

98. "I would love to share the benefits I have experienced since going vegan! My skin is glowing, I'm losing weight, my bowels move regularly, my hair stopped shedding, I have amazing energy, I'm happier, I'm calmer and I feel AMAZING!"

-- Azrielle A.

99. "Below are the benefits I've experienced from living vegan:

HEALTH. A. Since 2010 I had irritable bowel syndrome and of course I had to cut certain kinds of food. Among them were beans, lentils and greasy meat (sorry, I wasn't vegan yet). I just was drinking lactose-free dairy products, but still I was taking medication and feeling bad sometimes. Since I'm vegan (February 2016) I haven't taken any pill for this problem. Even I can eat beans, lentils, chickpeas and some others without a problem. B. I've lost about 10 lbs. being vegan, and I'm weighing the same since then. So, I can keep my weight without any problem. C. I have a chronic illness which is called "Interstitial Cystitis" since January of 2016. My two urologists have told me that, because I'm vegan, my illness is under control (although both are meat-eaters).

ETHICS A. Me and my husband decided to become vegans the same day, because when we watched *Earthlings* and saw what people do to animals every day, we said that we were not going to support that anymore, so we became vegans overnight even though I didn't know anything about how to be a vegan in the kitchen. B. We also said that it was ironic being a double moral person. I mean we said we loved animals, but we were eating them... that really doesn't make sense, don't you think?

SPIRITUALITY A. We are Catholics, and contrary to the majority of them, we don't believe that animals were for us. I mean what kind of god would ask you to kill them?

B. According to the Bible, in the book of Genesis, the lectures said that Adan and Eva in the paradise were eating just fruits, NOT animals... which means that humans decided to do it here in the earth, despite the fact that they knew how to grow seeds! C. When you are a god-believer, knowing that you don't kill anything to do your daily routine, survive or eat, you have a completely peaceful life.

MONEY A. Most people believe that being vegan is expensive, and I don't agree. Since we have become vegans we have spent less money on food, medical care, and personal stuff. I mean, I use synthetic shoes, and of course they are cheaper than leather shoes. B. I'm from Mexico, and I can tell you that veganism is relative new here. There are several misconceptions about it even. People believe that we are rich because we're vegans... and it's almost the contrary! The most expensive kilogram of veggies is about 30 pesos and the cheapest meat kilogram is about 70 pesos... so, who's the "rich" person?"

-- Yazmin G.

100. "Since I was a child, I didn't like meat that much. Sometimes it was even repulsive to me, but no one in my house was a vegetarian. My parents and sisters still eat meat nowadays. I am the only vegan in my family. Growing up as a kid eating meat daily was traditional for me, but I started noticing that I didn't like that, and this feeling grew a little bit bigger year by year, especially when I started cooking. I had to go grocery shopping and I didn't like to go to butchery section at the stores, but I had to because I wasn't buying food just for me.

At a young age, I left home to study in another city, so I started buying less meat and making meat dishes less often. One day I was cooking Chinese food for a bunch of friends. We bought chicken chest. I had to part it, set aside each muscle, cartilage and bone. I saw the rest of the blood in that and felt sick. It wasn't the first time I was doing that, I had done that a million times before, but that special time I felt too disgusted! I hid my feelings from my friends that night, but I never forgot how bad I felt... Disgusted and sorry for the dead animal! Then I quit chicken but I was still eating seafood, pork, and beef now and then.

A couple of months later, a friend showed me a video. It was Gary Yourofsky's video on YouTube called "Best speech you will ever hear". That video is about 1 hour long but I couldn't stop watching. It drew my attention so powerfully! I was amazed and terrified by everything that video was showing me. That was the day I quit milk, but I was still eating some meat, eggs, cheese and other dairy.

I kept asking myself how I could live a vegan life, because that seemed impossible to me! I would have to cook my own food every day, I'd never find vegan options in restaurants (I thought!), I wouldn't be able to go to my friends' celebrations and have barbecues with them... That seemed impossible, but it was so appealing to me! I couldn't feel okay knowing what animals go through for people to have them on their plates... I literally started asking the Universe to give me an answer! I prayed to God to help me become vegan and show me a way of doing it without having to move into the Amazon rainforest... I let it happen naturally. Sometimes I avoided every dairy, sometimes I avoided eggs, and sometimes I gave up buying a lotion because the brand tested on animals, so it was gradual and I felt so happy every time I did those things. I just wanted to feel that again, and again, and again, and lay my head in bed with a light and clean conscience.

One day I was making pizza for 60 people. It was a big event and I had to make some things in advance. One day before, I was chopping the food I would fry the next day. When I picked the piece of meat, red beef meat, I couldn't hold the knife! I immediately pictured a piece of a human's leg right in front of me and that felt like I was going to kill a person! I had a friend do that job for me that day and I just kept on with the veggies.

About 6 months later I definitely quit meat and became a vegetarian! It was really difficult for me to not eat meat those days. Not because I wanted it, but because I was never home, everything was far, and I was always buying food at cafés or bakeries, so only candies or a few other options didn't have meat in them. I didn't eat meat, but I started eating more candies, more sugar, and that was bad for my health. I decided to plan my weekly grocery shopping routine so that I'd have more fruit and vegetables instead of candies. All I needed was organization, and I made it, I felt happier! It wasn't so difficult, but I still wasn't vegan...

One day, I heard there was a vegan restaurant in a town nearby, but as I hardly ever used to go to that town, I didn't get around to going to this restaurant. About 8 months later I needed another job and I was really interested in cooking, but I had never worked with it. It was just a hobby. I was talking to a friend and she told me that a friend of ours was a waiter at that vegan restaurant, so I talked to him and he said they needed a bartender to make juices there. Within 2 weeks, I was there squeezing oranges at the restaurant bar! The owners of the restaurant are vegan, so they taught me a lot about veganism! I had never had vegan friends, but suddenly I was into that wonderful vegan environment! I was all about veganism! I learned so much from them! They were really friendly and nice people!

As I worked just making juice, I didn't know much about vegan gastronomy, but the chef noticed that I wanted to learn more about it, so she said, "The doors of my kitchen are open for you! You can use this restaurant as your lab to learn everything you want to learn!" I literally cried when I heard those words! I got so emotional and happy at the same time! I couldn't help crying! That was everything I wanted to hear! I hugged her and thanked her very much! For the next months, I woke up early twice a week to go learn vegan gastronomy in my beloved lab before my shift at the bar started. That restaurant was my final step on this transitioning path from carnivore to vegan.

There I learned pretty much everything I cook nowadays; there I got to know about online sources of very valuable information for vegans, and there I realized that being vegan wasn't impossible! Working there taught me that cooking vegan food is healthier, cruelty-free, more economic in every way, cleaner and even easier!

I couldn't wait anymore! I became vegan! The main reason that made me go vegan is the compassion and love for animals, but searching on YouTube videos, Facebook pages, websites, and so on, I saw that veganism isn't good only for animals! Veganism is a whole combination of benefits for the whole planet! For the plants, for the water, for the air, and for people too! When I realized that the amount of grains an animal has to eat for farmers to sell meat is that huge, the water wasted is that much, and when I knew about deforestation and air pollution caused by cattle breeding and livestock... I freaked! I realized veganism is the best solution to heal Earth in several ways -- and it's amazing! I want to encourage more and more people to go vegan! I understand it isn't easy. It wasn't easy for me, but I think that the vegan lifestyle and diet are so good, cruelty-free, and full of flavor! No one would miss out on anything by going vegan. Instead, people who go vegan have the amazing opportunity of finding out a beautiful new world of taste, compassion, peace of mind, and happiness."

-- Julia Kellermann de Moraes

101. "The most obvious thing for me is that being vegan has allowed me to eat in alignment with my own values -- the main value being that I love and care for animals. Also, the more I learn about the effects of animal agriculture on the environment, the prouder I am of the fact that I am vegan. Another bonus has been that, combined with a slightly more active lifestyle, I have lost a little over 20kg since becoming vegan. I also believe that veganism has allowed me to meet and connect with the most beautiful people on earth. I have found that the majority of the vegans I know share my values on things such as equal rights for women, marriage equality and equal rights for members of the LGBTQI+ community, animal rights, social justice issues, environmental impact and so many other things."

-- Corey S.

102. "I am an existential nihilist but I want to change this world to a better place by reducing pain. That's why I changed to vegan. After becoming a vegan, I also realized that a vegan diet helps the environment, species extinction and world hunger. So, I felt like veganism is the most important thing in the world and I could see that people are not realizing it. I started a vegan awareness program in my city. Now, after two years, I feel healthy too."

-- Steve A.

103. "Since I've become a vegan, I have been feeling better overall. I lost a lot of fat and sleep better too! I find myself feeling pure. Wild animals aren't afraid of me anymore for some reason either."

-- Simon L.

104. "When I switched to veganism, I immediately noticed that I had more energy. I was also able to eat a lot more with obviously more nutrition, but less calories since it was all plant-based whole foods. Going vegan also helped me spread awareness of course with what goes on in animal agriculture/factory farming. It was a dose of reality that I needed and I feel my eyes have opened immensely. I have more compassion and can also say that I have made the most ethical decisions. I want everyone to know going vegan is easy, affordable, practical, and basically the most humane lifestyle you can choose."

-- Ariel S.

105. "The biggest part of veganism is animal awareness: realizing that all lives are equal and our bodies are most certainly not meant to consume meat. We can thrive on fruits and plants! I am really starting to feel better within myself."

-- Jesse U.

106. "The changes brought on by veganism come in different stages. The first stage is the body. I feel healthier after being vegan. I did lose extra fat. I hope that soon I will be in a more beautiful shape.

The second stage is the mind... After being vegan you feel amazing inside of yourself, like a flower of love starting to bloom. You start loving and caring for all sentient beings. You realize how important this is for a beautiful life you always wished for. This realization gives you power.

Then the third stage comes when you feel inside compassion for all and love for all. You start loving beyond your wildest imaginations. You feel other's emotions and you are true to your own emotions.

I feel there is more levels beyond this. The more you experience, the more you learn."

-- Js Jags

107. "There are so many benefits to living vegan. More energy. Not being sick, so I don't have stress about the latest flu and sickness going around. I look vibrant and radiant, so my confidence is up. My perspective on animals changed. I don't see them as food. There's no more temptation. I see them as living beings like myself."

-- Jason I.

108. "The benefits of being vegan: Well, for me, the only benefit I really care about is the benefit to the animals that I don't eat, use or abuse. However, I have noticed I am losing weight easier now that I am vegan. (I have been vegan for just over a year now, after 30 years as a vegetarian). As for my health, it is difficult for me to assess the effect on that as I have many complicated health issues for which I am on numerous meds for. I do feel my energy levels have improved now that I am vegan, which have always been very poor. The biggest benefit for me personally is I just feel so much happier from a spiritual point of view living my life knowing I do not consume any animal suffering or cruelty. Another positive is making friends with so many other likeminded caring compassionate people."

-- Soosie W.

109. "Besides my feeling good about how my choices affect animal's lives, I don't get sick even when others around me are."

-- Anonymous

110. "When I started, it was with a total change in health focus... because I was fairly unhealthy back then and at too young of an age. I did all the nutrition research and such.... which l ended up at the idea of sticking with paleo for a while, but then added more and more raw vegan stuff to the point where at times I'm about sixty to eighty percent raw vegan! It's definitely easy in the summer, but not in the winter... and of course I always loved all creatures and it just all went together perfectly."

-- Usul M.

111. "I considered veganism at first, because a few of my friends were vegans and I thought that adopting the lifestyle would fit my personal feelings about things -- like fur and leather and animal testing already -- plus I was hoping for health benefits, as I suffer from a variety of different health complications.

The full conversion was admittedly health-based at first, but later, as I learned more about animal agriculture, it's not *only* about health, but also because I do not want to be a contributor to animal suffering and exploitation. Reasons to adopt a vegan eating lifestyle were because I have these health issues that are connected to or made worse by eating animal products: PCOS (polycystic ovary syndrome), which may have been caused by consumption of meat and dairy products in my childhood, and which contributes to (all of which I suffer/suffered from or were directly at risk for): Obesity, loss of scalp hair, infertility, higher risk of several cancers, organ malfunction (liver/kidneys no longer function at 100%), hormonal imbalance, higher heart attack risk, high cholesterol and type-2 diabetes.

I had hoped that switching to a plant-based diet would help with my health concerns, and I have seen that, yes, it certainly has! I was able to lose weight that I had been unable to lose before. My hormone levels seem to have come back to a more normal function, my diabetes is *gone* (had my A1C levels checked last month and the doctor said I no longer have diabetes), I have a lot more energy, I feel better in general (not as overall sick and fatigued), my acne is quite a lot better, I have my cycles back again and I feel very comfortable knowing that nothing I consume, whether I use it outside of my body or eat it for sustenance, has ever directly caused another being to suffer pain or fear."

-- Rachel L.

112. "I was vegetarian for a long time and made a gradual transition to being vegan. I'd say that since turning vegan I've met a lot of great people with whom I share a common ground. I've gotten to participate in and attend a lot of fun and inspiring events. I've learned that I'm not alone in my concern for animals."

-- Josh G.

113. "I look and feel younger and I'm more in tune with my meditation practice. My vibration is higher. My physical body feels better vegan and I have more mind clarity."

-- Tony T.

114. "My family and I first became vegans, because of our love for all animals. We soon realized that as a result we had more energy, felt lighter and better and our digestive systems worked much better. We also enjoy lower cholesterol and a better state of mind."

-- Dawn W.

115. "I'm a new vegan as I just started on April 1st. Before that, I was a vegetarian for 4 years. The best positive benefit is that my sleep cycle is much improved. For the

last 2 years, I've been sleeping from 3 to 5 hours and waking up from 3 to 5 times a night. Since I became vegan, it's like 5 to 7 hours of sleep a night and less waking up and I usually fall asleep much sooner!"

-- Vasu M.

116. "The main benefit of going vegan was having a clean conscience knowing that I wasn't intentionally creating any unnecessary harm. Secondary benefits were that my immune system improved greatly and I got sick A LOT less. I also stopped getting heartburn after giving up dairy."

-- Anonymous

117. "So many benefits:

1- All excess body fat has disappeared, without eating less, exercising or dieting.

2- Feeling more peaceful and connected with the world, and no feelings of guilt for hurting animals.

3- No colds or feeling ill and feeling more energetic."

-- Cazzie C.

118. "I have lost more than 30 kg of weight! At first, I was suffering from body pain, but then I realized that my body was detoxifying. My way of thinking has changed. It's really touching my soul."

-- Ramanathan U.

119. "I am a school teacher and, during a typical year, I would get sick 4-5 times. Since switching to a vegan diet, I got sick 1 time this year, total! I got strep because several of my students in class had it and, during that particular time period, I wasn't eating well. We were busy and junk food vegans, which I attribute to helping me get sick. I seriously saw a huge change in my ability to ward off colds and flus!"

-- Jenna V.

120. "I feel healthier. I don't get sick as much. I have seen people around me change because they saw me do it. I can feel like I make a difference in spite of my inept government. I know I am sparing animals from suffering. I am reducing my carbon

footprint. I am practicing what I preach. I am eating much better-tasting food, and enjoying more variety. I have the energy to care about getting more exercise and doing all the extra things to help the environment. I have connected to others who are like-minded and renewed my resolve to do everything in my power to reduce suffering, save the planet, and increase compassion and joy.

My reasons for going vegan were environmental, but learning about animal suffering and health benefits greatly strengthened my resolve.

Now I am vegan for the animals, the planet, my health, and so much more!"

-- Richard M.

121. "I've been vegan quite a while and I feel fabulous. I have lots of energy and rarely, if ever get sick or suffer from allergies, but most importantly, the feeling of knowing that I am not contributing to the abuse. My health is excellent. I'm 50 and I do not take any medication. I get all of my nutrients from eating a variety of good, clean food. Plus, your body eliminates more frequently so you never feel bloated or heavy. I tell people about the great organizations and people who I've met and the wonderful friendships I've made, both on and off of Facebook. This is a lifestyle that will benefit every soul on this planet, as well as the planet itself. Why cause harm and damage when we have so many wonderful options and choices?"

-- Bellene A.

122. "I am in better shape! Restaurants prepare me delicious meals if I give them enough notice! My skin is clearer! It feels amazing to not contribute to animal abuse and sacrifice for no reason! I wish I could do more about that."

-- Mick C.

123. "I was born a vegetarian and I used to wear long sleeves and long pants in summer, because mosquitoes loved to bite me. When I get bitten, the surrounding areas would get really red and itch like crazy for a few days! I'd still get mosquito bites after going vegan -- BUT! -- I would have no redness on my skin and the bites will only slightly itch for less than one minute! That is like paradise for me! I don't have to dread summer anymore!"

-- Wei C.

124. "I have been a vegan or vegetarian most of my life. The reason is based on me not wanting to eat my friends. I'm now a vegan and will be forever, mostly for

spiritual reasons. If there is suffering anywhere in the world, then we all suffer. I think when people can understand how universal energy works, it will be easier for them to be vegans. We learn compassion and love from animals -- plus the health benefits. Thank you for all you do."

-- Polly W.

125. "I've been vegan for 6 years and, when I just made the switch, I didn't know anything about nutrition or cooking. I literally lived off pasta and ketchup for a week, because I didn't know what to eat! My mom called me the only vegetarian that didn't like veggies (she didn't know the difference between vegan and vegetarian back then). That forced me into unknown territory and now I love all vegetables and know how to cook very well. I also have huge insight into nutrition, etc. I live much healthier now!

That's obviously just a side bonus. I went vegan because it broke my heart to see how we treated other animals. It's made me a stronger person to become vegan -- to stand up for something I believe is the only right thing, and the constant defending and debating with other people has made me a master of winning a discussion.

So, I live with a heavy heart knowing what is going on, but with a clean conscience and a purpose in life to make wrong right!"

-- Signe S.

126. "I feel better mentally and physically. I've always loved animals, so my life is more balanced with my psyche. I'm more tuned into who I am. I have been vegan for 4+ years now. It has deepened my disgust in the human race, which is not positive."

-- Karen J.

127. "I haven't gone totally vegan yet, but I don't eat red meat anymore. I just eat fruits and vegetables and fish and chicken. I love the healthy feeling my body has even for my age!

But even plants feel pain and express it. When grass is cut, the smell you notice is the grass crying out. Cucumbers have been recorded emitting whining when pruned. Trees communicate with each other, when threatened by a parasite.

My reason for going vegan would be the health benefits and letting other animals live, but eventually without the food chain, overpopulation in one species means the eradication of another."

-- Raymond D.

128. "My main benefit has been a clear conscience that I don't contribute to any animal suffering. Health-wise, I'm not sure as I've always looked after myself."

-- Michael W.

129. "Most obviously, on the outside I've lost 80 pounds and counting. I have more energy and I sleep better for sure. I feel better all-around and I know I'm making a difference. I have three different areas of knowledge that keep me vegan: environmental, health and political."

-- Jessica P.

130. "I started back in 2006 where I was looking after some sites on the Internet for animals in Denmark to find an organization in Denmark, where I live, where there would be some possibilities to be more active for the animals than just pay some charity money each month.

That's when I came across Anima. That was a horrible and cruel eye-opener for me and I stopped eating meat from that day forward and became a vegetarian in May 2006. During the past two years, I have become more and more vegan. Back then, between 2006 and until 2009/2010, Anima had local organization offices where I also was active in volunteering for activities on behalf of the animals in the agriculture industry and the fur industry. Plus, I've been spreading info about how to stop the mistreatment of the farm animals with flyers. We handed out information about how people could go vegan.

Besides my compassion and for the ethical reasons and my empathy for the animals, it is also for the environment and the climate plus nature. Health is just an added bonus!"

-- Marianne C.

131. "Since going vegan, my anemia from birth disappeared. My skin is beautiful as ever and I have more energy and a better life."

-- Anna P.

132. "First of all, I feel a lot more energized and healthy after getting rid of all animal products in my diet (I was vegetarian since I was young, and turned vegan last year).

Once I heard the truth about all of the food industries involving animals, I couldn't eat any meat, milk, dairy or eggs ever again. People would ask me if I missed eating all those foods, which I think is a common worry when considering going vegan, but I actually found so many other delicious and healthy foods and didn't even think about eating animal products again.

I discovered a lot about myself since going vegan, I became a lot more compassionate, not only towards animals but everything else in my life. I still think it's the best decision I've ever made and believe anyone who makes the choice to open their hearts to other beings on this earth will benefit a lot from it."

-- Shirel E.

133. "Besides increased health and a widened circle of compassion, I have a higher state of mind since going vegan."

-- Bennett R.

134. "I've been a vegetarian for a few years. I am a wildlife and aerial photographer. Since the years I've been a vegetarian, I've experienced a change in how animals react when they see me -- especially when I go for deep forest filming! There is definitely a change.

I guess the aroma our body gives plays a role from our meal pattern and its always pleasing to think that what we eat doesn't harm any animals."

-- Ranul T.

135. "The most positive effect I've had is how I naturally and effortlessly managed to reduce my weight from 82 kilos to 67. I've never been a health-conscious person and never really cared about my diet or nutrition, but I guess my diet must have become more balanced because I don't remember having to go to a doctor's office for seasonal viral infections. The most significant changes have occurred in my moral and ethical outlook, of course."

-- Rashid S.

136. "Well there are so many benefits, but for me the main one is that I don't have any guilty feelings about animals suffering for me to live."

-- Marie M.

137. "Since going vegan, I feel healthier, look healthier, look younger, have more energy, have a sense of doing something to help the bigger picture and being a part of such an amazing movement which will change the world as we know it."

-- Thomas N.

138. "I was vegetarian for thirty years and then went vegan at Christmas. I found, since going vegan, that I have lost weight and seem to have more energy. I feel better in myself! I went vegan because of the realization of what happens to cows and chickens. I found it harder to change from meat eater to vegetarian than vegetarian to vegan.

I had cancer of the uterus 2 years ago and, when reading about the causes, I did not meet any criteria. The only thing that I think might have contributed to it was dairy products, as I used to have a lot of cheese and semi skimmed milk and they give hormones like estrogen to cows for making more milk."

-- Valerie B.

139. "I'm only a vegan, because I'm a hedgehog."

-- Ticker

140. "My energy has improved as well as my depression. Having something to be passionate about is so powerful in and of itself. I eat much healthier now, I cook my own food, and I take better care of myself. More than that though, after going vegan I became more compassionate. Before, I was just awful to everybody. I had a bad attitude and distaste for everyone I met. I was pretty unlikeable. Being compassionate towards animals and caring for them has helped me to be compassionate towards other people as well. I'm friendlier and more approachable.

I'm also emotionally stronger! After the videos that I've seen of animal abuse, no insults get to me. I get called an ugly cunt on the daily and it couldn't bother me less. I care about ethics, and have a purpose. I was never someone who thought it was my job to change the world, and I always thought I would be fine with just living an average life. It was pretty depressing—I was pretty depressed—but I didn't put effort into anything and I didn't have anything I cared about. Someone could tell me their dad died or talk about child slavery and I didn't see why it was my issue. I've learned how to care, and I've learned that it's okay to care. Now, the suffering of others is my issue and something I'm so passionate about fighting. Honestly, whenever things get rough for me or whenever I'm going through turmoil, veganism helps me feel happy and giddy, because it's my passion and helping others is my dream!"

-- Mickey B.

141. "Becoming vegan is the best decision I've made! I have more energy; my gut health has increased and my soul is happy."

-- Rafael C.

142. "Benefits: serene peace, increased energy, constant energy (not a hyper-ness, but just the ability to keep going peacefully), feeling happier and more positive and upbeat and loving and patient with all things and beings, feeling like I am in a five year old's body, a lightness, little to no after meal tiredness, a feeling of rejuvenation after most meals, youthful appearance and demeanor, positive energy that attracts the positive energies of others, the knowledge that I am living up to the belief in kindness and love as much as possible... and, increasingly!"

-- Sophia A.

143. "Going vegan was the best choice I ever made. It was the most spiritually awakening and ego freeing transformation. I feel amazing. I feel great to know that I am trying my best to cause the least amount of harm to everything that is connected (animals, trees, land, water, my health and the starving).

My compassion, consciousness and love for everything has grown tremendously. For that I am grateful."

-- Christina L.

144. "I feel better physically. I was vegetarian for years, but the real benefits kicked in after giving up dairy as well. I didn't realize how badly it was messing with my tummy. Another obvious benefit is that I like myself more because I'm not contributing to animal suffering."

-- Trish J.

145. "There are literally no negatives in veganism. Just one example concerning personal health (and I've seen this shared by many) is the fact that my total cholesterol count fell from 300 to 200 in less than 6 months after eliminating meat and dairy."

-- Patrick O.

146. "The main reason for switching to veganism is that human food is only fruits and vegetables. All other items are non-food and pre-age people, create extra weight, cause disease, mucous forming, body odor, smelly bathroom trips, poor complexion,

lack of vitality, low energy, foggy thinking, aggressive behavior, and the list continues to go on."

-- Barry K.

147. "I became vegan to feel healthier and make a difference in the world."

-- Michael Z.

148. "I am FINALLY losing weight, I can finally cook, and I feel like I'm finally being a good environmentalist. My degree is environmental studies, so I needed to practice what I preach."

-- Melody A.

149. "Since becoming vegan, I am cleaner spiritually! It is lovely to know that I am living cruelty-free -- at least to the level it is possible."

-- Renata A.

150. "The benefits are rarely negative. Overall, eating vegan has made me more compassionate, has put perspective into my life and has allowed me to meet beautiful and caring people."

-- Dmitry M.

151. "I've noticed longer and stronger nails, skin glows and my skin cleared up a bit. I have more energy to get stuff done. I don't get sick that much anymore, like I used to."

-- Gianna G.

152. "The story begins from my school. I am a student who is often ridiculed by my friends because I am fat or maybe obese. So, I decided to become a vegetarian when I was 17 years old. I must lie to my parents that I have an animal protein allergy because my parents think meat is very good for health. They love me so much. Hahaha, kiss to my parents.

For me being vegan is not easy. Changing lifestyle and habits. Many processes I have to go through. I started with being a vegetarian and now I am vegan. I am an animal lover. I really love nature. I want to live healthy and loving life without killing just for food. Plants give me more love and energy for activity."

-- Dewi P.

153. "Veganism fixes mental issues, physical and spiritual issues and altogether improves one's outlook on life. In some ways, we join the world of nature more as animals live in it also. Yes, and I had "dermatitis", just another Latin name for a symptom of toxemia -- gone! Depression, gone. Other mental problems like "anger", gone. I credit those to raw veganism."

-- Colm R.

154. "Health benefits would be having more energy and not as tired or exhausted, less illness for sure, I am more focused at work, less bloating, and I actually get to eat more! Being vegan (or having a plant-based diet) has helped me to be more creative with food, to also realize how it heals and fuels my body better and knowingly understand that I'd rather put plants instead of animals that were killed inside my body.

For the animals, I feel like my eyes have been opened and I am able to respect, love and be more compassionate. It has awakened a part of me that I never knew was there. I feel more at peace knowing I'm not contributing to the slaughter of innocent animals that are here with us, for us to care for, love and cherish. No way in my mind is the animal agriculture right for them, for the planet or for us. I think a big benefit of educating myself about the animals is that it simply brings out the best in me for animals and for people. Being a lover and a giver. Not a life taker.

It's simply a WIN-WIN all around and I wish more people could open their eyes wider, stop shutting them so tight and getting on the defensive -- understand where we are coming from, it's a JOY!"

-- Danielle N.

155. "Although I didn't notice anything drastic because I was vegetarian for 20-ish years prior to being vegan, I did notice a reduction in anxiety and depression, and better skin. The more I learned about the animal agriculture industry, the more passionate I became about advocating for animals. I feel good about not contributing to their suffering for sure."

-- Jennifer D.

314

156. "Everything is positive knowing that you're not part of the broken system that abuses and murders animals. Helping yourself health-wise and benefiting the planet is a great thing."

-- Julie M.

157. "I have lost a lot of weight -- 50 pounds! I have more endurance in my workouts and I have more libido. I can eat a lot of food without worrying about gaining weight now."

-- Nikolaus V.

158. "I have been vegan for 14 years since I turned 30 years old. Reasons why I did it? My first reason is my love towards all living creatures. I always had dogs in my life, but long story short, I never made the connection until one day something happened that was my eye-opener. Health issues with my spleen got better... I have vegan children. My son is 5 years old and guilt-free.

I started seeing life with another point of view and I became a simpler humbler person. Materialistic things became something that was not my priority in my life. All I have from this are positive outcomes, even with a divorce on my shoulders, after I became vegan I was and still am a better human being."

-- Carmen C.

159. "I've experienced a lot of benefits. My acne has cleared up, less digestive issues, less brain fog, improvement in my mental state (has helped with my depression), it has helped with my PCOS (polycystic ovarian syndrome) and my conscience is clear."

-- Paige S.

160. "The change I felt after turning to veganism is that I feel like less of a hypocrite. Like I've finally aligned my actions with my thoughts and am not hiding behind any excuses anymore. Also, I feel I'm making a difference at an individual level and I feel inspired to stand up for animals. Also, physically I feel lighter. I've hit the gym lately as well. I'm less lazy.

Also, I find myself being more conscious about what I consume... and my food habits are becoming healthier."

-- Aura D.

161. "I switched to veganism 20 years ago. It was for health reasons, but after researching animal welfare shortly after the switch it changed. I am now living a cruelty-free lifestyle the best that I can and I am happy."

-- Mike V.

162. "I lost 50 lbs. My mood is so much more pleasant. My energy level is higher than it was when I was in my twenties and as a result of all those things... my sex life is better!"

-- Julie F.

163. "Going vegan has given me the kind of community and social support system that church gives religious people. You can't underestimate the power of a connection made through mutual love for the protection of animals. It's the same as joining the army or belonging to a religious group. Not only do you get to rest well at night knowing that you aren't contributing to a system of oppression, but being vegan in public leads to important connections and friendships that are invaluable."

-- Britty H.

164. "I took myself off blood pressure meds a year and a half ago when I became veganese. I'm not bloated, no headaches and now my eyes are wide open to a lot of things I was blind to."

-- Eva M.

165. "The main benefit of veganism is knowing that no animals suffered for me, plain and simple... its peace of mind."

-- Maryann H.

166. "I feel lighter and more energetic. I don't get sick like I used to, I rarely get colds anymore and if I do they last for a day instead of two weeks. Migraines are a thing of the past. I didn't care for at all, nor was I looking for 'health benefits' -- these are just a bonus. I have been vegan for 13 years now."

-- Bikky K.

167. "I can tell you about my health BEFORE going vegan: I was often very sick, had nausea, stomach and intestine problems, constipation and I easily became sick when the cold days arrived in September... I spent a lot of time at the doctor's, because I had multiple problems and also had many tests (like a camera in my stomach).

For my stomach pains and nausea, I tested out a lactose free diet when I was 12. Then later, as I was already a vegetarian, I tested out a gluten free diet. It was very expensive, but it did help.

3.5 years ago, I then became vegan for the animals. After about 6 months, my stomach pains, nausea and intestine problems disappeared altogether! I never went again to the doctor except for blood tests. In 3 years, I was sick once and it was just a little cold. My body odor also changed for the best -- people are telling me all the time! My skin became very soft. That's also a thing people are constantly pointing out! I also had suffered a lot of arthritis. I still suffer from it but much less!

My vegan diet also helped my dog Oslo, who suffered from many allergies and problems and also had many tests during the first 1.5 years I had him, because I did not know what he had. After I saw what veganism did to my body, I decided to try it for my sick dog so I started cooking vegan meals + buy vegan food for my dogs... Oslo did wonderful. After 3 months, all his problems also disappeared. He has wonderful fur and is no longer sick. I returned to the vet and he confirmed Oslo is allergic to animal protein (and peas), but the vet never did those tests because he believed that "a dog cannot be allergic to those things". I even found out that my second dog who also had allergy problems (but not as severe as Oslo) was also allergic to meat, so he also got even better and has a wonderful black fur now and loses almost no hair!"

-- Vanessa D.

168. "The benefits are, first of all, that I no longer participate in the torture, abuse, killing and exploitation of animals, and I am proud to be able to say that those who make money at the expense of the innocent ones will not get a cent from me. Then there is the ecological footprint which, for me, has been reduced by my choices. Last but not least, I'm healthy. I'm 53 and I have the body of an adolescent, perfect checkups, radiant skin, low weight but strong as an ox and my mood has improved because I'm doing the right thing."

-- Anim A.

169. "Switching to veganism has been the best thing for me. I started it because I got sick all the time and I never had energy. I'll admit, I did start for my health but the

animals are why I stay. Since going vegan, I've lost 60 pounds in the first 5 months! I have more energy and I don't feel foggy or weighed down. It's made me a lot more aware of what we put into our bodies. I used to get really bad headaches and, since going vegan, they've lessened greatly."

-- Kora C.

170. "I feel healthier and happier since I've been vegan. My karma now has much more positive sides and less negatives. Who could have asked for more?"

-- Erdal F.

171. "Physical benefits: Faster recovery (I am a marathoner and a weight lifter). It's anecdotal, but I always feel better now than I ever did on an omnivorous diet.

Emotional Benefits: I sleep well knowing that I am not contributing to the suffering of animals for my own selfish gain. I love my dog and cats at home so much and now I don't feel the hypocrisy of loving them, but eating animals just like them. I am now more aware of the way animals are treated and I go out of my way to ensure that everything I do does not contribute to that."

-- Mike S.

172. "I know that the amount of times I get sick has dramatically decreased, but I didn't go vegan for my health – it was strictly for the animals. The improved health was just a perk! I turned vegetarian when I was around 6 and I didn't even know what a vegan was back then. Then I began eating a little fish, chicken and turkey when I was around 19, because of the peer pressure of being a young mom. Then social media and videos "re-educated" me and I turned to veganism."

-- April P.

173. "There's a number of benefits I've experienced as a vegan: 1. It feels good looking back at all the years and calculating how many animals I've saved by not eating them. 2. I feel more inspired to eat healthy generally. 3. I don't work out, I drink lots of beer and *still* maintain a fit physique. 4. It seems there is a meat recall just about every year or so. Every time I hear this on the radio, I laugh free of stress and worry. 5. I feel happy about my environmental impact. 6. I feel like I've found a path of more connectedness and a better understanding of our reality."

-- Travis S.

174. "Since going vegan, I just have a new appreciation for life – for ALL life! Not only have I lost weight, but my skin has cleared. I just feel all around healthier and, most importantly, I have a better sense of self-worth knowing that I am not causing the death and / or pain and suffering of living beings."

-- Haley P.

Conclusion

In this book, you've discovered 200 different vegan recipes including everything from dinners, breakfasts and lunches to desserts, treats and smoothies! You have seen how to use any of the recipes in this cookbook to lose weight and get in the best physical condition of your life. You have also learned more about the science of *why* veganism is such a healthy lifestyle.

I would like to thank you once again for purchasing this book and taking the initiative to make not just your own life better, but to make the whole world a better place to live in. I challenge you to share the way this book and veganism itself has helped you, by telling those who you love the most about it. I would also very much appreciate it if you would help promote awareness about this book by writing an honest review for it on the Amazon sale's page or by promoting it on your blog, Tumblr, Pinterest or Facebook. Thank you for helping me save the world.

If you want to take your physique to the next level, I offer personal, customized diet plans and workout programs that are custom-tailored to *you* in order to fit your needs, your lifestyle and your goals. For a custom-tailored three-month total body transformation program, featuring three different phases of diet and exercise, I only charge $50. You can't beat that price! Most personal trainers charge that much or more for a single training session alone. If you want me to write you a personalized workout program and diet plan that is designed from the ground up for YOU and YOU alone, please contact me at jackalhead@live.com.

I look forward to hearing from you about the way this book has blessed your life and the lives of those around you and I look forward to being able to help you achieve your wildest dreams and goals – whatever they may be!

God Bless,

Jared

About the Author

Jared Bangerter has earned the reputation as a passionate leader in the health and fitness space. Throughout the span of over a decade, he has gained extensive expertise in the industry.

Starting out, Jared worked at Gold's Gym. He then obtained his NASM Certification in Personal Training. What fueled his drive the most was witnessing firsthand how his colleagues and clients underwent a colossal transformation, not only in body, but in mind and spirit through the power of nutrition and exercise.

Currently, Jared serves as a Nutritional Expert, where he is dedicated to creating customized diets for unique lifestyles. Most recently, he has been helping vegans across the globe unlock the secrets to the ins and outs of fat-burning and reaching peak physical shape.

Ultimately, Jared is on a mission to create lasting positive change in his community and the planet at large by making each and every person on it healthier and happier.

When he isn't helping people reach their full potential, you can find him in the great outdoors hiking, backpacking, and camping. He is also an avid advocate of animal rights. Jared happily resides in Pocatello, Idaho.

Total life transformation is just around the corner. Feel free to contact Jared Bangerter to begin paving the path to personal success.

Index

Barbecue-Style

Bean Burgers | 149
Carrot Dogs | 135
Spicy Chickpea Burgers | 183

Bars

Blueberry Bars | 272
Coconut Oatmeal Bars | 270
Davy Crockett Bars | 269
Dawn's Protein Bars | 268
Granola Bars | 271
Vegan Energy Bars | 61

Breads & Muffins

Apple & Bran Muffins | 53
Avocado Toast | 32
Carrot Cake Muffins | 70
Celiac-Friendly Banana Bread | 20
Chocolate Orange Muffins | 48
Cornbread | 161
Flax & Pumpkin Bread | 22
French Toast | 42
Fry Bread | 55
Sweet Potato Biscuits | 44
Tasty Banana Muffins | 60
Vegan Baguettes | 174
Vegan Drop Biscuits | 58

Cakes

Chocolate Cake | 262
Vanilla Cake | 261

Cookies, Donuts & Brownies

Almond Cookies | 267
Breakfast Oreo Donuts | 46
Brownies | 266
Chocolate Chip & Peanut Butter Cookies | 264
Cookie Dough Energy Balls | 74
Fudge Cookies | 263
Tickerdoodles | 265

Foreign Dishes

Akki Rotti | 38
Aloo Matar | 92
Face of Fasolia | 36
Fat Guy Panikeke | 30
Indian Lentils | 88
Indian-Style Stuffed Eggplant | 171
Muesli | 51
Scaloppini Cordon Bleu | 205
Super-Mangu | 35
Ta'ameya Falafel Balls | 105
Vegan Arepas | 83

Gourmet & Casseroles

Popeye's Casserole | 167
Shepherd's Pie | 144
Stuffed Zucchini | 150
Cheese-Stuffed Artichoke | 216

Ice Creams

Cherry Pie Ice Cream | 258
Choc. Chip Mint Ice Cream | 256
Chocolate Ice Cream | 260

Italian & Pastas

Butternut Squash Linguine | 190
Cauliflower Alfredo | 159
Garlic Pasta & Tomatoes | 181
Green Chili & Mac | 184
Lasagna Rolls | 210
Mac & Cheese-It Inferno | 217
Mac Without Cheese | 97
Parm & Pesto Breadsticks | 208
Pizza Pull Apart | 206
Ramen | 179
Spaghetti of Onion | 162
Stuffed Spinach Pockets | 214
Vegan Campanelle | 195
Vegan Lasagna | 146
Vegan Pizza | 154

Mexican

Avo-Tacos | 90
Black Beans Matter | 89
Breakfast Burrito | 72
Fajitas | 85
Great Northern Bean
Quesadillas | 157
Lime & Avocado Chilaquiles | 212
Paella | 152
Pasta Mexicana | 148
Red Cabbage Slaw Tacos | 202
Vegan Enchiladas | 169

Oatmeal & Cereal

Blueberry Pecan Granola | 33
Chia Oatmeal (Overnight) | 57
Choco-Cocoats | 43
Cinnamon-Quinoa & Oats | 66
Cornmeal Delight | 62
Fruity & Tangy Oats | 29
Good Morning Millet | 31
Porridge of Quinoa | 49
Slow Cooked Steel Oats with
Pumpkin | 63
Toasted Granola of Quinoa | 59

Potatoes

Artichoke & Olive Baked
Taters | 198
Greek Potato Salad | 165
Mashed Potatoes | 163
Potato & Zucchini Bake | 156
Potatoes au Gratin | 164
Rosemary Potatoes | 25
Sweet Potato Bakes | 188
Tater-Cakes | 28

Puddings

Breakfast Pudding with
Raisins | 21
Coconut Milk & Rice
Pudding | 254
Fruity Parfait | 75
Quinoa Pudding | 252
Raspberry Chia Pudding | 253
Tapioca Pudding | 255
Tea-ah-Chia Pudding | 56
Vegan Chocolate Pudding | 251

Salads

Barley Party Salad | 133
Breakfast Fruit Salad | 14
Fava Bean Salad | 118
Jicama Salad | 119
Mushroom Salad | 117
Roasted Mushrooms &
Eggplant | 107
Sweet Potato & Black Bean
Salad | 120

Sandwiches, Wraps & Pitas

Avocado & Tomato
Sandwich | 100
Chickpea Sandwich | 124
Sweet Potato PETA Pita | 103
Vegan BBQ Sandwiches | 91
Vegan Bagel Sandwich | 128
Vegan Crab Salad Sandwich | 204
Vegan Grilled Cheese | 203
Zucchini Wrap | 102

Scones, Pancakes, Crepes & Waffles

Cocoa Pancakes w/ Zucchini | 68
Chocolate Vegan Scones | 40
Lemon Scones w/ Poppy
Seeds | 50
Oatmeal Pancakes w/
Chocolate | 52
Protein-Packed Scones | 64
Vegan Cinnamon Waffles | 47
Vegan Crepes | 17
Vegan Pancakes | 16

Side Dishes, Dressings, Dips & Spreads

Avocado Tzatziki | 129
Green Chili Salsa | 125
Hummus Sandwich Spread w/
Tapenade | 99
Molten Hot Fava Spread | 24
Oatmeal Crackers | 122
Popeye Bites | 139
Seitan Pepperoni & Crackers | 137
Vegan Melted Cheese | 136
Vegan Pate | 106
Vidalia Salad Dressing | 121

Smoothie Bowls

Cherry Nut Smoothie Bowl | 248
Coco & Hazelnut Smoothie
Bowl | 250
Kiwi-Cado Smoothie Bowl | 249
Mango-Nut Breakfast Smoothie
Bowl | 67
Pitaya Smoothie Bowl | 247
Tahini Granola Smoothie
Bowl | 246

Smoothies

Almond & Blueberry
Smoothie | 232
Apple Pie Smoothie | 238
Beet & Raspberry Smoothie | 237
Blueberry & Mint Smoothie | 231
Butternut Date Smoothie | 245
Cacao & Kale Smoothie | 241
Cocoa Banana Nut Smoothie | 229
Coconut & Berry Smoothie | 227
Green Hulk Smoothie | 223
Green Smoothie-Sicles | 242
Hemp & Chocolate Smoothie | 228
Maca & Flax Seed Smoothie | 235
Mango & Chia Smoothie | 226
Oats & Strawberry Smoothie | 225
Peanut Butter & Jelly Oatmeal
Smoothie | 240
Pear & Apple Smoothie | 239
Popeye's Green Smoothie | 221
Pumpkin Smoothie | 236
Sesame Seed & Mango
Smoothie | 234
Sweet Avocado Smoothie | 224
Tropical Blast Smoothie | 220
Vanilla-Nut Smoothie | 244
Vegan Pina Colada Smoothie | 222
Walnut & Banana Smoothie | 233
White Bean & Coconut
Smoothie | 230

Soups, Stews & Chili

1-Hour Hot & Sour Soup | 108

Black Bean Soup | 110

Broccoli Soup | 112

Carrot Curry Soup | 114

Creamy Corn Chowder | 172

Garbanzo Bean & Kale Soup | 113

Portobello Stroganoff | 130

Red Lentil Curry Soup | 192

Red Lentil Soup | 111

Split Pea Soup | 132

Squash & Peanut Stew | 201

Three-Bean Chili | 194

Tofu Soup for the Vegan Soul | 115

Tomato Soup | 123

Winter Soup | 196

Spicy Curry & Stir-Fry

Coconut-Curry Quinoa | 93

Curried Chickpeas | 86

Ginger Stir-Fry | 87

Japanese Turnip Curry | 141

Noodles of Coconut & Spice | 197

Spicy Breaded & Fried Tofu | 78

Spicy Soba Noodles with Kale & Sea Veggies | 79

Vegan Stir-Fried Noodles & Tofu | 199

Vegan Egg Dishes

Popeye's Breakfast Quiche | 15

Scrambled Tofu | 19

Vegan Meat Dishes

Eggplant Bacon | 26

Vegan Seitan Makhani | 81

Sweet-Ginger Tofu Wedges | 95

Tofu Nuggets w/ Maple-Mustard Dip | 126

General Tso's Tofu | 176

Vegan Meatloaf | 178

Philly Cheese Seitan | 186

24569445R00187

Printed in Great Britain
by Amazon